Property and Trust Law in Hungary

Property and Trust Law in Hungary

Third Edition

István Sándor

This book was originally published as a monograph in the International Encyclopaedia of Laws/Property and Trust Law.

Founding Editor: Roger Blanpain
General Editor: Frank Hendrickx
Volume Editors: Alain Verbeke & Vincent Sagaert

Wolters Kluwer

Published by:
Kluwer Law International B.V.
PO Box 316
2400 AH Alphen aan den Rijn
The Netherlands
E-mail: lrs-sales@wolterskluwer.com
Website: www.wolterskluwer.com/en/solutions/kluwerlawinternational

Sold and distributed by:
Wolters Kluwer Legal & Regulatory U.S.
920 Links Avenue
Landisville, PA 17538
United States of America
E-mail: customer.service@wolterskluwer.com

ISBN 978-94-035-3608-8

e-Book: ISBN 978-94-035-3618-7
web-PDF: ISBN 978-94-035-3628-6

The Author

István Sándor, Dr habil. (born in 1970 in Vác, Hungary), is currently a professor of law at the Faculty of Law and head of the Department of Roman Law and Legal History, Eötvös Loránd University, Budapest (ELTE), where he teaches Roman law and trust law. He is also a visiting professor at the Faculty of Law of Károli Gáspár University of the Reformed Church (Budapest), where he teaches private law and was the head of the Department of Roman Law and Civil Law (2004–2012). He is also a practising attorney-at-law.

Curriculum vitae: diploma in law, ELTE (1995), diploma in political sciences, ELTE (1997), admitted to the Budapest Bar Association (1998), PhD, ELTE (2004), habilitation, ELTE (2014), doctor of the Hungarian Academy of Sciences (DSc).

He visited several universities and research institutes as a research fellow: Leopold-Wenger-Institute für Rechtsgeschichte, Munich (1992), Institute of Advanced Legal Studies, London (1996, 2012), Institut suisse de droit comparé, Lausanne (1996, 1997, 2012), Universität Trier (1998), Georg-August Universität Göttingen (1999), Università degli Studi di Padova (1999), Rijksuniversiteit Groningen (2000), Universität Wien (2000, 2001, 2004, 2010), Helsingin Yliopisto, Helsinki (2002, 2003), Max-Planck-Institut für Ausländisches und Internationales Privatrecht, Hamburg (2006), Humboldt Universität zu Berlin (2008). He was a lecturer at several domestic and international conferences, e.g., in Athens, Brno, Cluj Napoca, Dunajska Streda, Kuala Lumpur, Limassol, Limerick, Lisbon, London, Luxembourg, Lyon, Novi Sad, Prague, San Marino, Singapore, Tbilisi, Urbino, Vilnius, Warsaw.

He was a secretary and member of the working group named 'Law of Things' and, furthermore, a member of the working group named 'Legal Persons' (2010–2012) during the codification of the new Hungarian Civil Code (1998–2002). He was a member of the working group 'Representation' during the codification of the new Hungarian Code of Civil Procedure.

He is a member of the International Bar Association (IBA), Interlegal, International Federation of European Law, Society of Trust and Estate Practitioners, Selden Society and several Hungarian law and scientific associations. He is the chair of STEP Hungary.

He published more than 300 books and articles on company law, trust law, Roman law, legal history and private law. His most important books in the English language are: *Fiduciary Property Management and the Trust. Historical and Comparative Law*

Analysis, Budapest: HVG-ORAC Publishing House Ltd, 2015; *Business Law in Hungary*, Budapest: Patrocinium, 2016 (editor and co-author).

He was awarded the civilian section of the Knight's Cross of the Hungarian Order of Merit (2017) and the Academic Award of the Hungarian Academy of Sciences (2021).

Contact: Eötvös Loránd University, Faculty of Law, Department of Roman Law and Comparative Legal History (H-1053 Budapest, Egyetem tér 1–3.); Károli Gáspár Reformed University, Faculty of Law, Civil Law and Roman Law Department (H-1042 Budapest, Viola utca 2–4.), Kelemen, Mészáros, Sándor and Partners Law Office (H-1052 Budapest, Váci utca 24.). E-mail: Istvan.sandor@kelemen-lawfirm.hu, sandor.istvan@ajk.elte.hu.

Table of Contents

List of Abbreviations

ABGB	Austrian Civil Code (Allgemeines Bürgerliches Gesetzbuch, 1 June 1811)
AMF	Asset Management Foundation
BDT	Repository of State Judicial Orders ('Bírósági Döntések Tára'), Journal Published by Wolters Kluwer
BGB	German Civil Code (Bürgerliches Gesetzbuch vom 18. August 1896)
BH	Court Decisions ('Bírósági Határozatok'), Journal of the Curia of Hungary
Civil Code	Act V of 2013 on the Civil Code of Hungary
Criminal Code	Act C of 2012 on the Criminal Code
EBH	Principal Decision of the Curia (Supreme Court)
EU	European Union
Inytv.	Act CXLI of 1997 on the Land Registry
ITSZ	Provisional Rules of Jurisdiction of 1861
KGD	Case Law Report on Administrative and Economic Matters ('Közigazgatási-Gazdasági Döntvénytár'), Journal Published by Wolters Kluwer
MNV Zrt.	Hungarian National Asset Management Inc. (Magyar Nemzeti Vagyonkezelő Zártkörűen Működő Részvénytársaság)
Old Civil Code	Act IV of 1959 on the Civil Code of the Republic of Hungary
OR	Obligationenrecht (Switzerland 1881/83)
PPP	Public-Private Partnership
UCITS	Directive 2009/65/EC of the European Parliament and of the Council of 13 July 2009 on the Coordination of Laws, Regulations and Administrative Provisions Relating to Undertakings for Collective Investment in Transferable Securities
ZGB	Civil Code of Switzerland (Schweizerisches Zivilgesetzbuch, 10 December 1907)

List of Abbreviations

General Introduction

§1. General Background of the Country

I. Geography

1. Hungary is situated in Central Europe, in the Carpathian basin with an area of 93,028 square kilometres. The country borders Austria to the west, Slovakia to the north, Ukraine to the east, Romania to the southeast, and it shares the south border with Serbia, Croatia, and Slovenia. One of its main rivers, the Danube, divides Budapest, the capital city of the country, into two parts, namely Buda and Pest.

2. The Great Hungarian Plain, which lies east of the Danube River, dominates the country occupying 56% of its territory. The second main river of Hungary, the Tisza, flows across the plain and finally joins the Danube in Serbia.

Although most of Hungary's territory is flat, there are two mountain ranges; one of these is the Northern Mountains bordering the Great Plain on the north. The highest point of the country can be found in the Northern Mountains. This peak, the *Kékes,* with its 1,014 metres, is located in *Mátra* Mountain.

Lake *Balaton*, the largest lake in Hungary, can be found in the western part of the country. The 'Hungarian Sea', as it is often referred to, is also the largest freshwater lake in Central Europe. It is the most popular holiday destination for Hungarian people. The famous Benedictine Abbey of *Tihany* is located on the only peninsula of the lake.

The western part of the country is called Transdanubia. The Transdanubian Mountains are located north of Lake Balaton. The highest peak of this mountain range is in the *Pilis* Mountains.

The Little Plain of Hungary lies near the Austrian and Slovakian border. The climate is a bit different from the climate of the Great Plains. It is wetter and cooler here.

To the south of this part of the country lie the Mecsek Mountains. The southern slopes of these mountains enjoy sub-Mediterranean effects.

The small hills of the *Zala* area are not too high; the highest is about 301 metres. The waters of the small brooks here are collected by two rivers, the *Zala* and the *Mura,* and they finally flow into Lake Balaton and the River *Dráva*.

The wettest area of the country is located at the foot of the Alps along the west border. The highest peak here is *Írottkő* in the *Kőszeg* Mountain with its 882 metres.

The ten National Parks of Hungary offer stunning natural landscapes to visitors. As they are rich in natural treasures, several species of plants and animals can be found here.

The climate of Hungary is continental; there are four seasons: spring, summer, autumn, and winter. The summers are hot but the winters, which used to be cold, are getting milder nowadays.

II. Cultural Situation

3. Hungarian culture can be traced back to folk art in the form of ancient folk tales, folk music, folk dance, and folk poetry. Hungarian art music began with folk songs, which are usually on a pentatonic scale. Some famous Hungarian composers include Bálint Bakfark, Sebstyén Lantos Tinódi, and László Sáry. In the nineteenth century, the music of Ferenc Liszt brought Hungarian music onto the international stage, followed by Béla Bartók and György Ligeti in the twentieth century.

The tradition of Hungarian dance finds its roots in the regionally varied folk dances. Of the circle dances, the most well-known is the '*Karikázó*', performed by women, while among the two-person dances, the '*Csárdás*' is the most famous, and the '*legényes*' is the most well-known solo dance. The Renaissance brought new art dance forms, such as the Ungaresca and Hajdúdance. At the turn of the nineteenth-twentieth century, several initiatives were begun to kick-start contemporary Hungarian art dance. The first successful results were Béla Bartók's 'The Wooden Prince' and 'The Miraculous Mandarin'.

4. Hungarian literature can also be traced back to Hungarian folk stories and folk poetry genres. For example, the folk ballad '*Egyszer egy királyfi*' (Once upon a time, a prince), collected by László Arany and Pál Gyulai. The inception of Hungarian literary history can be traced back to 'Funeral Sermon and Prayer' (dated to 1192) for literature and to 'Lamentations of Mary' (around 1300) for poetry. After the impactful works of the Middle Ages, the first prolific period of Hungarian literature began in the Renaissance with the works of Bálint Balassi, followed by the poetry of Péter Bornemissza and the prose of Gáspár Heltai. After the Turkish occupation, Hungarian literature of the eighteenth century began with Ferenc Kazinczy's language reform. Besides lyrical poetry, the theatre, epics, and novels of Mihály Vörösmarty, Sándor Petőfi, János Arany, Imre Madách, and Mór Jókai became internationally recognized. In the twentieth century, the works of Mihály Babits, Endre Ady, Attila József, Frigyes Karinthy, Antal Szerb, Péter Eszterházy, and the Nobel Prize-winning Imre Kertész are most worthy of mention.

5. The number of notable Hungarian artists in the fine arts is also exemplary. In painting, romanticism was represented by Mihály Zichy and Viktor Madarász, academic art by Bertalan Székely, wall painting by Károly Lotz and Mór Than, historical painting by Mihály Munkácsy, plein air by Pál Merse Szinyei, secessional expressionism by Tivadar Kosztka Csontváry, and the post-impressionist József Rippl-Rónai.

Hungary's architectural achievements are also outstanding, e.g., the Buda Castle District which is a Unesco World Heritage site, the Danube banks, *Andrássy* Street, *Hollókő* village, the *Aggtelek* Karst, the thousand-year-old *Pannonhalma* Archabbey, the *Hortobágy* National Park, the Coptic Christian cemetery in *Pécs*, the *Fertő* culture region, and the historic *Tokaj* wine county.

The representatives of Hungarian film culture have been successful internationally many times, e.g., István Szabó's film 'Mephisto' won the best foreign movie Oscar in 1982, while most recently, László Jeles Nemes's movie 'Son of Saul' won the best foreign-language movie Oscar in 2016.

III. Political System

6. Since 23 October 1989, Hungary has been a constitutional parliamentary representative democracy. Hungary's political system was developed in 1989 based on the West-German model.

The Hungarian parliament sits in a single chamber; parliamentary representatives are chosen through direct elections by Hungarian citizens. Representatives of political parties and independent candidates can stand for election. The National Assembly consists of 199 members. The party (parties) that achieve(s) the most votes can form a 50% + 1 majority, which then chooses the Prime Minister, who forms the government.[1]

There are currently nine parties in the National Assembly: the governing Fidesz (Hungarian Civic Alliance) and the Christian Democratic People's Party, as well as the opposition, the Hungarian Socialist Party, the Democratic Coalition (DK), the Dialogue, the Jobbik for Hungary Movement, Politics can be Different, Együtt (Together, Party of the Epoch Change), Our Country. There is also a nationality (National Self-Government of the Germans in Hungary) and an independent representative in the Parliament.

7. Of the five legal authorities, the President of Hungary is the foremost, who expresses national unity through Hungary's Fundamental Law and guards the democratic processes of Hungarian democratic governance. The President is elected for a five-year term by the National Assembly.

The Hungarian Constitutional Court restricts legislative power through a judiciary system. The Hungarian Constitutional Court was formed as part of the constitutional reforms during the regime change, based on the model of other countries, primarily Germany. The Hungarian Constitutional Court is the main body defending the Fundamental Law. Its task is to make sure legislation adheres to the Constitution and to protect constitutional order and the fundamental rights provided by the Fundamental Law. The Hungarian Constitutional Court is not part of the justice

1. For detailed analysis of the Hungarian constitutional system, *see* Zsolt Szabó, *The Constitutional System of Hungary*, in *Business Law in Hungary* 39 ff. (István Sándor ed., Patrocinium 2016); *The Basic Laws of Hungary, A First Commentary* 1 ff. (Lóránt Csink, Balázs Schanda & András Zs. Varga eds, Clarus Press 2012); Bálint Ablonczay, *Conversations on the Fundamental Law of Hungary* 10 ff. (Elektromédia 2012).

apparatus. The Hungarian Constitutional Court has fifteen members elected by a two-thirds majority in the National Assembly for twelve years. The members cannot be re-elected, and their mandate expires if they reach seventy years of age, even if they have not yet completed their terms. The National Assembly chooses the President of the Hungarian Constitutional Court from the presiding Constitutional Judges, who then carries this position until the end of their term. The Vice President of the Hungarian Constitutional Court is chosen secretly by the Constitutional Judges.

The National Audit Office is the National Assembly's primary financial and economic monitoring institution, which is subordinate to the National Assembly and monitors the management of public, government, and local government funds. The primary task of the National Audit Office is to monitor the management of public finances and national assets. The National Audit Office monitors adherence to the accounting processes of public finances and the proper functioning of the internal control system for public finances.

The task of the commissioner for fundamental rights is to ensure the protection of fundamental rights and to make sure that the actions of the authorities do not compromise the constitutional rights of the people. The commissioner is politically independent. No one can give him orders, and he answers only to the National Assembly. He has a ministerial rank and salary and parliamentary immunity. The ombudsman is selected by the National Assembly, based on the recommendation of the President of the Republic, with a two-thirds majority, for six years.

8. Within local administrative organizations, Hungarian local governments have the right and opportunity to govern and manage a significant proportion of local administrative tasks for the people. Hungarian administrative areas have two main levels. On a regional level, there are nineteen counties and the capital (Budapest), while at the local level, there are 3,154 towns and small municipalities. In terms of municipalities as a whole, 328 are towns, and the rest are small municipalities. The cities include twenty-three county capitals and the capital, which consists of twenty-three districts. These individual areas have local governments. Budapest has a two-level local government system, consisting of the Budapest City Council and the district local governments. There is no hierarchical relationship between county and municipality local governments.

§2. Legal Background of the Country

9. Within the continental European legal systems, the Hungarian one most resembles the German legal family. Due to geographical and historical factors, the development of Hungarian law was most influenced by Austrian, German, and Swiss law.[2]

2. In connection with the development of Hungarian law, *see* Gábor Hamza, *Le dévelopment du droit privé européen* 54 ff. (L'Université Eötvös Loránd Faculté de Droit 2005); *Magyar jogtörténet* (*Hungarian Legal History*) (Barna Mezey ed., Osiris 1996); Károly Szladits, *Magyar Magánjog. I. Általános Rész, Személyi Jog* (*Hungarian Private Law, Vol. I, General Part, Law of Persons*) (Grill

I. Legal Family or Tradition

10. After the foundation of the Hungarian State by St. István I in 1000, the kingdom consisting of tribal alliances was formed into a Christian monarchy. The history of Hungarian private law can be divided into several periods. The main periods are identified as follows:

- Period until Werbőczy's Tripartitum (1514).
- Period until the laws passed in 1848.
- 1848–1861, the National judicial conference.
- 1861–1945.
- 1945–1989.
- 1989 until today.

Creating periods is arbitrary in certain respects since the development of private law did not necessarily mesh with the above periods; therefore, these periods are merely a reference and a starting point.

A. *Period Before Werbőczy's Tripartitum*

11. Before István Werbőczy (approximately 1458 – Buda, 13 October 1541), unwritten laws of custom were primarily prevalent in Hungarian private law, which was chiefly characterized by royal donation, aviticity, and serfdom. Aviticity was the passing of family assets from the first holder down through the family lineage. There is very little information about the tribal laws of the founders of Hungary. During the reign of the kings of the Árpád House, private law was very much exercised in an unwritten form, while the laws passed by the Árpád House kings did not deal much with private law. The St. István (Stephen) laws were not primarily related to private law either. St. István's laws lay the foundation for a unified Hungarian legal system while preserving national traditions.[3]

The private law based on custom law in the Middle Ages was greatly influenced by contact with Western states, Roman law influenced contract law, Canon law influenced marriage laws and burial rights, Czech-Moravian law affected the comitatus, German law influenced municipal law and contract formats, while Lombard feudal law affected aviticity and the development of landowners' authority. King Mátyás' book of laws (Decretum Maius) in 1486 can be considered a collection of law to some extent, primarily containing litigation rules from a private law perspective.

1941); Lajos Vékás, *Történeti visszapillantás a magyar magánjog kodifikációjára* (*Historical Flashback on the Codification of the Hungarian Private Law*) 66 (Jogtudományi Közlöny 2011); János Zlinszky János, *Werbőczy jogforrástana* (*Werbőczy's Tenet of Legal Sources*), in *Tanulmányok Werbőczy Istvánról, Studien über István Werbőczy* (Gábor Hamza ed., Magyar Felsőoktatás 2001).

3. Gábor Hamza, *Szent István törvényei és Európa, Sain Étienne et l'Europe* (*Saint Stephen's Laws and Europa*), in *Szent István és Európa* (*Saint Stephen and Europe*) 19 (Gábor Hamza ed., Magyar Felsőoktatás 2001²).

B. Werbőczy's Tripartitum

12. István Werbőczy, the national court's master judge (protonotarius Judicis Curiae Regiae), was entrusted by Vladislaus II to compile complete materials on Hungarian law and custom law. The result was a legal book (domestici juris compendium), which approached statutory law from literary, scholastic, and didactic perspectives. The book was written in Latin, titled: *Tripartitum opus juris consuetudinarii inclyti regni Hungariae*. Werbőczy presented it to the king in 1514, who put it in front of the national assembly; in turn, they asked the king to sanction and proclaim it in Decree LXIII of 1514.[4] The king sanctioned it, but the law was not printed (sealed and distributed); this was initially due to technical reasons (copying the large material), but it was then hindered by the nobleman's party because the code assumed the equality of all nobles. In 1517, Werbőczy had the Tripartitum printed at his own expense, and so it lived on as written custom law. Law XXXI of 1525 hastens the sanctioning of the Tripartitum and the unifications of royal decrees in a corpus Decretum but in vain.[5]

The Tripartitum reflects the Hungarian feudal custom law of the time. It deals primarily with noble law and only briefly discusses municipal law, serf law, and particular law. Besides common law, the Tripartitum contains numerous penal and litigation rules. Although the structure of the Tripartitum – *de personis, de rebus, de actionibus* – follows the tradition of Roman law, it only superficially adheres to the institution system. Concepts and legal principles known from Roman law were also only formally adopted, while, e.g., custody in the case of testamentary, legal, or ordered custody, as well as certain rules regarding testamentary law, are direct reflections of Roman law. Therefore, the Tripartitum is a bill, but it did not aim to supplement or change previous laws; instead, it was intended to summarize contemporary custom law at the time.[6]

The development of Hungarian private law was greatly influenced by judicial practice, especially in the period after the Court of the Seven (1715) and the Royal Court (1723), which includes the Court of the Seven and the Royal Court of Justice too. The *Planum Tabulare* contained the Court of the Seven and the Royal Court decrees between 1715 and 1768, which Maria Teresa summarized in 1769 before being sanctioned by the Queen. The Planum Tabulare shows the rather advanced

4. Ferenc Eckhard, *Magyar alkotmány – és jogtörténet* (*History of Hungarian Constitution and Law*) 188 ff. (Politzer 1946); Gábor Hamza, *Origine e sviluppo degli ordinamenti giusprivatistici moderni in base alla tradizione del diritto romano* 142 ff. (Andavira editora 2013); Gábor Hamza, *Entstehung und Entwicklung der modernen Privatrechtsordnungen und die römischrechtliche Tradition* 139 ff. (Eötvös Loránd Universitätsverlag 2009).
5. Bishops Zakár Mosóczy & Miklós Telegdy edited the Tripartitum and published it in Nagyszombat in 1584, after which it became public property. The 1628 second (Vienna) edition was titled 'Hármaskönyv' (Tripartitum). Márton Szentiványi's third, 1696 edition first held the title *Corpus Juris Hungarici*. János Szegedi's fourth edition was published in 1742; this is the final version of the work. Further editions were only updated with current laws.
6. Zlinszky, *supra*, 171 f.

level of legal practice at the time. From 990 decrees, 698 can be considered substantive private law and contain almost every law in force, adapting the Tripartitum rights to the changed economic and social conditions.[7]

C. Significance of Laws Passed in 1848

13. The struggles for reforms that led to the 1848 revolution and freedom fight began in 1825. At this time, the efforts headed by Count István Széchényi in order to abolish aviticity and restructure the property system are most worthy of mention. In principle, Act XV of 1848 abolished aviticity and the royal donation system. Act IX of 1848 stopped serf relationships with possible reimbursements for landowners. Act XV of 1848 directed the ministry to develop a Civil Code.

Losing the 1848 freedom fight was also a great loss to the Hungarian private law system as well. By using old Hungarian legal material, Hungarian lawmakers would certainly have come up with an independent civil law system. Erasing ancient institutional principles interrupted the gradual reforms in the name of legal continuity but did not necessarily mean that Hungary's legal development would stray under the influence of foreign thought. Fundamental legal system reform was unavoidable by 1848. However, the transformation destroyed Hungarian law more quickly than its construction could begin. The gap this destruction left was quickly filled by institutions of Austrian law, which made it impossible to form a Hungarian legal system based on ancient laws.[8]

D. Period after 1848

14. After the defeat of the freedom fight, the aviticity order and feudal patents (1852–1853) put an end to serfdom and aviticity. Simultaneously, the 1811 Austrian Civil Code (Allgemeines Bürgerliches Gesetzbuch, (ABGB) came into effect (29 November 1852), with the exception of certain decrees relating to marital rights. The land registry decree from 15 December 1885 promulgated the Austrian land registry system in Hungary, followed by the Austrian mining law and bankruptcy law. The Hungarian bill of exchange law was replaced by the general German bill of exchange law. The land registry only came into effect in Transylvania, the military frontier and Fiume much later. The significance to the public law of the October Diploma from 1860 was the change from a centralist government structure to a federal one.[9]

---

7. Szladits, *supra*, 80.
8. Szladits, *supra*, 83. According to the impact of the Austrian private law on the Hungarian law, *see* Franz Wieacker, *Privatrechtsgeschichte der Neuzeit unter besonderer Berücksichtigung der deutschen Entwicklung* 337 (Vanderhoeck & Ruprecht 1996^{2}).
9. *See also* Miklós Ujlaki, *A magyar jog sorsa az Ausztriához és Lengyelországhoz csatolt területeken* (*Fate of the Hungarian Law on the Territories Annexed to Austria and Poland*) 24 ff. (Grill 1932).

As a result, the pre-1848 laws were reinstated, including the Royal Court and the Court of the Seven. Hungarian courts began working from 1 May 1861. Considering that Hungarian courts could not have operated based on foreign law, József Ferenc (as an un-crowned king) convened the National Judicial Conference with an imperial announcement alongside the October Diploma, consisting of the judges in the Court of the Seven and notable scholars of the time. The National Judicial Conference took place from 22 January to 4 March 1861 and created an extensive work titled: 'Temporary laws recommended by the National Judicial Conference.' Considering that public law affairs were disorganized, the national assembly was incomplete, and a king was yet to be crowned, no law could be passed on this. The house of representatives announced in their meeting on 22 June 1861, and this was confirmed by the Upper House on 1 July that Hungarian private law would be reinstated, but the work of the National Judicial Conference could be used temporarily as an aid. At the meeting of the Royal Court on 23 July 1861, it was announced that these rules would be considered 'a permanent benchmark' in judgments; thereby, the Provisional Rules of Jurisdiction of 1861 (ITSZ) became written custom law.[10]

With regard to the partial reforms to private law that were accepted, it is worth noting Act XVI of 1876 on the format of a will, the custody law (Act XX of 1877), and the law on matrimonial law (Act XXXI of 1894). Furthermore, Act XXXVII of 1875 should be mentioned, the Commercial Law Code (Kt.), of which not only the trade law parts but also the sections relating to private law became important factors in legal practice (e.g., protection of rights acquisitions in good faith, purchase transactions).

Austrian law, though only in effect temporarily, still had a major impact on Hungarian private law. Austrian law brought German-Roman legal thinking into Hungarian law, which was useful, but also tore Hungarian legal thinking away from the culture of old Hungarian private law and directed it towards pandectic knowledge.[11]

E. Plans for the Codification of Hungarian Civil Law

15. The preparation of the private law code began following the 1867 agreement, primarily in the form of partial plans.[12] The development of the General Private Law Code in 1871 is most associated with Pál Hoffmann, Istvány Teleszky's inheritance law draft in 1882, István Apáthy's law of obligations draft in 1882, Endre Halmossy's law of things partial draft in 1882, and Béni Grosschmid's marital, personal, and property law draft. In 1895, Sándor Erdélyi, Minister of Justice, created a committee to prepare a unified plan for the Civil Code. Its members included Gusztáv Szászy-Schwarz, whose name is associated with developing the

10. The ITSZ not only extended to private law but also to civil and penal procedures, bill of exchange law, bankruptcy, trade law, serfdom, mining law, land registry law and custody. Part I, point (a) of the ITSZ covers substantive private law (civil private law, substantive part), while part I, point (b), Ch. XII (formative part) covered the land registry. ITSZ jurisdiction only extended to the mother country; the Austrian ABGB was used in other areas of pre-Trianon Hungary.
11. Szladits, *supra*, 96.
12. *See also* Wieacker, *supra*, 484.

draft for inheritance law. The bill in 1900 primarily reflected the influence of the German Civil Code (Bürgerliches Gesetzbuch vom 18 August 1896) (BGB) and consisted of four parts: personal and family law, the law of obligations, the law of things, and inheritance law. The bill did not contain a General Section; regulations relating to this are found in the law of obligations section. The German BGB had even more influence on the 1913 bill, but it did not include a General Section either.[13]

Of the drafts, the 1928 'Recommendation for a Private Law Bill' (Private Law Bill) was not accepted either, though courts often refer to it and essentially consider it law. The Private Law Bill strongly reflects the Swiss ZGR and Obligationenrecht (Switzerland 1881/83) (OR), which had a large impact on legal practice and the creation of the Civil Code.

F. First Codification of Hungarian Civil Law, Act IV of 1959 (Old Civil Code)

16. A socialist political system was created in Hungary after the Second World War, which meant Soviet law had a major impact on the legal system. The committee entrusted with creating the Civil Code was convened in December 1953. The committee members included university lecturers from law faculties, employees from the Institute for Political Science and Legal Studies of the Hungary Academy of Sciences, the Supreme Court, the Prosecutor General, and representatives from the Ministry of Justice. The Civil Code was put in front of the National Assembly as a bill in 1959. The code was accepted as Act IV of 1959 and entered into force on 1 May 1960.[14]

In spite of its basic socialist features, the Civil Code also reflects the influence of the German BGB, the Swiss OR, and the Civil Code of Switzerland (Schweizerisches Zivilgesetzbuch, 10 December 1907) (ZGB), as well as Hungary's 1928 Private Law Bill. Of all the socialist civil codes at that time, the creators of the code drew on the 1922 Soviet Civil Code, the 1950 Czechoslovakian Civil Code, the 1955 Polish civil code bill, and the 1950 Bulgarian law governing property.[15] The codification of Act IV of 1959 took place amidst an economic environment where private ownership, as personal ownership, was dwarfed in comparison to the primacy of state ownership. Professor Lajos Vékás aptly described the situation when he said that 'socialist civil law was private law without private ownership'.[16]

---

13. *See also* Hamza, *Entstehung supra*, 378 f.
14. *See* István Sándor, *Az 1959. évi IV. törvény megalkotása és módosításai 1989-ig* (*The Creation and Amendment of the Act IV of 1959 and Its Modifications until 1989*), in *Tanulmánykötet az 1959-es Polgári Törvénykönyv előkészítéséről, alapvető intézményeiről és fejlődésmenetéről I–II* (*Volume of Studies on the Preparation, Basic Institutions and Development of the Civil Code of 1959*) 40 ff. (Tamás Sárközy ed., Magyar Közlöny Lap- és Könyvkiadó Kft 2018).
15. Gábor Hamza, *Az európai magánjog fejlődése* (*Development of the European Private Law*) 177 (Nemzeti Tankönyvkiadó 2002); *see also* Hamza, *Origine*, *supra*, 351 ff.; Hamza, *Entstehung*, *supra*, 388 ff.
16. Vékás, *Történeti*, *supra*, 268.

After the old Civil Code Book was adopted, it was modified several times. Significant modifications before the regime change included the changes accepted in 1967 and 1977.

G. *Legal System after the Transition*

17. The processes implemented in Hungarian society during the 1980s brought about significant changes. The earlier socialist statist economic mechanisms were replaced by a need for a free-market economy in the political will, as a result of which related legal regulations underwent a change. Alongside devising laws for political and societal order in a democracy and creating conditions for balancing power and parliamentary democracy, an important role was played by private law legislation aimed at restricting the government's role in the private sector. This was also connected to the newer external factor of adhering to the legal harmonization required for integration into the European Union (EU).

As a result of the regime change, the equality of private ownership with public ownership was constitutionally recorded, and – after numerous social and political debates – the victims of the Second World War, socialist privatizations and cooperatives were reimbursed. The other important factor in the reorganization of ownership was dismantling state ownership, which manifested as government-led privatization.[17]

Economic laws provided the legal framework for the transition to a free-market democracy, within which the opportunity to establish and manage privately funded businesses emerged. The fundamental laws of the market economy are corporate law, competition law, the law on foreign investments, stock exchange trading, and the laws underlying the banking system. The political regime change, the transition from a planned economy to a market economy and the creation of certain laws governing the economy (e.g., the law on business organizations, the law on unfair trading practices, the credit institutions law, the securities law, and then the stock market law) also led to some significant changes in the Civil Code after the regime change. However, there was no doubt that the changed social and economic conditions required a new private law codex. Therefore, preparation for the codification of the new Civil Code began in 1998. Hungary joined the EU in 2004, which meant that legislation in Brussels is now also in effect in the Hungarian law.

II. Relation and Hierarchy Between the Sources of Law

18. For Hungarians, a legal source is considered to be a legislative institution with the power of the state, which passes laws (fontes originis); furthermore, a law

---

17. In detail, *see* Jenő Czuczai, *A magyar privatizáció alulnézetből. Múltja, jelene, jövője* (*Hungarian Privatization Viewed from Below: Its Past, Present, and Future*) 77 ff. (Agrocent 1994).

proclaimed by the legislative institution with the power of the state (fontes cognoscendi). Virtual legal source is the general term for legal regulations, while we consider named regulations concrete, so the law is generally a virtual legal regulation, and the Civil Code is a concrete law.[18]

Primary legal sources are regulations adopted by supreme legislative bodies, and secondary legal sources are laws made by those subordinate to these organizations. Acts are considered primary legal sources, while secondary legal sources are government, ministerial, and local government decrees. Based on section 26 of Act CXXX of 2010, laws have to be promulgated in the official Hungarian Gazette, the 'Magyar Közlöny'. From 1 January 2012, laws can be found in a standard format and are freely accessible in the National Legal Archive (www.njt.hu).

A. *Fundamental Law*

19. On 18 April 2011, the National Assembly adopted Hungary's Fundamental Law, which came into force on 1 January 2012 to replace Act XX of 1949, the previous Constitution. The Fundamental Law declares several fundamental principles relating to private law, especially under the title of 'Freedom and responsibility'.

In world legal history, fundamental rights are the acquis of the French Revolution, which were primarily formed to create civilian equality and force back the police state. In this vein, Hungary's Fundamental Law ensures absolute rights. Of course, fundamental rights are not directly sanctioned legal norms, so some argue they do not even belong directly to the legal sources for private law. Under such an approach, a correct analysis of fundamental rights is that they should be interpreted and applied to the relationship between citizens and the state, giving rights to the people vis-à-vis public bodies.

At the same time, in the hierarchy of legal sources, the Fundamental Law determines the main regulations, and subordinate sources of law cannot contain contradictory provisions. Thus, the subordinate civil law sources of law convey the basic rights enshrined in the Fundamental Law and import those civil law sources of law into a private law context. As a result, provisions that contradict the Fundamental Law constitute a breach of law that must be considered in terms of civil law relations as well. However, fundamental rights play an important role when interpreting civil law norms and in the case of legal loopholes.[19]

18. Regarding the private law sources in detail, *see* Ádám Boóc & István, *Előadásvázlatok a polgári jog általános tanaiból* (*Lecture Notes on the General Part of the Civil Law*) 75 ff. (Patrocinium 2014^5).
19. According to the role of the constitution on the field of private law, *see* Barnabás Lenkovics, *Polgári alanyi jogok – alkotmányos alapjogok (Alapvető kérdések az alanyi és az alapjogok körül) Subjective Rights – Constitutional Fundamental Rights (Basic Questions Around the Subjective Rights and the Fundamental Rights)*, in *Alkotmányosság a magánjogban* (*Constitutionalism in the Private Law*) 107 ff. (Adrás Sajó ed., Complex Kiadó 2006).

B. Acts and the Civil Code

20. In terms of civil law – in accordance with the traditions of legal systems in continental Europe – the acts, and particularly the prevailing Civil Code, form the basis of legal practice.[20] The new Civil Code is the result of fifteen years of planning following the regime change. The National Assembly adopted the Civil Code on 11 February 2013, Act V of 2013 on the Civil Code of Hungary (Civil Code). The new Civil Code was published in the Hungarian Gazette on 26 February 2013.[21]

The structure of the new Civil Code predominantly follows the institution system. The creation of the codex aims to uniformly regulate commercial and civil law (monist system), targeting a unified voice in private law, including private law terminology. Without a doubt, the fundamental changes experienced by Hungarian society and its economy in the last twenty-seven years required the creation of a new Civil Code. Also indubitable is the fact that the new Civil Code was created based on the results of legal science and judicial practice.

The Civil Code is split into books by the Dutch codification example. Book I of the Civil Code contains introductory provisions and general civil law principles in six paragraphs. Book II, titled 'Man as a subject of law', contains the laws relating to natural persons. Book III contains laws relating to legal persons, as well as corporate law. Book IV covers family law, which was previously in a separate act (Act IV of 1952 on Marriage, Family, and Custody). Book V is titled 'Law of things,' instead of the previous 'Ownership rights,' which better reflects the dogmatic approach to this area of law. In accordance with the demands of technology and scientific developments, the legislator loosened the approach towards things and further strived to clearly define the spheres of state and private property. The legislators also included apartment building regulations in the new Civil Code, while the land registry was regulated in more detail. The placement of liens in this book got rid of the fragmented regulation and organized this legal institution in a dogmatically correct manner. The law of obligations is in Book VI, containing the general regulations for contracts and agreements, detailed regulations for certain contract types and the legislation for compensation liability. Book VII contains inheritance law, while Book VIII contains the closing provisions.[22]

---

20. *Szakértői Javaslat az új Polgári Törvénykönyv tervezetéhez* (*Expert Proposal for the Draft of the New Hungarian Civil Code*) (Lajos Vékás ed., Complex Kiadó 2008).
21. *See* Lajos Vékás, *Az új Ptk. Szakértői javaslatának elvi kérdései* (*Theoretical Questions of the Expert Proposal of the New Civil Code*), 55 Magyar Jog 65 ff. (2008); Lajos Vékás, *Bírálat és jobbító észrevételek az új Ptk. kormányjavaslatához* (*Criticism and Betterment Comments to the Draft of the New Civil Code*), 55 Magyar Jog 577 ff. (2008); Imre Vörös, *Az új Ptk. tervezetének szakértői javaslata* (*The Expert Proposal of the Draft New Civil Code*), 63 Jogtudományi Közlöny 571 ff. (2008); Ádám Boóc, *Észrevételek az új Polgári Törvénykönyv tervezetéhez nemzetközi magánjogi szempontból* (*Remarks to the Draft of the New Civil Code from Private International Law Aspect*), 8 Polgári Jogi Kodifikáció 3 ff. (2008).
22. The chief themes of the codification of the new Civil Code can be followed in the journal titled 'Polgári Jogi Kodifikáció' (Private Law Codification) that has been launched in 1999. It is also worth mentioning professor Lajos Vékás' theoritical volumes, Lajos Vékás, *Az új Polgári Törvénykönyv elméleti előkérdései* (*Theoretical Premises of the New Civil Code*) (HVG-ORAC 2001); and Lajos Vékás, *Parerga. Dolgozatok az új Polgári Törvénykönyv tervezetéhez* (*Parerga: Studies for the Draft*

21. Private laws have geographical, personal, temporal, and material scopes. Geographical scope means the geographical unit in which civil law norms are applied, which is primarily the territory of Hungary. There are also certain laws, e.g., government decrees, which target a particular unit and are only effective within certain administrative units (such as local government decrees on housing). Civil law norms are effective for all legal subjects, including legal persons as well as people. The temporal scope of civil law norms is usually defined in the norm itself. The general legal principle in private law is that a law cannot have a retroactive effect, and existing rights cannot be encroached upon by new laws. The material scope of the Civil Code covers all legal subjects and their material and personal relations.

Individual rights, though creating an absolute legal relationship, exhibit a strong similarity with the law of things' rights, yet nonetheless, they are treated as a separate legal area. People's property and individual rights are effective towards the state, too, since the state, as a legal person, can only be subject to civil law contracts and civil law rights, and therefore, from this perspective, is the same as an individual person in the eyes of the law. Due to the equality and interdependence recorded in the Civil Code, the state is subject to civil law obligations in the same way as to procedures, actions, and failings derived from public administration and public law functions, just like other subjects of the law.

Equality and interdependence are manifested in civil law processes, and therefore, Hungary's constitutional order must be taken into account when proceeding according to the Civil Code. According to section 6 of Act CXXX of 2010, Hungarian laws extend to all private persons, legal persons, and organizations without legal personality within the area of the country.

The Civil Code's temporal scope is determined by section 8:4, which came into effect on 15 March 2014. Section 7(1) of Act CXXX of 2010 also applies to civil law regulations, based on which the day a law comes into effect must also be determined. It is also possible for individual provisions of a certain law to take effect at different times. The general principle is that the law cannot take effect before its promulgation and cannot deem any behaviour unlawful.

---

of the New Hungarian Civil Code) (HVG-Orac 2008). Certain issues of the codification are also worked out in detail in the following volumes: György Bíró & József Szalma (eds), *Kötelmi jog kodifikációs tanulmányok (2003–2005)* (*Codification Studies on the Law of Obligations*) (Novotni Alapítvány 2005); *A magánjogi kodifikáció eredményei* (*Results of the Private Law Codification*) (Réka Gondosné Pusztahelyi ed., Novotni Alapítvány 2008); *Bank- és hitelviszonyok. Kodifikációs tanulmányok az új Ptk. születése kapcsán* (*Bank and Credit Relationships. Codification Studies related to the Birth of the New Civil Code*) (Judit Barta ed., Novotni Alapítvány 2009); *A magánjogi kodifikáció eredményei* (*Results of the Private Law Codification*) (Réka Pusztahelyi ed., Novotni Alapítvány 2010); *Merre tart a magyar civilisztikai jogalkotás a XXI. század elején?* (*Where Is the Private Law Legislation Go at the Beginning of the 21st Century*) (Mónika Csöndes & Zoltán Nemessányi eds, Pécsi Tudományegyetem Állam és Jogtudományi Kar 2010). *See also* Attila Harmathy, *A polgári jogi kodifikációról* (*About the Civil Law Codification*), in *Liber Amicorum, Studia L. Vékás dedicata* 325 ff. (András Kisfaludi ed., ELTE ÁJK Polgári Jogi Tanszék 2009). Lajos Vékás, *Az új Polgári Törvénykönyv tervezetének néhány elméleti és rendszertani előkérdéséről* (*About Some Theoretical and Systematic Preliminary Questions of the Draft of the New Civil Code*), in *Sárközy Tamás ünnepi kötet* (*Sárközy Tamás Festal Volume*) 263 ff. (Kinga Pázmándi ed., HVG-ORAC 2006). Particular fields of the new Civil Code are also presented in the volume, *Business Law in Hungary* (István Sándor ed., Patrocinium 2016).

Other than the Civil Code, there are numerous laws relating to civil law, e.g., bankruptcy law, company law, competition law, and consumer protection law.

C. Legislation in Decrees

22. The government can pass a decree in areas it is responsible for or based on permission given by law. Ministers may pass decrees in areas they are responsible for or based on permission given by law or in a government decree. A local government can pass a decree based on statutory authorization for the detailed regulation of their local area and resolve societal issues not governed by higher-level legislation.

So based on the above, other laws with private law content should be taken into account, in addition to the Civil Code, including decree laws still in force, government decrees, ministerial decrees (e.g., the recently repealed Decree No. 1/1965. (I. 24.) IM on Bills of Exchange) and local government decrees (neighbour rights).

D. Judicial Practice and the Curia

23. There is essentially no precedent law in Hungary, but judicial practice does still play a major role. Rulings ensuring uniformity are especially important as tribunals and courts must consider them when passing judgments.[23]

Based on the Hungarian Fundamental Law, the Curia ensures the law is applied uniformly and adopts uniformity rulings that are binding for tribunals and courts. Chapter III of Act LXVI of 1997 on the Organization and Administration of Courts states that the Curia can adopt a uniformity ruling in the context of a uniformity process, which aims to ensure uniform case law by courts and tribunals. A uniformity process is justified if a uniformity ruling is needed in a matter of principle to further legal practice or to ensure uniform case law or if one council of the Curia wants to deviate from a ruling of another council of the Curia in some legal issue.

Each decision in each individual case published in the Official Gazette of the Curia, i.e., the Collection of Court Decisions (BHGy),[24] took precedence from 1 April 2020. As a rule, judges must not only deviate from the findings made in the unity rulings but must also follow all the legal interpretations expressed in the curiosity decision published in the BHGy. With this, the individual Curia resolutions, previously published for the purpose of recommendation or information only, now amounting to thousands of legal disciplines, have become precedents.

Beyond uniformity rulings and precedents, we have collegial positions, principles, and decisions too. These are also meant to ensure uniformity in case law and in the courts' application of the law. After the new Civil Code entered into force, the Curia's uniformity ruling of 1/2014 revised its previous guidelines relating to substantive law and determined the ones that were still relevant.

---

23. According to the Hungarian judicial system *see* Sándor Udvary, *The Organization of the Administration of Justice*, in *Business Law* 50 ff. (István Sándor ed., Patrocinium 2016).

24. *See* https://birosag.hu/birosagi-hatarozatok-gyujtemenye and s. 346(3) of the Civil Procedure Code.

The courts apply the laws in the court cases and they interpret them, of course; therefore, the law is replaced by court decisions. Law in action means case law, which is comparable with written law or legal regulations.

E. Role of the Hungarian Constitutional Court

24. The role of the Hungarian Constitutional Court, which basically controls norms from the perspective of fundamental rights, should also be mentioned. Decrees of the Hungarian Constitutional Court can only annul certain laws, but this serves to further the law, with particular regard to the legal reasons given in the reasoning for its rulings.

Based on Act CLI of 2011 on the Hungarian Constitutional Court, it has the power to carry out proactive and retroactive norm controls. Proactive norm controls are an option for laws that have been approved but not yet promulgated, while retroactive norm controls can also be applied during specific judicial proceedings.

The presiding court is duty-bound to request the complete or partial annulment of anti-constitutional or anti-Fundamental Law actions in a retroactive motion if they detect that the law used in the given case contradicts the Fundamental Law. In this case, the presiding judge suspends the court proceedings and initiates a Hungarian Constitutional Court procedure, while any person who thinks the law being applied in the given case contradicts the Fundamental Law can move for judicial proceedings. If the Hungarian Constitutional Court determines that the law or any other legal tool of the state contradicts the Fundamental Law, the said law or other legal tool of the state must be partially or completely annulled. The annulment of law or other legal tool of the state does not affect legal relations established prior to the promulgation of the ruling or the rights and responsibilities derived therefrom.

Furthermore, anyone can turn to the Hungarian Constitutional Court with complaints of rights enshrined in the Fundamental Law being violated, who was wronged because of a regulation being applied that contradicts the Fundamental Law and who has exhausted all other legal remedies, or who does not have any other legal remedies at his/her disposal. When examining the constitutional law complaint, the Hungarian Constitutional Court may not only examine the consistency of the law applied in the individual court case with the Fundamental Law but also whether the actual court ruling adopted in the given case is consistent with Fundamental Law.

F. EU Law

25. Community law and EU law are also important to note. Section 8:1(2) of the Civil Code specifically declares that for the purposes of the new Civil Code, any directly applicable Community legislation that is binding in its entirety shall also be construed as part of the legal system.

Under EU law, Council regulations are directly applicable in the Member States (e.g., Regulation on European companies), so according to the Civil Code, they are to be considered civil law. In terms of directives, Member States have a harmonization obligation (e.g., consumer protection), while recommendations are left to the sovereign discretion of the Member States, so the Member States may decide whether to apply them or not. A decision determines a right or obligation for the addressee; it has no direct implications for the other Member States.

Legal acts of the EU are important with regard to the Hungarian legal system for two reasons. EU regulations are directly applicable in Hungarian law, while Hungarian legislators have a harmonization obligation with regard to directives. Accordingly, section 8:6 of the Civil Code lists the EU legislation that the Civil Code complies with. However, when creating laws, the legislators have an obligation to harmonize bills with EU institutions and the Member States.

G. *Other Legal Sources*

26. International agreements concluded by the Hungarian State are also considered legal sources if their content is applicable in civil law. Of course, international agreements become part of Hungarian law by being accepted as Hungarian legal regulations.

Tools governing public law organizations, normative decisions, and normative orders (previously referred to as other tools of the state) are not considered legal regulations. Tools governing public law organizations, e.g., are resolutions by the National Assembly, the government, local governments, and the President of the Central Statistical Office.

§3. Introduction to the Law of Property and Trust

I. Historical Origins and Evolution

27. Before 1848, private law was typically rank law, which made significant distinctions between nobility, urban citizens, and peasants. The pre-1848 property law was based on real property law, the tenure system. Municipal law is a separate, closed legal system; noble and peasant law were based on serfdom.

The three fundamental institutions of noble law were royal donations, aviticity, and serfdom.[25] The royal donation system was developed at the time of the Anjous; apart from original domiciles, all land belonged to the holy crown. Royal law *(jus regium)* governed the ownership of all real property (bona et jura possessionaria). There were royal rights only the king was entitled to (bona coronalia), and there were lands that the king gave to others for management and sovereign purposes. In reality, the country was split into noble lordships, which were donated by the king. Lands that were separate from cities or regions were under landlord control. Donations were made with a bill of donation to a defined group of individuals with male

25. On the concept of ownership in Hungary in the Middle Ages, *see also* András Téglási, *A tulajdonhoz való jog alkotmányos védelme* (*The Constitutional Protection of the Right to Ownership*) 56 ff. (Pólay Elemér Alapítvány 2013).

lineage inheritance; female lineage inheritance was the exception, promoting the last daughter to a son (praefectio). Once the circle of heirs died out (defectus seminis), the property was returned to the king (devolutio); the same thing happened in the event of crimes punishable by loss of property or with infidelity (nota infidelities) too. The property was returned (*bona fiscalia*) but had to be donated again.

Ancient assets could not be freely disposed of; only the things were personally gained. The men inherited first, and this was compensated for by the maiden quarter (quartillium, one-fourth of the value of an asset, if the girl did not marry a nobleman or landless noble, with her father's and siblings' consent) and maiden right (jus capillare, orphaned maidens received a house, maintenance, the chance to marry, and an endowment from her male siblings).

Serfdom meant the superiority of landowners over common people. Landowners received a manor in exchange for military service; other crown rights had to be handed over to the landowners for management. Maria Theresa's Urbarium, as well as Act IV of 1836, set forth the rules of serfdom. There were two categories in serfdom: the thralls (people with land, coloni, subditi), who lived off their own labour; and cotters who could be housed (inquilini) or unhoused (subquilini, renting). The thralls enjoyed usufruct over the landowner's property (cessio), peasant economy, roughly half a hectare of living space (house, garden), 8–20 hectares of arable land and 3–11 hectares of meadow land, the size of which changed by region, the right to graze, cut wood, cut reeds, pannage, distill fruit brandy, and open shops. A thrall property could be split into four; the smaller properties were then considered cotter properties. The landlord's duties included paying taxes in cash (tax per house, smoke tax, fruit brandy tax, shop tax) and taxes in kind (e.g., Lajos Nagy created the ninth hill tax for grapes). Furthermore, there was a 'robot' manual service, which meant one day's yoke work or two days' walking work. Further public taxes included the priest's tenth and other church taxes (e.g., parochial wage).

28. In principle, Act XV of 1848 abolished aviticity and the royal donation system. Act IX of 1848 stopped serf relationships with possible reimbursements for landowners. In the second half of the nineteenth century and the first half of the twentieth century, Hungarian property law transitioned between the feudal tenure system and equality of ownership.

29. The Hungarian property system was significantly impacted by the introduction of the socialist political system following the Second World War, which went hand-in-hand with the nationalization of private ownership. The socialist legal system notably transformed private law towards public law, and private law fields increasingly narrowed. This did not mean the complete end to private ownership, but it severely limited it.[26] There were three known forms of ownership: state ownership, cooperative ownership, and personal ownership. With regard to personal ownership, there were significant restrictions in terms of both size and composition.

26. István Szászy, *A Szovjetunió magánjogának alapelvei* (*Basic Principals of Private Law of the Soviet Union*) 17 ff. (Józsa Béla Athenaeum 1945).

Under the socialist political system in Hungary, private law was placed on the back burner from 1949 to 1989; the political changes occurring in the second half of the 1980s brought significant changes.

30. The regime change in 1989 made private ownership equal to public ownership on a constitutional level, and there was a political will – following numerous social and political debates – to compensate the victims of the Second World War as well as the socialist nationalizations and cooperatives. Based on the compensation laws, the ownership conditions prior to the Second World War were partially restored in the Hungarian economy. The other important factor in the reorganization of ownership was the dismantling of state ownership.

This process began with spontaneous privatization, though it is important to note that 'semi-privatisation' already existed in the 1980s, with contracted transactions in the Hungarian economy.[27] The ad hoc privatization that took place in the late 1980s was finally regulated by Act VII of 1990, which aimed to stop the 'wild west' approach to privatization.[28] From then on, privatization was allowed within the confines of Act LXXIV of 1990 (small privatization law) and the Transformation Act (Act XIII of 1989), under increasingly sophisticated organizational and procedural rules and privatization techniques (Acts LIII, LIV and LV of 1992 on Privatization and the 1995 privatization law).

The introduction of foreign capital played a large role in all of this, which ensured one of the most investor-friendly regulatory environments of all Central and Eastern European nations. The introduction of local government ownership played a large role in restructuring ownership rights based on Act LXV of 1990 and Act XXXIII of 1991 on the Transfer of Certain State-Owned Assets to Local Governments.

Compensation, privatization, and asset transfer laws created a radically different ownership situation in Hungary. Compensation laws helped to achieve the restoration of pre-Second World War conditions, while privatization laws helped to develop the new ownership structures. The laws that partly restored and partly reorganized the legal environment can be considered revolutionary since they achieved fundamental change in the country compared to either the pre-1949 or even the pre-1989 ownership structure.

II. The Concept of Ownership

A. *Unity and Fragmentation*

31. The law of things constitutes a significant portion of private law. The regulations found in this book of the Civil Code determine how to acquire an ownership right or possession over which assets. This book also regulates what rights the

27. Tamás Sárközy, *Rendszerváltás és a privatizáció joga* (*System Transition and the Law of Privatisation*) 195 (Közgazdasági és Jogi Kiadó 1997).
28. Ferenc Mádl, *Privatizáció Magyarországon. Az európai örökség útján* (*Privatisation in Hungary: On the Route of the European Heritage*) 347 (Athenaeum 1995).

owner or possessor has vis-à-vis the given property and what legal protection they have.[29] The law of things is part of property law, in which the rights and obligations of a legal subject in respect of a thing are governed in relation to other individuals. Ownership rights are an important part of private law and also the law of things; regardless, the Civil Code considers this under the law of things.

32. Acquiring ownership means: 'acquiring goods required for one's existence, keeping them under one's power and using them to satisfy human needs'.[30] Under this approach, property, therefore, belongs under material relations, and certain elements have legal ramifications.

33. Any person, both a natural person and a legal person, can be the subject of an ownership right. The right to own is universal, equal, and unconditional; an owner can even be a foetus (theoretically) or the state. The ownership right receives constitutional and private law protection as well.[31] Any contract or unilateral statement restricting ownership is null and void.

34. Absolute legal relations prevail in the field of the law of things; the subjects are persons, and the direct objects are the rights and responsibilities, while the indirect object is the thing. The unique aspect of absolute legal relations is that, in theory, they contain rights enforceable against everyone, as opposed to relative legal relations.

The classic categories of the law of things are rights over one's own property (ownership right) and rights over the property of someone else (limited in rem rights, *jura in re aliena*), which the Civil Code follows consistently.

35. Within private law, separate principles were devised owing to the unique regulation of the law of things. The closed number principle applies within the law of things, i.e., the in rem rights' *numerus clausus*, the standardization requirement of the law of things, according to which only the law can qualify something as having an absolute effect. Based on the principle of set content, the content of an individual in rem rights is set by law. In accordance with the absolute effect principle, the person in the authorized position is defined and may exercise this right vis-à-vis anyone. According to the principle of publicity, everyone is entitled to know the holder of the in rem right. The principle of uniqueness, the indirect object of the in rem right, can always only be one specific thing.

---

29. Three main commentaries of the new Hungarian Civil Code are the followings: *A Polgári Törvénykönyvről szóló 2013. évi V. törvény és a kapcsolódó jogszabályok nagykommentárja* (*The General Commentary of Act V of 2013: On the Civil Code and the Related Legal Provisions*) I–IV (András Osztovits ed., Opten 2014); *A Polgári Törvénykönyv magyarázatokkal* (*The Civil Code with Explanations*) I–II (Lajos Vékás and Péter Gárdos eds, Wolters Kluwer 2013); *Polgári jog – Az új Ptk. magyarázata* (*Civil Law – Explanation of the New Civil Code*) I–VI (György Wellmann ed., HVG-ORAC 2013).
30. Barnabás Lenkovics, *Tulajdonjog* (*Ownership Right*) 7 (Tankönyvkiadó 1991).
31. In connection with protection of the ownership in the practice of the Constitutional Court, *see* Téglási, *supra* 119 ff.

The absolute effect of the ownership produces a subjective right, the abstract legal expression of traditional private ownership and also property law relations. The direct object of the ownership right is found in human behaviour and everyone must respect the rights of the owner. The indirect object of the ownership right is the thing. 'The content of an ownership right can best be defined by the regulations giving the owner freedom, and the limitations of this freedom.'[32]

36. From another perspective, ownership rights are defined by the rights and obligations stemming from the ownership right relationship. Ownership rights comprise the right to possess, use, utilize, and collect proceeds, as well as the right of disposal. The right of disposal states that the owner is legally allowed to alienate or burden the thing, use it contrary to its designated purpose, and even destroy it. The rules of Roman law manifest themselves significantly in Hungarian private law through German and Austrian law. As a result, the concept of shared ownership rights derived from common law and equity, as known from Anglo-Saxon law, does not exist.

37. With regard to international trends, the new Civil Code introduces the institution of fiduciary asset management, which fulfils the trust function in Hungarian private law. Hungarian private law does not recognize split ownership; therefore, a thing can only be owned by one person. Of course, there is an opportunity for ownership rights to be allotted to multiple persons, i.e., for joint property to emerge. In the case of joint property, the joint owners are all allowed to exercise their ownership rights, but only in proportion to their ownership.

38. Special attention must be paid to the public law limitations on ownership rights, which manifests as the legal subject's responsibility towards the public. This is demarcated by just about every constitution, but there is no doubt that ownership rights, as the most important subjective private right, have been steadily narrowed by state constraints. Furthermore, there are substantial private law limitations too, manifesting mostly in neighbour rights. The French and Belgian Civil Codes consider neighbour rights a sort of easement, which owners create over their real property voluntarily. Conversely, the German and Swiss laws do not treat this as an easement but have developed it as part of ownership rights. By comparison, when we speak of tolerance on the part of the owner relating to an encumbrance on their own property, where the owner establishes a limitation not of their own free will but not as a limitation defined a priori either, this is an intermediary system. The implicit limitations of ownership rights are also manifested when the law forbids or at least does not condone improper use of ownership rights. The BGB specifically

32. Attila Menyhárd, *Dologi jog* (*Law of Things*) 142 (Elte Eötvös Kiadó 2010).

states that a right may not be exercised if its purpose is merely to harm other persons.[33] The ZGB further states that everyone is compelled to exercise their rights in good faith and that the law does not support improper legal practice.[34]

The legislative question relating to the public law limitation of ownership drew attention to how assets, plena potestas, and ownership right limitations are regulated at the level of concept and ownership right content. According to Winscheid's pandect law definition: 'Das Eigentum ist als solches schrankenlos, aber es verträgt Beschränkungen.'[35] By borrowing from Swiss and German literature, we find that Peter Liver arrived at unlimited ownership and complete personal rule over a thing based on the concept, not the content.[36] The owner has the right to use the thing and dispose of it based on the statutory limitations, and this also belongs to the content of ownership rights. This formal/abstract definition of ownership right prevailed for a long time and led Arthur Meier-Hayoz to the conclusion in the 1966 Berner Kommentar[37] that the concept of ownership was immanent due to its inherent limitability and not the numerous individual limitations.[38] With this, he reworked the immanence concept of forty years earlier by Robert Haab and Erwin Ruck, according to which obligations, which burden the owner through neighbour rights and public law, are conceptually immanent. Consequently, the content of ownership and its limitations are part of its concept. Liver found fault with the immanence theory from a formal/logical perspective, since, according to his interpretation, the concept of ownership includes use, possession, and freedom of disposal but not the denial thereof, so limitations are not part of the concept of ownership.

In the eighteenth century, civil codes tried to define the limitations of ownership by providing lists of limitations for individual things. In the nineteenth century, comparably abstract and vague definitions were given for the limits of ownership rights, essentially planting a Renaissance sfumato painting technique in the field of legal regulation.[39] ZGB mentioned abusing property rights; the Italian Codice civile discussed the limitations supported by law.[40] The Dutch Civil Code of 1992 uses limitation terminology based on unwritten law.[41] Accordingly, ownership rights – and property rights too – are only definable by thoroughly examining the entire legal system.[42] This is why, with a slight exaggeration, almost all public administration

33. *'Die Ausübung eines Rechtes ist unzulässig, wenn sie nur den Zweck haben kann, einem anderen Schaden zuzufügen'*. BGB, Art. 226. *See also* Jürgen F. Baur & Rolf Sturner, *Sachenrecht* 268 ff. (Beck 1999[17]); Hans Josef Wieling, *Sachenrecht* 81 ff. (Springer 1997[3]).
34. *'Jedermann hat in der Ausübung seiner Rechte und in der Erfüllung seiner Pflichten nach Treu und Glauben zu handeln. Der offenbare Missbrauch eines Rechtes findet keinen Rechtsschutz'*. ZGB, Art. 2.
35. Bernhard Windscheid & Theodor Kipp, *Lehrbuch des Pandektenrechts* 857 (Frankfurt a. M. 1906[9]).
36. Heinz Rey, *Dynamisiertes Eigentum*, 96 Zeitschrift für Schweizerisches Recht 65 (1977).
37. Berner Kommentar, *Kommentar zum schweizerischen Privatrecht* IV/1 (Arthur Meier-Hayoz ed., Schultess 1966).
38. Rey, *supra*, 66.
39. Antonio Gambaro, *Perspectives on the Codification of the Law of Property: An Overview*, 4 European Review of Private Law 499 (1997).
40. Codice civile, Art. 832.
41. Dutch Civil Code of 1992, Art. 5.11-2.
42. 'Property rights themselves are none other than a set of limitations, and these limitations are to be found throughout the whole complex of the legal system, and it is better to leave them just where they are, with all their variety and flexibility intact.' Gambaro, *supra*, 500.

law is part of civil law, or at least separating the two is difficult.[43] From a different approach, we also see that ownership limitations emerge not only in tolerance but also in positive performance obligations. These obligations – e.g., construction requirements for properties – prescribe *eo ipso* action obligations. However, if we move on to another step, Sontis drew the conclusion that ownership can be considered a legal relationship.[44]

In short, we find that unlimited static ownership rights without content must be strictly separated from dynamic ownership handling limitations immanently. From Rey's thought processes, we can conclude that the choice of definition already defines whether the legislator asserts a dynamic or static concept of ownership rights because if we choose ownership rights with itemized limitations or even performance obligations, then it will be dynamic and prevent the legislator from exercising greater influence over the property.[45] The main limitations of ownership rights can be split into two parts: private law limitations and public law limitations.

39. Private law limitations include neighbour rights (e.g., neighbour's excavations, fruit fallen from an overhanging branch, public utility works, keeping animals, maintaining a fence, animals on private property), encroachment and the restraint on alienation and encumbrance. Public law limitations include limitations on acquiring ownership, restrictions on use and utilization, right of disposal limitations and expropriation.

B. *Immovable and Real Property (See Also* Part I)

40. Everything that can be possessed can be the subject of an ownership right. Consequently, anything that can be the subject of an ownership right is a thing, and the basic legal relationship under the law of things is an ownership relation. The thing, as the subject of the ownership right, has two qualities: one, that it is a physical object, and two, that the object can be possessed; it follows that intangible property, such as rights (e.g., ownership rights, liens), claims, and contractual positions are not things because these are neither physical objects nor can they be possessed, so they cannot be subjects of ownership rights. This does not mean that the holder of the intangible property is not protected from others or that this property cannot be transferred because they are not subjects of ownership rights. Both protection and transferability come under the law of obligations to some extent, as well as private law provisions; for example, with regard to claims or contractual positions, assignment, contract amendments, and transferring holdings in business organizations, corporate law provisions apply, while individual rules pertain to the portfolios of insurance companies, credit institutions, and investment service providers.

---

43. '[T]he whole government system – financial, military, judicial – is part of the law of private property.' Frederick William Maitland, *The Constitutional History of England* 23 (Cambridge Univ. Press 1908[1]).
44. Rey, *supra*, 69.
45. Rey, *supra*, 71.

The difference between things and intangible properties eligible for sale is that while transferring the ownership of a thing requires handing over possession of the thing or changing the rights to them in the relevant registry, transferring ownership of intangible property that is eligible for sale does not require the taking of possession as they cannot be possessed.

The Civil Code does not define the concept of a thing; it merely contains limitations, according to which something capable of being possessed must be a physical object. Whether something can be possessed is not a legal but a physical property in that the object can be spatially defined. However, spatial presence is only one of the conditions for possession because there are spatial objects which, according to current science, cannot be possessed, though they are spatial things according to their physical properties. Such are, e.g., the nitrogen and methane surrounding the largest moon of the planet Saturn, Titan, or the hydrocarbon fields that cover its surface, so currently, these cannot even be considered things. From the perspective of spatial limitation and the ability to take possession, things may be solid, liquid, or gas in form. Gas and liquid things can be considered things if they are spatially limited because only then can they be possessed – e.g., ocean water confined to an aquarium can be possessed and is considered a thing, sleeping gas can be possessed in a cylinder and considered a thing, just like liquid oxygen can.

41. The difference between real property and movable property is significant in many private law cases. Real property is considered to be the surface of the earth and whatever is permanently attached to it. Real property can only be partially linked to natural properties; from a legal perspective, what matters is how it is designated in the land registry. By oversimplifying, we can state that all independent properties in the land registry can be considered real property.

Furthermore, the components of real property are also considered real property and share the same legal fate. The physical connection of a building to the ground does not determine whether it is real property or movable property, e.g., a pavilion on public land – despite its mechanical connection to the ground – maintains its movable property status. If the ownership right of the building matches that of the land, the building cannot be transferred without the land. The ownership right to a building (structure) may be transferred validly by itself if it previously constituted a separate land registry unit in the land registry; it is separately registered; for lack of this, the land and the building (structure) form a unit.[46]

C. *Movable and Personal Property (See Also* Part II)

42. Immovable property is everything that is not real property and is not permanently connected to the ground. From a law of things perspective, the definition of movable property does not depend on the size, weight, movability, value or other properties. Anything which can be possessed and is not real property is considered movable property.

46. BDT 2004/1054; BDT 2007/1597.

43. The Civil Code goes further and specifies that a physical object cannot be considered a thing if it cannot be owned. For example, the human body, since a person is a legal subject and not a legal object. A person's body can be physically possessed, but it does not qualify as an object, and thus, there can be no ownership right on it. Furthermore, the various obligation rights (e.g., usufruct, liens.), claims (e.g., demands based on money or securities), and holdings in business organizations (e.g., business shares) cannot be considered things.

III. Estate and Patrimony

A. *Unity and Fragmentation*

44. Ownership rights can be clearly distinguished from the estate (Vermögen, patrimoine, patrimonium), the latter extending beyond ownership rights and even the law of things to also include the law of obligation rights and responsibilities.

European continental law does not apply the concept of estate as often as Anglo-Saxon common law, but it still plays an important role at times, e.g., in relation to general estate and separated estate (Sondervermögen, Patrimoine distinct ou autonome). The general estate of a legal subject is the sum of their rights and obligations, which, depending on the proportions of the two, can be either active or passive estates. The issue of separated sub-estates emerges, e.g., in fiduciary asset management, where asset managers are obliged to separate managed estates entirely from their own assets.

Ownership rights and contracts are the foundation of financial life and one of the most important benchmarks for the social structure of a state from a legal perspective, seeing how these regulations develop, including state recognition and protection. The most important component of the concept of an estate is ownership. The indirect object of ownership is the thing, which primarily means tangible objects and, in certain cases, intangible things too. By contrast, estates are the sum of the estate law rights and obligations a person has. Thus, estates also include the law of obligation rights, over and above rights to things.

B. *Trust and Fiduciary Mechanisms (See Also* Parts IV and V)

45. The duality of common law and equity is not manifested in Hungarian private law; therefore, split ownership rights do not exist. The institution of trusts in Anglo-Saxon law is not recognized, but the Civil Code introduced fiduciary asset management contracts, which, functionally, are very similar to the institution of trusts.

Hungarian trusts also include regulations from Anglo-Saxon trusts, such as the separation of the managed estate from the assets of the settlor, the trustee, and the beneficiary, as well as the recognition of the trustee as an office. The possibility of tracing also applies if a third party gains from the trust assets for free or in bad faith.

IV. Possession and Title

46. Ownership rights must be kept sharply distinct from possession. Ownership rights ensure complete power over a thing and have a legal impact, mainly through the protection of possession. The possession and the possessor are primarily a question of fact. We consider the possessor to be the entity that has physical power and rule over the thing.

The Civil Code defines possession from the legal situation of the possessor, considers it a subjective right, and separates the identities of the main possessor and sub possessor. Physical rule over a thing must be defined based on common sense. This can mean physical contact (e.g., in someone's hand or pocket), but it can also be expressed in a manner that the possessor holds the tool necessary for physical possession of the thing in their hands (e.g., a person holding the key to a locked flat, in which the thing is located).

The legal grounds for possession of a thing express the fact that the person actually holding the thing has permission from its owner or based on other legal means to have that thing (e.g., someone rents something from the owner or the tenant places the rented object as collateral, or someone finding something keeps it as per the law). By contrast, a wrongful possessor is someone who has no legal ground for possession.

47. The Civil Code regulates the following cases of possession, based on the previously mentioned definitions of possession.

A possessor is someone who keeps the thing as his or her own. In this case, two conditions have to be fulfilled. The possessor must have the ownership right, or at least the possession must be considered final and exclusive. Furthermore, they must have actual physical rule over the thing.[47] The intent to own, keeping the thing as one's own, is partly a subjective element, signifying the possessor's mental state towards possession. In this respect, it is important to consider whether, given the care generally expected in the given situation, they knew or should have known that they did not have the right to possess the thing. With regard to this last condition, the title and grounds for the possession must be examined.

Actual physical power is an objective condition; it expresses to the outside world that the thing is under the rule of the possessor. That said, this latter condition does not have to prevail constantly in the case of the main possessor; giving someone else (secondary possessor) the right to possess it does not change the possessor's position. A possessor is also someone who keeps the thing based on his legal right to do so. In this case, the possessor does not keep the thing as his own, but he must have the legal title for possession. If someone genuinely keeps physical power over the thing without the right to do so, they qualify as a wrongful possessor.

The difference between a possessor and a secondary possessor relates to the legal title to the possession of the thing and is evaluated only in the context of the legal relationship between them. According to the explanation above, the possessor has appropriate legal grounds for possession, even if the thing is not under his direct rule. By contrast, the secondary possessor can keep the thing under his physical rule,

47. Vékás, *Szakértői supra*, 587.

but the right to possession stems from the main possessor. Unlike the internal legal relationship between possessors, all possessors are considered possessors in the eyes of third parties.

Legal grounds for possession are significant in this respect if the person with the legal right to possession and the person actually having physical power over the thing disagree on who has more of a right to possession. In this case, the legal grounds and not the actual possession are used to determine the individual rights.

48. Acquiring possession can happen through one's own actions or by transferring to another's possession. Gaining possession of a previously unpossessed thing happens through actual physical power, for which the cooperation (handover) and willing transfer of a third party are not needed. Taking possession of lost or otherwise unpossessed things, therefore, depends entirely on the person wishing to gain possession. The case differs when possession is gained from someone by transfer of the thing by the new possessor. Besides gaining possession through individual legal acts, this can also be done by transferring the thing.

There are two legal conditions for transferring possession. There must be an agreement on the transfer of possession between the transferor and the person acquiring possession. The rules on the creation and validity of the contracts must be applied correctly to the agreement. Apart from the agreement, the actual transfer of power over the thing is necessary too. This is a broader category than simply handing over the thing and can occur in different forms.

The Roman law cases of *brevi manu traditio* and *constitutum possessorium* are regulated in the Civil Code by stating that agreement between the parties is sufficient to transfer possession if the person acquiring possession is already a secondary possessor of the thing (*brevi manu traditio*) and the transferor maintains possession as the secondary possessor of the thing (*consitutum possessorium*). Since both the possessor and secondary possessor are considered possessors, we believe there is no actual transfer of possession in the scenario described above, only a change in the legal title of the possession, which is effective only in the internal relationship between the possessor and the secondary possessor. The corporal element is also missing when the transfer of possession takes place with a simple agreement and the relinquishing of power over the thing by the transferor. This complies with *longa manu traditio* from Roman law. The legal situation is similar if the transfer of possession takes place upon the transfer of a claim for recovery of the thing, for which agreement between the parties is sufficient (*cessio vindicationis*). In this case, it is not the possession but the possession claim that is transferred; however, based on the regulatory logic of the Civil Code, this is also considered a transfer of possession because someone who does not have physical power over the thing but is otherwise entitled to possession qualifies as a possessor.

49. Legislators use several areas of law in cases where possession ceases to exist. The possession of the thing can cease with and without legal succession. In this case, if the possessor has an appropriate legal title to possession (e.g., ownership right, lien, deposit, rent), the cessation of physical power over the thing does not equate to the loss of title to possession. If the previous possessor subsequently finds the thing, he may lay claim to have the original possession reinstated. Without a legal successor, possession ceases when possession of the thing is definitively relinquished (possession derelictio). In this case, as opposed to a loss, the possessor's intent to possess ceases, i.e., they willingly cease the state of possession. Willing cessation of possession can occur with the intent of keeping the legal title related to the thing and only wanting to temporarily cease direct physical power over it. This is what happens in so many different and common cases (e.g., someone puts their bike down in front of the shop while they go inside). When relinquishing possession of the thing, it can be determined based on the possessor's intent and expression whether this is temporary or permanent. A typical example of this from Roman law is when the cargo of a ship caught in a storm is thrown overboard. After the storm passes, they naturally intend to collect the cargo. Resolving this situation is helped by the rule whereby possession is not lost simply by the possessor being temporarily unable to exercise power over it.

Possession is lost with legal succession if possession of the thing is transferred. Possession is equally lost with legal succession in the event of the possessor's death, or if it terminates without succession, possession would be due to the legal successor. Please note that besides the aforementioned reasons, possession can cease due to its subject or object as well.

Possession ceases due to its subject if the possessor dies. In this case, the possessor's successor gains the right of possession. Possession also ceases if the thing possessed is destroyed. Of course, possession of the thing's surrogates – if any – remains.

Part I. Immovable Property and Real Property

Chapter 1. General Classification

50. Real property is considered to be land as well as everything permanently associated with it. The Civil Code contains uniform rules on ownership rights for both real property and movable property; only with the detailed rules do we encounter some differences. In terms of land registries, we are familiar with the further breakdown for real properties: land parcel (e.g., an unbroken area of the earth's surface that is not interrupted by an administrative or inner-urban border) and other independent properties (e.g., building, cellar, underground garage, and other structures, etc.).

§1. The Extension of the Ownership

51. The principle of the 'unrestricted nature' of ownership rights prevails only with severe constraints in modern legal systems, which is why boundaries must be set both upwards and downwards in the case of real property. Thus, the rule of 'cuius est solum, eius est usque ad coelum et usque ad inferos' is no longer applicable under today's conditions. The Civil Code does not set a lower limit for real property, but there is one restriction in that the ownership of the land shall not extend to the treasures of the earth, nor does it extend to natural resources. The legal fates of land ownership as well as the 'treasures' and 'natural resources' found in the earth and only determined in general can differ. The Civil Code does not define treasures of the earth and natural resources; this is entrusted to legal practice. It is generally accepted that this includes subterranean waters, mineral materials, gases, and radioactive materials.

Legal literature offers three different theories in this respect:

(1) The so-called cone (or pyramid) ownership theory, according to which the real property ownership right extends down to the centre of the earth, narrowing from the borders of the land, while above the earth, in a similar fashion, it broadens out from the borders of the land to infinity.
(2) According to the so-called interest theory, the vertical borders of the property are linked to the use of the property or extend for as long as is justified by the

economic use of the property (this was the approach of the 1928 Hungarian Private Law Bill, and is currently followed by the Swiss ZGB).

(3) Under the third theory, the real property ownership right only covers the surface of the earth; the owner of the property does not own the parts above and below the earth's surface, only the right (privilege) to use them.[48]

In countries with civil law systems similar to Hungary's, it is likewise the interest theory and versions thereof that primarily apply. The German BGB treats the space above and below the ground as part of the real property ownership right but states that the owner may not prohibit influences that are exercised at such a height or depth that he has no interest in excluding them.[49] By contrast, the Austrian ABGB enables the owner to prohibit influences both above and below the ground as the owner physically uses the property.[50] Similarly, the Swiss ZGB draws the borders for property ownership above and below the ground in accordance with the land owner's legitimate interest in using the property. The owner's interests are defined by whether he can exercise his rights over the given space.[51]

The current Hungarian Civil Code does not specify the vertical extension of real property in detail. It is generally accepted in legal literature that the owner of the real property must tolerate influences on the property if they are at such a height or depth that they do not disturb the proper use of the property.[52]

I. The Relevance of the Land Registry

52. For land, the land registry provides some guidance, and the rules are set forth in the Civil Code and also in the relevant other laws.[53]

The basic elements of the land registry are the title deed, the map, and the archive. In the land registry, the data on the real property, the rights, and legally significant facts associated with the real property, as well as the beneficiaries and their data, must be entered on, recorded, or transferred to the title deed. Title deeds are numbered in sequence, starting from one and separately for each municipality. Alongside the number of the title deed, every title deed must also contain the name of the municipality. In the computer system for the land registry, the number of a property's title deed is the same as the topographical lot number or the unique identifier of the real property. The rules for determining the topographical lot numbers for real properties are set forth by the relevant minister in a decree. In view of the special

48. Menyhárd, *supra*, 71 ff.
49. BGB, Art. 905.
50. ABGB, Art. 297. *See also* Helmut Koziol & Rudolf Weber, *Grundriss des bürgerlichen Rechts* 251 ff. (Manz 2002).
51. ZGB, Art. 667; Menyhárd, *supra*, 72.
52. *See* Menyhárd, *supra*, 72. *A Polgári Törvénykönyv magyarázata* (*Explanation of the Civil Code*) 328 (György Gellér ed., Közgazdasági és Jogi Kiadó 2001); Ferenc Petrik, *Tulajdonjogunk ma* (*Our Ownership Right Today*) 83 (HVG-ORAC 2007).
53. Act CXLI of 1997 on the Land Registry (Inytv.), and Decree 109/1999. (XII. 29.) of the Ministry of Agriculture and Rural Development implementing Act CXLI of 1997 on Real Estate Registration (Inyvhr.).

registration needs of certain properties, the title deed for such properties may be kept in two integral sections, consisting of a primary title page and an auxiliary title page.

The purpose of the title deed is to record the data on the real property, the rights, and legally significant facts associated with the real property, as well as the beneficiaries and their data. This is information that is available to anyone.

53. The written form is a key criterion of the land registry. Recording a right or a legally significant fact in the land registry may only take place based on a written document or using a court or other official resolution. Rights may only be registered in the land registry based on documents specified by law, which means a public document, a private deed representing conclusive evidence, or copies of such witnessed by a notary public.

54. Alongside the registration principle – and this is why registration is so important from a law of things perspective – Hungarian law also has the *nemo plus iuris* principle because, e.g., in the case of a registered usufruct, it is clear to a third party that the real property may only be sold with the usufruct.[54] The essence of the land registry as a public register is that if the land registry contains some fact or right, nobody can say that they were not aware of such facts or rights. Of course, this does not simply apply to the land registry but also to the company registry as a public record.

55. The authenticity principle applies to margin notes and provisionally registered claims too, which is essentially for preventative purposes to avoid someone being able to say, after ignoring a margin note, that such does not need to be taken into consideration.

56. The constitutive rule means that the right of the person registered definitely precedes the person who perhaps has a right to the property, but it has not been registered. On the basis of rights registered and facts recorded in the real estate register, it is to be presumed that such registered rights and recorded facts pertain to the holder thereof until proven otherwise. A party acquiring a right outside the land registry may not request that its ownership right be recorded in the land registry if, after acquiring ownership, the ownership right of another person acting in good faith was registered in the land registry or if their application for the registration of their ownership right precedes the former in the ranking.[55]

57. The authenticity comes with a burden of proof: anyone contradicting the authentic data in the land registry must provide evidence they are right. The authenticity concept is consistent with the protection effect of the land registry: A person

---

54. In connection with the principles of the land registry, *see* György Kampis, *Telekkönyvi jog* (*Law of Cadastre*) 72 ff. (Közgazdasági és Jogi Kiadó 1963); Ferenc Petrik, *Ingatlan-nyilvántartás, Kommentár a gyakorlat számára* (*Land Registry, Commentary for the Practice*) 35 ff. (HVG-ORAC 2015).
55. BDT 2008/1920.

holding some right under substantive law or who is expected to obtain some right upon the cancellation of an entry may bring a cancellation. This action can be initiated against a third party who acquired a right in good faith[56] for a consideration and based on an unlawful entry or an entry that subsequently became incorrect, relying on the completeness and the probity of such entry, within six months from the date of delivery of the resolution on the originally invalid entry. If the delivery did not take place, the action for cancellation may be brought within a period of three years from the effective date of the entry. These deadlines are preclusive, i.e., they do not lapse.

58. The Civil Code connects the authenticity of the land registry with the requirement of good faith, which is still a basic principle of the Civil Code. In exercising rights and in fulfilling obligations, the requirements of good faith and fairness must be observed. This requirement is considered breached if a party's exercise of rights is contradictory to his previous actions, which the other party had reason to rely on. Good faith and fairness can be approached in two ways: as an external limitation of subjective rights and as a self-limitation of subjective rights. Thus, good faith and fairness imply a prohibition of the unlimited exercising of subjective rights, and in this respect, overlap with the rules on the prohibition of abusing rights. The requirement of good faith and fairness is also a standard in cases where the law does not specifically determine how to behave in a given situation. The concepts of good faith and fairness cannot be separated from one another, and so in both cases referred to above, the habits of those dealing fairly must be taken as the benchmark. This is manifested in the obligation to tell the truth. According to the general rule, the existence of good faith shall be examined at the time when the application to register the acquisition of a right in the land registry is submitted. If an agreement to change a right is concluded after the effective date of registration, then to determine whether good faith prevails, the conclusion date of the agreement must be examined. If the party acquiring the right is aware that the actual situation differs from that registered in the land registry, this results in the loss of good faith.

The law does not define the concept of bad faith; according to judicial practice based on general belief, bad faith is when someone knows of the existence of a right not registered in the land registry or fails to become aware of it because they did not take the necessary care. In this respect, there needs to be a separate examination and evidence provided from case to case in order to determine what 'necessary care' is.[57]

59. The principle of completeness is very similar in nature to the basic principle of authenticity, and the essence is that the land registry contains complete information. Namely, if there is a registered fact or right in the land registry, it must be assumed that the beneficiary is entitled to such until proven otherwise.

According to the registration principle, rights are created when recorded in the land registry. For a constitutive entry, two conditions must be met: registration in

56. In connection with good faith in the Hungarian private law, *see* András Földi, *A jóhiszeműség és tisztesség elve* (*The Principle of Good Faith and Honesty*) 91 ff. (ELTE ÁJK 2001).
57. BH 2000/159.

the land registry may be carried out if the grounds for change are verified and the registered holder of the changed right consented; a right may be deleted with the holder's consent. First of all, there needs to be a suitable legal title on which to make the registration. If we are talking about registering ownership, e.g., then this could be a sale/purchase, a gift or an exchange. According to standard court practice, the document underlying the registration must clearly show these legal titles. The other important formal condition is the explicit consent of the registered beneficiary. This must also be evident from the document underlying the registration. In the case of a property sales contract, it is possible that we find the approving consent to the registration of the ownership right transfer in the contract itself. This generally happens when the contract is also performed upon being signed, i.e., the customer pays the purchase price in one lump sum. In many cases, though, the payment is deferred, even using a bank loan. In such cases, one of the most important forms of security for the vendor is only transferring the ownership right when the purchase price has been paid in full. This constitutes separate registration consent when the approval of the registration is not included in the contract but in a separate document (It is another issue altogether that the registration consent in practice is often signed at the same time as the contract – in a separate document – but this document is retained by the lawyer drafting it until the full purchase price is paid.)

60. It is also important to distinguish between the concepts of ranking and hierarchy: Ranking is mainly a substantive law concept, whereas hierarchy stems from procedural law. Ranking means that in the event of entries that preclude each other, the later entry is effective, while in the case of registering related rights, the right in the earlier hierarchy precedes that in the later one. The hierarchy concept is defined in the Act CXLI of 1997 on the Land Registry (Inytv.), according to which the ranking of an entry in the land registry and thus the hierarchy of the entries is determined by the filing date of the registration application. A ranking may be established solely on the basis of an application for which a document serving as grounds for the registration has been attached.

II. Totality of Things

61. Here, it is worthwhile touching upon the totality of things too. The simple object category suggests that the given thing forms a unit based on its nature, such as a tree, a bush, a cane, etc. A complex thing is made from several different things that originally formed individual units, e.g., a table, which is made from wood, nails, and glue. Complex things are significant in the event of commixtures when public opinion treats certain independent things under a common name, for example, a flock, herd, or library. In these cases, the things belonging to the totality of things maintain their independence, but applying this concept in a legal transaction makes it easier to dispose of all the things in the totality of things. By totality of things, we mean objects that are not constituent parts of each other and instead have only a functional connection (i.e., physically separable but representing a whole unit in economic circulation). One example of a totality of things is a factory with the associated properties, buildings, equipment, and machinery, etc.[58] However, the objects that are part of the totality of things do not form an ownership unit; they are still separate parts of the ownership right even if the owner has them at his disposal at the same time. Consequently, the totality of things does not mean that individual items of the movable property need to be reclassified as immovable.

58. 2/2009 PK (Supreme Court's Civil Collegium) opinion, point 9.

Chapter 2. Legal Interests

62. It is commonplace and generally accepted in everyday life if someone keeps with them a thing that they own, i.e., the ownership right and the actual physical rule over the thing coincide. The supreme right over a thing is the ownership right; it follows that the owner is also due the right of possession over the thing. From another perspective, the owner's right of possession has to take priority over the rights of all others. Consequently, the owner has the right to protect possession.

In this case, if the thing is not possessed by the owner, then in terms of the owner's right to protect possession, we have to examine whether the possessor is legally entitled to possess the thing, which enables us to decide who is entitled to the right of protection of possession. While Anglo-Saxon law speaks of a bunch or bundle of rights to a thing, according to the understanding based on Roman law traditions, if there is a right to a thing, this is an ownership right, which comprises certain partial rights. There may only be one ownership right for one thing, while the owner is entitled to transfer partial rights to others. Ownership rights can be contrasted with rights over the property of someone else, which demonstrate the individual sub-rights of ownership. It should be noted that the special rules on state property are found in different laws.

63. The laws apply the terminology for national assets and state assets in respect of state property.[59] Unless otherwise provided for by law, the ownership rights and obligations of the Hungarian State regarding national assets are exercised and discharged by the minister responsible for the supervision of state assets; these duties are carried out via the Hungarian National Asset Management Inc. (Magyar Nemzeti Vagyonkezelő Zártkörűen Működő Részvénytársaság (MNV Zrt.)), the Hungarian Development Bank and the organization exercising the ownership rights.[60]

§1. Rights of the Owner

64. The owner has the right to use, possess, and profit from the thing and enjoys a right of disposition over it. Additionally, the owner enjoys in rem property protection based on his legal title.[61]

65. The owner is entitled to use the thing. This is important for two reasons. First, in the vast majority of cases, an owner generally intends to use a thing in his own interest and for himself after acquiring the ownership right. The ownership right is the highest legal title for using a thing. From a different perspective, the

59. Act CXCVI of 2011 on National Assets governs the basic rules for national assets. The rules of Act CXCVI of 2011 also cover the exercising of ownership rights over assets owned by the Hungarian State (national assets) and the related organizational framework, as well as the management of such assets.
60. This is all provided for by Act CVI of 2007 on State Assets.
61. According to the ownership rights, *see* Menyhárd, *supra*, 173 ff.; Ferenc Fábián, *Előadásvázlatok a dologi jog köréből* (*Lecture Notes on the Law of Things*) 34 ff. (Patrocinium 2015).

owner may decide whether someone else can exercise the right of use or whether to exclude others from using the thing, which falls under the right of disposition.

66. Alongside using the thing, the owner is entitled to reap the benefits of it. The right to reap the benefits (fruits), which is dealt with separately in the dogmatics of Roman law (*jus utendi, jus fruendi*), states that the owner is entitled to the accretions and yields of the thing too. The benefits may arise in a natural way, from the nature of the thing, which using Roman law terminology is referred to as natural fruits (*fructus naturales*) (e.g., the nuts on a walnut tree). Benefits may also be derived from the utilization of the thing, which we call civil fruits (*fructus civiles*) (e.g., renting out a tractor). In this latter case, we not only reap the benefits but also utilize (profit from) the thing, which is permitted by the Civil Code under the right of disposition.

67. The owner must bear the cost of damage to the thing if others cannot be obliged to do so. The Civil Code is based on the Roman law principles of *casum sentit dominus* or its equivalent *casus nocet domino*. The owner can demand compensation from others for damage to the thing based on contractual and non-contractual damage liability and indemnification rules, while contracts may also shift the damage onto others.

68. What really differentiates an ownership right from rights over the property of someone else is the right of disposition. The owner has the right to surrender the possession, use, or beneficial enjoyment of a thing to another person, to pledge it as collateral or encumber it in another way, and, furthermore, to transfer or abandon ownership.[62] Based on the classic content of a right of disposition, the owner may transfer the thing to other people, and in the event of death, he may encumber the thing – establish a right over the property of someone else – and may use it in a way other than for its original purpose, which can also result in the destruction of the thing.

The owner's right of disposition crops up in four typical ways: ceding the exercise of certain rights, transferring the ownership right, establishing a right over the property of someone else, and abandoning the ownership right over the thing. With the latter, the owner is legally entitled to use the thing other than for its original purpose or even to destroy the thing and give someone else permission to do so. It should be noted, however, that ownership rights over property may not be abandoned, i.e., ownership rights over property may only be terminated by transfer.

When looking at rights of disposition with regard to ownership, we must distinguish between the categories of eligible and not eligible for sale. Eligible for sale is the legal category affecting the thing's transferability and, in certain cases, its use or earning from it.

Owners of things eligible for sale (*res in commercio*) are free to dispose of them. By contrast, the law limits the owner's right of disposition over things that are not eligible for sale (*res extra commercium*). Such restrictions are included in public law

62. According to s. 5:30(1) of the Civil Code.

rules (e.g., for assets owned exclusively by states or local governments), but transactions between legal persons may also specify this, with restraint on alienation and encumbrance, for instance. Under Hungarian law, things not eligible for sale principally include public things, which may only be transferred based on defined conditions, primarily with an act of public law. For lack of such an act, the transaction to transfer the ownership of the thing not eligible for sale is null and void.

Restraint on alienation and encumbrance can limit a right of disposition. Exercising a right of disposition may also not be abusive. For example, an owner may not enter into a fraudulent contract by making reference to his right of disposition.[63]

§2. Protection of Ownership Rights

69. In Article V, under the title 'Freedom and responsibility' of the Fundamental Law, it is stated that everyone shall have the right to repel any unlawful attack against his or her person and/or property or one that poses a direct threat to the same.[64] Article XIII states that property may only be expropriated exceptionally, in the public interest and in the cases and ways provided for by an Act, subject to full, unconditional, and immediate indemnification.

70. An ownership right is an absolute right, i.e., an owner may take action against others and receive protection in order to protect his rights. However, we also have to take into account that the owner's claim derived from a violation of his ownership right may be enforced against the person violating the property.

Ownership claims may be enforced against the perpetrator. Ownership claims still do not lapse based on the Civil Code; they do not cease to exist over time. From another perspective, the possibility of adverse possession does limit this rule to a certain extent. The protection of ownership rights means the owner may demand the termination of illegal intrusions or influences and demand the surrender of the thing from the wrongful possessor. If the secondary possessor unlawfully ceded possession of the thing to a third party, the owner shall be entitled to demand, in the name of the secondary possessor, that the third party return the thing to the secondary possessor. If the secondary possessor refuses to receive the thing, the owner shall be entitled to demand the surrender of the thing to himself.

As regards the owner's request for having the thing surrendered, where the owner acquired ownership without an effective transfer by way of assigning a claim for the thing, the possessor of the thing shall be entitled to all the objections he would have been entitled to against the claim of the owner for having the thing surrendered. Pursuant to the rules on the protection of possession, the owner may arbitrarily restrain or prevent any and all illegal intrusion or influence that impedes, restricts, or renders impossible the exercise of his ownership rights. The protection of ownership rights is ensured by arbitrary action, protection designed to prevent illegal intrusion, ownership legal actions to reclaim possession of thing and land registry

63. BH 2003/449.

64. *See* András Téglási, *The Constitutional Aspects of Ownership*, in *Business Law* 168 ff. (István Sándor ed., Patrocinium 2016).

claims. The owner is entitled to take arbitrary action based on the rules for protecting possession if the illegal intrusion or influence of others prevents, limits, or renders impossible the exercising of his ownership right. Such illegal intrusion or influence can take place in many ways.

71. The owner's claim may also extend to receiving state protection against illegal intrusion or influence (*actio negatoria*). In this case, based on the legal title to the ownership right, the owner can receive protection against the person who has no legal grounds to intrude on or influence the thing or to conduct any disruptive activity.

72. The owner no longer in possession of the thing may take action against the person who is in possession of the thing (rei vindicatio). Here, when ruling on the claim to have the thing surrendered, the relationship between the legal title of the owner and the legal title and legal grounds of the possessor must be examined. The owner's claim to surrender the thing is only recognized if the possessor is obliged to surrender it based on the legal title to the thing. If the possessor has an appropriate legal title to the thing, e.g., chattel mortgage lender and usufruct holder, then he clearly cannot be compelled to surrender it. In this respect, the Civil Code contains a new rule for when the secondary possessor holds the thing from the owner, as the main possessor, under an appropriate legal title, but then the secondary possessor passes the thing onto a third party without the consent of the owner. Here, the owner may step into the secondary possessor's legal status and may demand the thing be surrendered to the secondary possessor, or if the secondary possessor refuses to take possession, then it goes back to the owner himself. For example, if a chattel mortgage lender leases a thing without the consent of the owner, the owner of the thing may take action against the lessee to have the thing surrendered back to the mortgage lender.

73. There is a separate rule for the legal situation that arises if the owner did not acquire the ownership right from a direct transfer of the thing but only received a claim for surrender from the transferor. In this case, the possessor of the thing may enforce any and all objections vis-à-vis the owner of the thing that the original owner was entitled to as well. As a general rule, transferring the ownership right of a leased thing does not terminate the lease contract; thus, the lessee may refer to lawful possession based on the lease contract in dealings with the new owner. If the owner of real property acquired the ownership title outside of the land registry, he may request to have his ownership registered in the land registry.

74. For property transfers, acquiring ownership requires an entry in the land registry to be valid under the Civil Code. By contrast, however, there are ways to acquire ownership where an ownership right is established on the real property without this being subject to entry in the land registry. Typical examples include adverse possession, official resolutions, auctions, inheritance, expropriation, marital property community, etc. In these cases, the owner's ownership claim may extend to the ownership right being registered in the public land registry so he can easily demonstrate his legitimate ownership right vis-à-vis third parties.

Chapter 3. Equitable Interests

75. Hungarian law does not recognize equity-based judgments known from Anglo-Saxon law, so the category of equitable interests is not applied.

Chapter 4. Limited Interests

76. Under rights over the property of someone else, Hungarian law differentiates between rights of use, easements, and security rights. For rights of use, the obligee is entitled to in rem protection for a thing owned by another person based on a legal relationship. In Hungarian law, this includes usufruct, use, and land use.

By contrast, there are relationships entitling use, e.g., leasehold or lease contracts, where the given person only has relative rights to the given thing, i.e., they do not fall under the law of things within Hungarian law.

Security rights comprise the various forms of lien, including security deposits. These are discussed in Part V.

§1. Usufruct

77. Usufruct falls into the category of personal easements, based on which the usufruct holder may possess, use, utilize, and reap the benefits from a thing owned by someone else.

I. Establishing and Subject of Usufruct

78. Usufruct may be created by legal regulation (e.g., widow(er) right of surviving spouse), court judgment, and contracts. As regards contractual usufruct, it should be highlighted that alongside concluding the contract (origination of other legal titles), it is also important for possession of the thing to be transferred. If we are talking about real property usufruct, the usufruct must also be entered into the land registry. It is crucial to note that failure to make the entry in the land registry means the usufruct can only be enforced against someone acquiring the real property for free or in bad faith.

79. Usufructs primarily relate to some movable or real property, but the Civil Code also allows for usufructs to be established on individual rights and receivables.

Usufruct shall not cover the increment in the object of the usufruct, which is gained after the commencement of the usufruct unless the increment results from the use of the usufruct object within the framework of prudent management. Given that the usufruct holder clearly has a right to reap benefits and collect proceeds, we cannot dispute whom the usufruct for the increments gained under prudent management must be assigned to.

II. Content of Usufruct

80. The usufruct holder is entitled to possess, use, utilize, and reap the benefits of the thing. Thus, from the classic trio of ownership rights (possession – use, utilization, right of disposition), the usufruct holder enjoys all of them apart from the right of disposition, meaning that the owner is left only with the ownership right (*proprietas nuda*).

81. Understood as an absolute right, usufruct creates a negative obligation for everyone vis-à-vis the usufruct holder – including the owner – i.e., the owner must refrain from any and all conduct that prevents or jeopardizes the exercising of the rights under the usufruct.[65] Of course, it also follows that the owner has a right of disposition over the thing, yet if he wants to transfer the thing, he can only do so together with the usufruct given the *nemo plus iuris ad alium transferre potest, quam ipse haberet* principle.

The usufruct shall remain in force even if the owner of the property changes. It is also possible for a property subject to usufruct to become part of a company's assets, e.g.,[66] property subject to usufruct can be contributed in kind as well, since it is just as eligible for sale as any other property, provided such eligibility for sale is not ruled out in a manner indicated in the land registry.

82. Usufructs are always set for a fixed period, and in the case of a natural person, at most until their death. Usufruct may be assigned to legal persons too for a fixed period but for not more than fifty years.

83. In Hungary, usufructs for legal persons were very common as part of some Public-Private Partnerships (PPPs), where private equity was brought in to achieve a public task – building and running a higher education institution, for instance – as part of a public procurement procedure. Thus, as part of a public procurement procedure, e.g., the contractor carried out the requested building development and operated the building, while in return, the higher education institution periodically paid a fee.[67] To secure the rights of the contractor/operator, a usufruct is often registered on the property.

84. The essence of a usufruct as a legal institution is that it is personal, which is why Roman law refers to it as a personal easement. It follows that usufruct is partly a right that is not eligible for sale because it cannot be transferred. At the same time, the rights of possession, use, and utilization may be transferred by the usufruct holder to a third party. If this happens free of charge, the usufruct holder may do so without any further action or approval, but the owner must be informed. What is much more common than a free transfer is when the usufruct holder wants to do this for some consideration. In this case, the owner has a pre-rental right in that the

65. BH 2010/147.
66. KGD 1997/4.
67. In connection with the construction of PPP, *see* particularly: Gyula Koi, *A PPP elméleti és terminológiai megalapozásának kérdései a nemzetközi szakirodalom tükrében* (*The Theoretical and Terminological Questions of the Foundation of PPP in the Mirror of the International Literature*), in *XIV. Országos Jegyző-Közigazgatási Konferencia, Államreform-Közigazgatási reform* (*14th Notary-Administrative Conference, State Reform – Administration Reform*) 215 ff. (Ferenc Gyergyák ed., Közszöv-KSZSZ 2006).

usufruct holder must first ask the owner whether he wants to take advantage of the opportunity under the same conditions; only then may use of the thing be transferred to a third party for consideration.

III. Rights of Usufruct Holder

85. During the usufruct, the usufruct holder is entitled to use the thing under the rules of prudent management. The nature of the thing subject to the usufruct determines exactly what prudent management means under the given situation. In the case of premises used as an apartment, there are models developed by practice and everyday experience, which help define the scope of prudent management, but if we are talking about a specific thing, for instance (e.g., a factory or a particular software program), defining this context is a task for those applying the law. In this respect, one issue is the extent to which the usufruct holder may change the economic purpose of the thing. Here, the usufruct holder may change the economic function or may convert or considerably alter the thing insofar as maintaining the economic function or leaving the thing subject to usufruct unaltered contradicts the requirements of prudent management.

It follows from the specific nature of a usufruct that the usufruct holder is obliged to bear the burdens associated with the thing – apart from extraordinary repairs and maintenance – along with the obligations related to the use of the thing. If the usufruct holder does not use the thing, he still has to pay the maintenance costs unless someone else undertakes this based on a separate contract. Consequently, if we are talking about the usufruct for an apartment building, the usufruct holder is obliged to pay the common charges.

86. If the usufruct holder decides to transfer use to the owner free of charge, who pays the costs, and then the usufruct holder changes his decision, it follows from the rule that the costs paid by the owner will have to be reimbursed.

87. The usufruct holder must notify the owner of risks threatening the thing and the damage sustained. This includes cases where a third party prevents him from exercising the usufruct. Furthermore, the usufruct holder must tolerate the owner taking the necessary measures to prevent the risk or eliminate the consequences of the damage. Given that, in most cases, the usufruct holder actually wants to use the thing subject to usufruct, it is in his own interests for the owner to prevent a possible emergency situation at the owner's own expense. The usufruct holder only has to pay the costs related to the proper maintenance of the thing. It is clearly the owner that has to carry out and pay for extraordinary repairs or restoration work – e.g., if the usufruct object is damaged or breaks down. At the same time, there can easily be a situation where the owner is not able to remedy the problem for objective reasons, and in this case, the usufruct holder can do it instead. Before the usufruct holder orders the work or has it carried out himself, he must inform the owner, and he only becomes entitled to act if this notification is unsuccessful. This – and verifiable proof the notification took place – is significant because it could be important during a subsequent settlement whether the usufruct holder was in fact entitled to carry out the unscheduled repair.

IV. Irregular Usufruct

88. Irregular usufruct – or the *quasi-ususfructus* known from Roman law – relates to the usufruct of things which, by virtue of their nature, can be consumed or expended. The usufruct holder is entitled to use the things subject to the irregular usufruct to the extent justified under the rules of prudent management. If the replacement or reimbursement claim of the former owner of a thing that was sold or consumed in the course of a usufruct is considered to be at risk, the owner may demand adequate guarantees.

V. Rights of the Owner

89. Since the thing is used by the usufruct holder, the owner only keeps the ownership right along with a related inspection right. The Civil Code prescribes that the lessor shall have the right to inspect use without causing any unnecessary disturbance to the lessee. The term ‘unnecessary disturbance’ is not used for usufruct, but it follows from the other rules in the law that the owner’s inspection right may not impair the usufruct holder’s use of the thing. Among other things, this means in practice that if the usufruct holder uses a given property as his usual residence under the usufruct, then the owner may only inspect it in a manner that takes the usufruct holder’s form and style of life into consideration in all respects. That said, there can be a situation where the usufruct holder does not use the thing for its original purpose, damages it, or possibly changes its purpose illegally. Initially, the owner is entitled to object to this.

In the event the thing subject to the usufruct is destroyed – in contrast to the owner’s intent – the owner is not obliged to restore it. If he does so, the usufruct is reborn, but the owner is then entitled to limit the usufruct in proportion to the amount spent on the restoration. If the owner does not restore the thing, the usufruct is terminated; if the object of the usufruct is replaced by another thing or receivable, the usufruct shall extend thereto.

VI. Termination of Usufruct

90. One typical example of when a usufruct is terminated is upon the lapse of a fixed period: In the case of a natural person with a usufruct until they die, or in the case of a legal person, the termination of the said person without a legal successor. The confusion arises when the usufruct holder acquires the ownership right to the thing (*confusio*).

91. When the usufruct is terminated as part of a legal transaction, it is absolutely necessary for the usufruct holder to provide an explicit waiver in which it relinquishes the usufruct in a legal statement to the recipient.

If the usufruct is registered in an authentic public registry – the land registry in the case of real property – a termination statement must be made in writing, and the usufruct must be deleted from the registry in order to terminate the usufruct.

92. If the subject of the usufruct is a right, then the rules applicable for transferring rights must be applied to the relationship between the usufruct holder and the obligor. If the usufruct relates to a receivable, the usufruct holder will be entitled to claim the receivable. This is similar to the usufruct for consumable things, where consumption of the thing means proper use. If the lender needs to waive the receivable for it to fall due, then the usufruct holder is entitled to exercise said right of the lender. One important liability rule is that if the receivables are collected by the usufruct holder, he shall be held liable for the enforcement of the receivables in respect of the lender, according to the principles of non-contractual liability. Other acts of the usufruct holder relating to the receivable shall be null and void. If the debtor fulfils its obligations, the object is acquired by the beneficiary of the receivable, whereby a statutory usufruct is established for the usufruct holder upon said performance.

§2. Building and Planting Rights

I. Land Use Right

93. Land use right is essentially derived from Roman law. Roman law recognized and regulated the legal institution that is similar – but not completely identical – to our land use right today under the title of *superficies*. Superficies was a broad right in Roman law, very similar to ownership right in many respects, relating to a structure erected on land owned by someone else – for lease or other reasons – and which was enjoyed by the beneficiary and his legal successors for a long time, but at most until the structure was destroyed.[68]

The Civil Code follows the *aedificium solo cedit* principle known from Roman law as the main rule, meaning that the legal fate of the structure shares that of the land. It follows that the ownership right to a structure built on a piece of land belongs to the owner of the land. In practice, however, there are many cases where someone builds on land owned by another. Different rules can be established for such cases.

Roman law, superficies, and the structural law applied in Hungary prior to the Second World War provided a right over the property of someone else to the superficiary on the land. The old Civil Code rule deviated from this and managed this issue through land use. By contrast, the new Civil Code amendments make it easier for the land owner and the building owner to agree to the building being entered into the land registry as separate property.

---

68. András Földi & Gábor Hamza, *A római jog története és institúciói* (*History and Institutes of Roman Law*) 368 (Nemzedékek tudása 2015[20]).

94. According to the current rule, if a building and the land on which it stands belong to different people, the owner of the building shall have a right of use to the land to the extent required for normal use of the building for as long as the building exists. The land use right covers the fact that the building owner is entitled to use the land and reap the benefits to the extent necessary for using the building. This also means though that he must pay a proportionate amount of the costs related to the upkeep of the land, in line with said use.

95. The ownership right to a building (structure) may be transferred validly by itself if it previously constituted a separate land registry unit in the land registry. For lack of this, the land and the building (structure) form an ownership unit.

The builder does not obtain the ownership right of the building without a written agreement with the land owner and its filing in the land registry, and therefore, he cannot exercise a pre-emption right for the land. In the case of sales following a contract that was concluded by violating the pre-emption right, the right to pre-empt does not arise anyway and may be converted into a compensation claim.

That said, based on the old Civil Code, a building could only be included as a separate property in the land registry if it was built on land owned by someone else. By contrast, the new Civil Code allows existing buildings to be registered as separate properties in the land registry.

96. If the ownership right to the land parcel and the structure on it are separated, the owner of the land parcel is due a fee for land use. It is conceptually impossible to enter into a lease contract for the land occupied by the structure, as this is only possible if the owner also has a right to dispose of possession of the thing. However, the right of use of the structure's owner to the land below the structure is not based on an agreement between the parties but is based on law.

The contract between the land owner and the building owner only governs the internal relationship between the parties. For the content of the contract to be applicable to third parties too, there needs to be a note added to this effect in the land registry. For lack of this, the land use right only originates rights and obligations between the parties, meaning the land use, as a right over the property of someone else, only becomes absolute when noted in the land registry.

The Civil Code provides a mutual pre-emption right for both the land owner and the building owner. The statutory pre-emption right is justified for reasons of economic efficiency. By providing a mutual pre-emption right, the legislator wants to make it possible for the land and the structure on it to be owned by the same person.

II. Encroachment

97. During construction, it is possible in practice for a builder to erect a building that stretches across the land's boundary, generally because such boundaries were not surveyed properly. In the event of such encroachment, the building is erected on two different land parcels according to the land registry. We note here that under normal court practice, the rules of encroachment must be applied not only for buildings but also for all structures. Properly applying the rules of encroachment can be an issue when building fences, e.g., in this situation, the legal consequences differ depending on whether the encroachment was in good or bad faith.

A. *Encroachment in Good Faith*

98. Encroachment in good faith means that the builder acted as could generally be expected in the given situation when taking into account the boundary to the neighbouring plot of land during the construction. In the event of encroachment in good faith, the neighbour may choose from three different legal consequences:

(1) He may request indemnification from the encroaching builder for the use of the occupied land and the depreciation in value caused thereby.
(2) He may request that the occupied land be bought if the land can be divided in accordance with the relevant zoning rules.
(3) The neighbour may request that the encroaching builder buy the entire plot of land.

This latter alternative is only applicable if the remaining part of the land becomes unusable because of the encroachment or if some right or occupation related to the land cannot be exercised because of the encroachment or such becomes significantly more expensive. Only the neighbour may request the application of legal consequences; they may not be applied at the request of the encroaching owner.

The court may decide on consequences for the encroachment that differ from what the neighbour selected and may even apply legal consequences that the neighbour did not ask for unless both parties object to this.[69]

B. *Encroachment in Bad Faith*

99. Encroachment is considered to be in bad faith if the builder knew, or taking due care, should have known that the construction extends beyond the boundaries of the plot onto the neighbour's land. In such cases, in addition to the three legal consequences for encroachment in good faith, there are another two possible legal consequences that can be applied under the Civil Code. Alongside dismantling the building and restoring it to its original state, the neighbour may ask for the encroaching builder's land and building to pass into his ownership upon payment of the consideration.

The costs of dismantling the building and restoring the original state must be paid for by the encroaching builder, but he is also entitled to keep the materials used.

It should be emphasized that while the court is not compelled to follow the parties' requests in the case of encroachment in good faith and can adopt a different decision, in the case of encroachment in bad faith, the court must apply the legal consequences

69. BH 1982/370; *see also* BDT 2002/634.

specified by the neighbour. Naturally, in such cases, the court must follow general basic principles other than encroachment rules when ruling on requests (e.g., requirement for good faith and fairness, prohibition on abusing rights), i.e., the encroachment in bad faith may not turn into a situation putting the neighbour at an unjustified enrichment or the encroaching builder at an unjustified disadvantage.

§3. Leasehold Interests: Chattels Real (*See Also* Part II)

100. In Hungarian law, lease contracts only have a legal impact *in personam*. For lease contracts, please *see* Part I, Chapter 4, §4.

§4. Emphyteusis and Rent Charge

101. Hungarian law does not recognize the concept of emphyteusis, but it does contain a similar aspect of leasehold contracts. The main difference between the two is that leasehold only creates a contractual, i.e., *in personam* relationship, between the parties. At the same time, a leasehold contract provides many additional rights for the leaseholder when compared to a simple lease relationship.

I. Leasehold Contract

102. Under a leasehold contract, the leaseholder shall be entitled to temporarily use an economically viable thing or to exercise an economically viable right and to reap the benefits thereof, and he shall be obliged to make an appropriate leasehold payment for this. A leasehold is a particular type of lease contract, which essentially differs from a lease in terms of its objective and subject. The subject of a leasehold is always an economically viable thing, most frequently agricultural land, while the purpose of the contract is to use the economically viable thing and collect the proceeds. The rules relating to leases constitute the legislation behind leaseholds, i.e., for lack of any provision to the contrary, the rules for leasing things may be applied accordingly for leaseholds.

A. Content of the Contract

103. The subject of a leasehold contract can be any economically viable thing, and here, the emphasis is primarily placed on the leasehold of arable land and on agricultural production.[70]

Leasehold agreements tend to be concluded for lengthy periods, and so, given the generally long nature of the relationship, the owner's risk includes whether he will

70. Accordingly, the rules in Ch. IX of Act CCXII of 2013 laying down certain provisions and transition rules in connection with Act CXXII of 2013 concerning agricultural and forestry land trade contain further provisions on the leasehold of arable land, within the framework of the Civil Code.

receive the subject of the leasehold back in a condition suitable for further use. At the same time, the leaseholder has to undertake to pay a larger portion of the upkeep costs and maintain the profit-generating status, as this is largely in his own interests too. The primary difference between a leasehold and a lease is that while a lease only provides the lessee with a right of use, based on a leasehold contract, the leaseholder is not only able to use the thing but also collect the proceeds. This is essentially the difference that defines the different rules of leaseholds from leases.

The subject of a leasehold is primarily an economically viable thing, but it can be an economically viable right as well.[71]

The Civil Code prescribes formal requirements and the written form for concluding a leasehold contract, owing to the lengthy term, nature, and economic significance of the legal relationship. Based on a leasehold contract, the leaseholder acquires a temporary right of use over the thing. Such contracts can be for fixed or indeterminate durations. Apart from using the thing, the leaseholder is entitled to collect the proceeds from the thing and reap its benefits.

B. Rights and Duties of the Parties

104. The leaseholder is entitled to the natural accretions (fruits) of the thing and owns them once they separate from the thing. However, since the leaseholder only has a temporary right based on the leasehold, the right to collect proceeds can mean that he tries to realize as much profit as possible from the thing, possibly at the expense of the thing's state or condition. In this respect, the law specifically states that the leaseholder may only use the thing and collect the proceeds in accordance with the rules of prudent management.

105. Leaseholders of agricultural land are not just entitled but indeed compelled to cultivate the land in accordance with its designated purpose. In the course of this work, they must preserve the fertility of the land.

106. In terms of collecting the proceeds, costs and expenses related to the thing differ slightly from the rules on leases; such obligations for leaseholders are higher. With a lease, the lessee only has to pay smaller expenses related to the upkeep of the thing, while a leaseholder has to pay all of the necessary renovation and repair costs connected to preserving the thing, along with related taxes and levies.

The owner only has to pay the costs of extraordinary or unscheduled renovations and repairs.

107. Incidentally, the owner has an obligation to warrant title and quality – under lease rules – for the proper and unrestricted use of the thing.

108. A leasehold is a contract for countervalue, so the leaseholder has to pay a leasehold payment. (If it is free, it is a lending arrangement.) The parties enjoy a

71. *See* Act LV of 1996 on the protection of game, game management, and hunting or Act XLI of 1997 on fishery and fishing contain provisions on the leasehold of rights.

great deal of freedom with regard to the consideration paid in exchange for use: they can agree on a leasehold payment in cash, but there is nothing to stop them from agreeing on use in return for a certain proportion of the yield (sharecropping). Depending on the agreement between the parties, the leasehold payment can be defined in cash, yield, or a mixture of the two. In contrast to leases, the leasehold payment is not made (settled) in advance but periodically in arrears. This is because the leaseholder tends to live from using and reaping the benefits from the leasehold thing, from working with it or on it, so only by exercising the leasehold can he create the means with which to make the leasehold payment.

In the case of agricultural leaseholds, in years where the crop yield is below one-third of the average due to a natural disaster or some other extraordinary event, the leaseholder is entitled to request a reduction in or relief from the leasehold payment. The owner must be informed of such a request prior to the harvesting of the crop in question. Reduced or cancelled leasehold payments may not be demanded from crop yields in subsequent years.

The owner is entitled to a statutory lien up to the level of the leasehold payment in arrears, in the same way as a lessor. This lien applies not only to the owner's assets on the thing subject to the leasehold but also to the proceeds of the thing.

C. *Termination*

109. The leasehold is terminated at the end of the contractual period when the circumstances set forth in the contract occur or if the parties decide to terminate the leasehold contract by mutual consent. For leasehold contracts concluded for an indeterminate duration, the notice period is one month; for agricultural leaseholds, however, they can be terminated with notice of six months at the end of the financial year. The owner shall also have the right to terminate the leasehold contract if the leaseholder fails to cultivate the arable land despite being requested to do so or engages in conduct that seriously jeopardizes the success of the production, the fertility of the land, the livestock, or equipment.

110. Following the death of the leaseholder, the heirs of the leaseholder may also terminate the contract if his death occurred within the last six months of the financial year. However, the heirs may only exercise this right within thirty days of the legally binding completion of the probate proceedings. If there are no probate proceedings, the thirty-day deadline shall start from the death of the testator.

111. Under certain circumstances, the owner may terminate the leasehold contract without notice in the case of both fixed-period and indeterminate contracts. For leasehold contracts on arable land, termination without notice is an option if the leaseholder:

- fails to comply with his utilization obligation despite written notices or engages in cultivation that jeopardizes the fertility of the land;

- transfers use of the land to a third party without the owner's consent or deviates from such consent, uses the land for other purposes, changes the agricultural classification or uses the land for purposes other than those defined in the Act on Protecting Arable Land;
- engages in activity that deviates from the provisions established based on nature conservation regulations or nature conservation authority rules, or which adversely influences the state or condition of the area, furthermore, if the preservation of natural values is in any way threatened; or
- does not make the leasehold payment or pay taxes connected with the land when they fall due, despite written notification, and within fifteen days of receiving said notification.[72]

112. If the leaseholder of agricultural land is a natural person, they may terminate the leasehold with immediate effect owing to poor health or any permanent change in their family and/or living conditions.

113. Upon the termination of an agricultural leasehold contract, the land and the other leased things shall be returned in a condition that allows production to be continued immediately in an appropriate manner. The owner and the leaseholder must settle with one another if the contract is terminated for whatever reason. Any prior agreement for the exclusion of such settlement is null and void.

Unless otherwise agreed, upon the termination of a leasehold contract, the leaseholder:

- may remove the equipment and accessories he has created;
- may demand the actual value of equipment installed with the consent of the owner which cannot be removed, plantations he planted, perennial crops and plants, as well as soil protection, enhancement and other interventions and facilities designed to preserve and improve the quality of the soil; said values shall be determined based on agricultural and other documents existing at the time of the contract termination; and
- must dismantle and remove any structures he built at his own expense and without any indemnification.

II. Lease Contract

114. Under a lease contract, the lessor enables the lessee to use something temporarily in return for a lease payment. So, based on a lease contract, the lessor waives his possession and use of the thing – for a fixed or indeterminate duration – and in return, he receives a consideration. A lease contract also only results in a contractual relationship; the law of things impact of this is only evaluated in terms of protection of possession. The essence of the lease is the right of use, but the use of the thing is governed and ensured by other legal relationships. Such rights of use

72. *See* s. 58(1) of the Act CCXII of 2013 laying down certain provisions and transition rules in connection with Act CXXII of 2013 concerning agricultural and forestry land trade.

are provided by lending arrangements, where the lender is obliged to hand the thing over for use by the borrower for the period set forth in the contract and for free, while the borrower is obliged to return it at the end of the contract. So similarly to a lease, a lending arrangement means the temporary possession and use of a thing (which is clearly not yet used), but not with a contract for countervalue, based on a gratuitous contract. Both contracts, however, are fundamentally different from loans because with loans, the borrower acquires ownership of the lent thing, and upon the termination of the contract is obliged to transfer the same type, quality, and quantity of the thing; a lease is a legal title that does not involve the transfer of ownership.

Under a lease contract, it is conceptually impossible for the ownership right to be transferred. A leasing contract focuses on the same temporary possession and use of a thing, based on which the lessee is temporarily entitled to possess and use the thing in exchange for the lease payment defined in the contract; however, in contrast to lease contracts, the lessee bears the risk of damage and as a general rule is responsible for preserving the thing as well as paying maintenance costs.

115. With a lease contract, the lessor is responsible for keeping the rented thing in a state fit for use, and he is responsible for damage to the thing that cannot be passed on to anyone else. The Civil Code does not contain any rules on operating leasing; for lack of any separate rule in this respect – and based on the definition of lease contracts – the Civil Code rules on lease contracts must be applied. The Civil Code governs financial leasing as a separate financing tool, which means the rules on financial contracts are applicable here.

116. Legal relationships established by lease contracts are always temporary. The Civil Code does not recognize the concept of emphyteusis or long-term leases, which would encumber the leased object in a manner incompatible with market conditions.

The common feature of usage obligations is that the service or use in question is always irreversible, which means it is conceptually impossible with these services to restore the original state (*restitutio in integrum*) (it is not possible to withdraw from the contract; if it is considered invalid, legal consequences may only be imposed looking forward, etc.).

A. Creating Lease Contracts

117. As a general rule, there are no formal requirements for a lease contract: the agreement between the parties can be created in writing or through implied conduct (The exceptions to this main rule are the individual forms of residential rental contracts). The law contains no particular constraints for the parties to the lease agreement (or does not provide for such), and as a result, essentially, any legal subject can occupy the position of lessor and lessee. Due to the nature of the legal relationship, however, the lessor has to have a right of disposition over the thing; this means the lessor is generally the owner of the thing but can be the usufruct holder, or in the case of subletting, the main tenant, as long as the right of disposition, or the usufruct or the main tenancy prevails.

B. Content of Lease Relationship

118. The lessor's main obligation is to transfer the thing (hand over possession) and accept that the lessee can possess and use the thing undisturbed for the entire duration of the lease agreement. It follows from this that during the lease, the lessee is entitled to the protection of possession, even vis-à-vis the lessor. The lessor must not just tolerate undisturbed use but ensure such. He must warrant this not only when handing over the thing but also during the entire duration of the lease contract. This warranty obligation goes both ways:

- Given that the lessor has to ensure undisturbed use, it follows that he is responsible for guaranteeing that third parties have no right to the leased thing that limits or prevents use by the lessee.
- The leased thing must be in a state suitable for its designated use throughout the lease agreement; it must comply with statutory and contractual requirements for which the lessor undertakes a warranty of quality.

It follows from the lessor's warranty obligation that he is responsible for the extraordinary or unscheduled renovation and repair costs and must pay the necessary expenses spent by the lessee on the thing too. This is because the major expenses either stem from faults in the leased thing, for which the lessor has given a warranty or are expenses which the lessor will also benefit from after the contract expires. However, the lessee is responsible for smaller expenses related to the upkeep of the thing. When using the thing, there are inevitably smaller costs and expenses that are primarily related to its upkeep. These cannot be passed on to the lessor and must be paid by the lessee, mainly because the frequency and volume of such expenses largely depend on the careful use by the lessee and the degree of use. However, the lessor's warranty does not cover providing a new thing in place of a destroyed one, not even in the case of replaceable things. Thus, in terms of ownership rights, the lessor is exposed to the risk of destruction, and in terms of the rental right, it is the lessee; with regard to the lease payment, the lessor carries the risk. In his capacity as owner, the lessor is responsible for paying taxes and duties on the thing unless the parties agree otherwise in the contract. However, the fact that the lessor and the lessee agree differently in their contract from the general rules on tax and duty payments does not necessarily mean this will be accepted by the beneficiary of such payments unless the consent of said beneficiary is obtained in accordance with the rules on debt assumption.

The lessor must take into account and ensure compliance with the deadlines defined in the contract regarding transfer and return of the thing as well as inspections of proper use. Based on the obligation to cooperate that covers all civil law relationships, the lessor must inform the lessee of all important features of the thing that are required for its proper use.

119. Under the lease contract, the lessee is obliged to receive and take possession of the leased object. The lessee's main service is the lease payment. As a general rule, the parties are free to set the level of the lease payment. Lease payments are generally made periodically in advance, but there is nothing to stop the parties from agreeing on payment in arrears, or not on a periodical basis, but in one lump sum, either in advance or in arrears. The lease payment is an obligation to pay money, but there is nothing to stop the parties from agreeing on a consideration that is not money, e.g., the supply of some crop yield.

The agreement between the parties may compel the lessee to pay a security deposit. The security deposit, as a collateral obligation securing the contract, is designed to make it easier for the lessor to recover any receivables; namely, if the lessee does not pay or does not pay in line with the contract, the lessor may settle his receivable directly from the amount of the security deposit. The deposit is generally cash or securities. The security deposit is returned if the contract is terminated without the lessor having legal grounds to satisfy any claims from the security deposit.

120. No rent is payable for any period during which the thing cannot be used for reasons beyond the lessee's control. This obviously may only happen for objective reasons and not for reasons within the lessee's control (e.g., illness). However, in the event that the lessee is unable to use the thing for reasons within the lessor's control or for reasons beyond both of their control, then the lessor is not due payment of the rent for the period when use is not possible. Failure to make the lease payment can prompt the lessor to terminate the agreement with immediate effect, provided that the lessee was notified in writing about payment of the arrears by an appropriate deadline and with a warning of the potential consequences and the lessee failed to pay by this deadline.

121. The security for payment of the rent in the case of real property rentals is the statutory lien, which the lessor is entitled to from the lessee's assets in the leased property, up to the level of the lease payment and additional charges. The thing must be in possession of the lessor for the lien to be created.

122. The lessee is required to use the thing in accordance with its designated purpose and the lease contract. Since the lessor does not possess the thing in the course of the rental agreement, the lessee must tolerate the lessor inspecting said proper use without causing any unnecessary disturbance to the lessee. In the event of use that is not in line with the designated purpose or which violates the contract, the lessor may ask for such use to stop and for the damage resulting from such use to be compensated. If this improper use continues, or if demanding that the lessee cease such activities would not serve the purpose owing to the severity of the risk, the lessor may terminate the contract with immediate effect and demand compensation.

123. The lessee may not transfer the use of the thing to a third party without the lessee's consent, neither for subletting nor for other purposes. If a third party is given use with the consent of the lessor, i.e., legally, the lessee is responsible for the conduct of said third party as for his own. If, however, a third party is given use of the thing illegally, then the lessee is liable for all damage that would not have happened had said use not been provided, which can even extend to include *vis major.*

124. After the lease contract is terminated, the lessee must return the thing. Anything installed at his own expense, the lessee may remove; if the thing was converted, its condition prior to the lessee taking possession must be restored. At the end of the legal relationship, the lessee may have counterclaims against the lessor (e.g., necessary costs and practical expenses that would benefit the lessor). To ensure and recover these, the lessee may choose from the following rights at his disposal:

- withhold the thing and not use it;
- continue to use it and offset the accruing lease payment against the claim.

The lessee is entitled to remove everything that he installed in the leased thing at his own expense, provided that doing so would not damage the condition of the thing. If removing it without damage is not possible, then according to the rules on cost distribution, the lessee may demand compensation if the parties cannot agree.

C. Termination of Lease Contract

125. Depending on their agreement, the parties may enter into a lease contract for a fixed period or for an indeterminate duration. If the scope of the contract depends on the occurrence of some future event (termination condition), then this is also considered a fixed-term contract.

If the lease contract is concluded for a fixed period, the contract terminates without any further legal act upon the expiry of the said term or the occurrence of the event.

The lease contract shall also terminate if the leased thing is destroyed, regardless of whether anybody is responsible for this or not.

Termination of the contract is not influenced by whether the destruction of the thing was the result of actionable conduct by the lessor, the lessee, or any third party (impossibility of performance). If, when concluding the contract, the parties do not know or do not want to set the term for their (long-term) legal relationship, the contract is concluded for an indeterminate period.

This unlimited term does not signify a contractual relationship until the end of time; with all contracts entered into for an indeterminate duration, and therefore lease contracts too, either party may terminate the agreement with notice (the inevitable way to terminate contracts of indeterminate duration).

126. There are no formal requirements for terminations; the contract terminates when the notice period expires. The parties may agree on a notice period, failing which the contract will terminate fifteen days after the notice period is given, in accordance with the Civil Code's default rule.

If, after the termination of a fixed-term lease contract (when the fixed period elapses), the lessee does not return the thing to the lessor and continues to use it, the contract turns into an agreement of indeterminate duration unless the lessor objects to this within fifteen days (The fifteen-day deadline provided for the lessor to object is a preclusive deadline). This is because if the parties express, by means of their uniform conduct once the fixed period has elapsed, that they wish to maintain the situation created by their lease contract, this essentially means the lease contract is amended by virtue of implied conduct.

If the lessee dies, the heirs taking his place as legal successors may terminate a fixed-term contract by giving notice. It would be unjustified to compel them to maintain a contract that they do not need. Nonetheless, the lessor's interest is protected by the provision, which states that the heirs may exercise this right within thirty days of the grant of probate becoming final. If there are no probate proceedings, the thirty-day deadline shall start from the death of the testator (lessee).

127. Terminating the contract with immediate effect (without notice) is an option for both fixed-term contracts and contracts of indeterminate duration in the event of a serious breach of contract.

128. If the lessor sells the thing in the course of the lease contract, a peculiar situation arises. In light of the obligatory nature of a lease agreement, it has no absolute effect, which means the lessor position, in theory, does not pass over to the customer (the 'Kauf bricht nicht die Miete' principle applies). The general liability obligation of the original lessor applies to all of the obligations that were transferred to the new owner upon assigning the lease contract and thus the change in the person of the lessor.

D. Special Rules of Residential Rental Contracts

129. If the object of the rental contract is residential property, then the general rules for rental contracts must be applied, but property rentals require special rules in comparison to general rules, primarily owing to the special interests related to the use of the rented thing. The different regulation of property rentals – in view of the social role and significance of property rentals – is mainly aimed at protecting tenants.[73] In addition to this, local government decrees apply for properties in local government ownership, while ministerial and asset management decrees apply for properties in state ownership.

130. The subjects of residential rental contracts are, of course, the landlord and the tenant. The special feature of the landlord position is the local government or state ownership, while on the tenant side, it is the multi-tenant situation, given that properties are generally used by families. Rented properties can be in the state, local government or private ownership. Properties in private ownership can be owned by private individuals, companies, cooperatives, apartment buildings, or other organizations.

73. Although not specifically stated by the Civil Code, rules of a separate law pertain to property rental contracts, Act LXXXVIII of 1993 on the Rules and Alienation of Residential and Non-Residential Property. The underlying legislation for this Act is the Civil Code.

131. According to general rules on rental contracts, the tenant shall be entitled to remove any and all items he added to the thing at his own expense, without causing any damage to the thing. In the case of an apartment, the tenant may not exercise his right of removal if the landlord offers appropriate indemnification to compensate for his right of removal, and this does not harm the tenant's lawful interests. The rule assumes that movable property represents a higher value inside the rented property than when removed. This is why the law enables the landlord to provide compensation. This right of the landlord only covers things that are actually fitted to the apartment, i.e., physically connected. The landlord's right does not cover things where there is no such physical connection, even if there used to be a physical connection, but the tenant has since taken them down.

To protect the tenant, the contractual limitation or exclusion of the removal right and compensation claim are linked to the proper compensation of the related inconvenience, i.e., the parties may only limit or exclude the removal right or the compensation claim in their contract if they agree on appropriate compensation for the inconvenience caused. Appropriate compensation can mean any benefit provided to compensate for the inconvenience incurred by limiting (excluding) the removal right and the compensation claim, e.g., a reduction of the rent, a longer notice period agreed by the landlord, indemnification, or the landlord agreeing to some other collateral obligation.

§5. Use and Habitation/Occupation

132. Use is a category that stretches back into Roman law, known as *usus* as well as *ususfructus* (usufruct). Although the rules of usufruct must principally be applied for use, there are two very important exceptions: one is utilization or exploitation (right to reap benefits), and the other is the transferability of the right.

In the case of a right of use, the use and exploitation right is limited; namely, the authorized person may only use and exploit the thing to the extent required for his and his family members' needs, no more. The other main difference is that in contrast to usufruct, a right of use cannot be transferred to others. Use arises most often in practice with regard to real properties. Based on the latter rule, the person with the right of use may only use the property in question personally or with the family members co-habiting with them when the right arises.

If the person with the right of use is a legal person, then such legal person shall be entitled to use the thing arising from the right of use and enjoy its proceeds in accordance with the purpose and activities set out in the instrument of the constitution. The agreement does not have to be in writing for a contract establishing a property use right to be valid, but it does have to be entered into the land registry. In terms of who pays which costs in relation to rights of use, it is essentially the rules of usufruct that must be applied.

§6. Easements and Profits

I. Land Easement

133. Based on land easement rights, the possessor of the dominant estate may use the servient estate to satisfy certain economic requirements. The possessor of the dominant estate is always the beneficiary of the easement, who cannot achieve or reach an economic objective with his estate alone, and therefore, it is necessary to use the normally neighbouring or nearby estate.

134. The Civil Code only provides some examples of easement rights, stating that easement may be granted for right-of-way, the installation of water pipes or water conduits, constructing cellars, poles for aerial lines, building abutments, or for other similar purposes to the benefit of the dominant estate. The easement can also be construed in a negative way, whereby the beneficiary of the easement demands that the possessor of the servient estate should refrain from some otherwise rightful conduct. It is important to emphasize that the Civil Code always refers to the current possessor of the estate, not the owner. It follows that the easement on the estate may be granted to anyone lawfully using the land. Thus, anyone using the dominant estate as a favour would also be authorized to fully exercise the easement right.

135. The extent of the easement is determined by the economic need. The court decision that statutory easement generally only means right-of-way by foot applies in this respect. The beneficiary has to prove that he has a greater interest in being able to cross the estate by car than the person granting the easement has in using his own property without allowing cars to cross. The growing significance and expansion of motorized traffic are not necessarily sufficient per se for the statutory easement to allow the beneficiary a right-of-way by car.[74]

A. Granting a Land Easement

136. Easements are primarily granted in a contract, though it is also possible for someone to grant an easement with a unilateral declaration, for which rules on contracts must clearly be applied. This latter opportunity was not regulated by the old Civil Code, but the practice was recognized and applied. If the easement is granted in a contract, the Civil Code states that the rules for establishing usufruct shall be applied.

137. Easements may also be established based on law or court rulings. Easements and easement rights are most akin to usufruct. That said, we must draw a distinct line between easement and rights of use. The main difference in terms of the legal subjects for a property use right established by contract and a land easement right is that the person authorized for use may only be the person in the contract,

74. BDT 2000/224.

while a person benefiting from easement can be anyone else who legally possesses the property, not just the person concluding the contract.

An easement may be granted via adverse possession too. One new rule compared to the old Civil Code is that the deadline for the adverse possession of an easement is fifteen years. This is subject to the possessor of the other property not objecting to its use for a period of fifteen years. In terms of legal title, however, it is very important that exercising rights extended as favours or rights extended until withdrawn may not result in adverse possession. The adverse possession of a land easement is only possible in the event of easement-like use. Exercising a right may not be considered easement-like use if the owner provided a right-of-way to the public too, and so it was not exclusive for any user or with a view to obtaining an easement. In terms of the adverse possession of a land easement right, it makes no difference whether the adverse user acted in good or bad faith if such use did not constitute a crime and did not take place in an underhand manner. Use out of favour or use rights extended until withdrawn do not result in an easement obtained through adverse possession. However, if the conditions specified in the law are met, the user may ask for the easement to be granted based on a court ruling.

B. *Exercising Easement Right*

138. Easement can significantly restrict the use of the servient estate, but exercising the easement may never harm the rights of the person using the thing subject to easement unnecessarily. Accordingly, in order to judge what is an unnecessary grievance, all of the circumstances of the given case must be known. However, if exercising the easement right comes at a cost, then for lack of any agreement to the contrary, the costs of maintenance shall be split between the person granting and the person benefiting from the easement in line with the extent to which they use the equipment or installations giving rise to the costs.

C. *Termination of Easement*

139. If the parties want to terminate the land easement by means of a legal transaction, there are two conditions: one, a written cancellation statement addressed to the owner of the dominant estate and written to the owner of the servient estate, and two, consequently, the deletion of the easement from the land registry. Of course, decisions on whether the easement is needed for the use of the thing in line with its designated purpose must be made on a case-by-case basis, and sometimes, an expert opinion is required in light of the type of easement.

II. Use for Public Purposes

140. According to the rules on use for public purposes, easements or other rights of use may only be granted for properties, in the public interest, and for the persons specified in separate legislation. In light of the public interest, appropriate indemnification must be paid for limiting the ownership right to the property, such as via easement or right of use. The rules on expropriation must be applied here according to the Civil Code.

§7. Construction Right

I. Introduction

141. Construction right, as an in rem right, was introduced into Hungarian private law in the summer of 2023 (section 93 of Act XXXIX of the Civil Code) with the aim of ensuring an appropriate legal background for the changed technological conditions and economic needs. Construction right enables investments in the construction of various buildings, artefacts, and technical equipment to be financed with appropriate loan collateral. It provides a typical and specific opportunity for credit institution financing to be implemented, especially for solar power plant investments. The construction right, as a right that can be encumbered, provides an opportunity for this, which serves as the basis for a mortgage right that can also be registered in the real estate register. In a similar way, the construction right that can be encumbered with a mortgage right can satisfy a significant national economic demand as a loan security in the case of financing construction concessions affecting public lands, construction projects planned under or above public lands (e.g., highways, tunnels, bridges, underground parking garages, etc.).

Construction right was already a well-known legal institution in Hungarian private law before the Second World War, and its previous rules were renewed and modernized by the legislator. In addition to land use, the rules of construction right would provide another alternative for encumbering real estate with a limited in rem right for the purpose of construction.

II. Content

142. Construction right is a transferable, inheritable and encumbered limited real (in rem) right relating to real estate, which is established by the agreement of the owner of the real estate and the holder of the construction right, by registration in the real estate register (with constitutive effect), and is charged to the property for which this right was registered. The construction right is perhaps most comparable to the right of usufruct relating to real estate, but it gives the building owner an even stronger right beyond the right to use and utilize, by providing, on the basis of this right – within the framework of the agreement with the owner – the right of free disposal of all the building and to its constituent parts, which he creates or created in the exercise of his construction right. The construction right – in contrast to the usufructuary right – can be transferred, encumbered and subject to legal succession, so it can be considered a more substantial right of property value than the usufructuary right in this respect as well.

On the basis of the construction right, the holder of the right may construct or use a building on the land or under its surface. The construction right can be established not only for the establishment of a building but also for the utilization of an existing building that has already been created. The construction right allows the construction, operation and utilization of buildings on the land used for this purpose, which would otherwise not be listed as independent properties in the real estate register, and consequently, the rules regarding the separation of the building and the land would not be applicable.

The construction right also covers the building established or utilized on the basis of it and its components. In the case of the transfer and encumbrance of the construction right, or in the case of legal succession with respect to this right, the constructed or utilized structure is also transferred or encumbered together with the construction right, as a component of it, i.e., the structures affected by the construction right – during its existence – share the fate of the construction right.

The exercise of the construction right is governed not only by private law but also by construction rules, within the framework of which the contract establishing the construction right may establish additional restrictions and requirements. The construction right can therefore be exercised – among other things – in addition to the requirements of reasonable and normal management in accordance with the sectoral construction regulations. In the contract establishing the construction right, it can be stipulated that the construction right can be alienated or encumbered by the holder only with the consent of the owner of the property.

III. Creation

143. The construction right can be established in several ways: with a unilateral declaration, a contract, or even a will, but by definition, it would not be excluded that such a right could be created by legislation or an official decision based on it under certain conditions. The construction right can only be established in writing and for a fixed period of time, up to fifty years. There is, of course, no obstacle to renewing the construction right encumbering the real estate by means of a new agreement between the owner of the land and the construction right holder under the same or different conditions, i.e., establishing the construction right for a new fixed period of time. The construction right can be established free of charge or against a return, in which latter case the building owner is charged with a one-time and/or periodically recurring payment obligation ('construction fee') in favour of the property owner, which must also be defined in the contract establishing the construction right.

The construction right can only be established for a fixed period of time, thirty-five years, with regard to national property. In the contract on the establishment of the construction right affecting the national property, the parties must also agree on the physical characteristics of the building that can be erected by the holder on the property or under its surface, as well as the conditions of utilization. In the event of national property being involved, the construction right can only be established against a fee, by paying the turnover value of the building right.

An important limitation is that a person who is considered a consumer cannot grant a construction right on the property he owns, and he cannot acquire such a right either by founding or by transfer.

IV. Termination

144. The construction right may be terminated if the right holder does not exercise this right for fifteen years. The construction right can also be terminated if the right holder waives this right with a written statement addressed to the owner of the encumbered real estate, and in view of this, this right is deleted from the real estate register. The construction right may expire after the deadline for which it was established. Finally, in the event of a serious violation of the law or breach of obligations, the construction right can be terminated before the specified time or fifty years have passed, if the owner of the property applies to the court with reference to the termination of the construction right, and the court – having established a serious violation of the law or breach of obligations fact – decides on the termination of the construction right in accordance with the claim. The contracting parties themselves can define the question of what constitutes a serious violation of law or a breach of obligation on the part of the building owner in the contract, thus reducing the scope for judicial consideration.

§8. LICENCES

145. Various issues may arise in connection with licences when acquiring the ownership rights to real property. As a general rule, Hungarian citizens may acquire ownership rights to real properties without restriction. That said, we do encounter cases where acquiring ownership is subject to obtaining a licence.

I. Acquisition of Property in Hungary by Foreigners

146. Foreigners require a licence to buy non-agricultural land in Hungary.[75] The following are exceptions to the category of foreign citizens:

- citizens of EU Member States and their organizations with and without legal personality;
- citizens of countries party to the agreement on the European Economic Area (Norway, Liechtenstein, Iceland) and their organizations with and without legal personality;
- citizens of Switzerland;[76]

75. *See* Government Decree 7/1996. (I. 18.) on the acquisition of property by foreigners.
76. It is based on the agreement regarding the free movement of people promulgated with Act CXXV of 2006.

- dual citizens, if one of the citizenships is Hungarian or of a Member State, and the property acquisitions of Hungarian citizens living abroad;
- furthermore, in the case of succession; and
- the acquisition of property required for the business activity of the Hungarian branch office of a foreign enterprise registered in a country not part of the EEA, in the cases specified in international agreements, or if there is reciprocity in this respect between the state of the foreign enterprise and Hungary.

II. Other Licences

147. Aside from the above, government office permits are required in all cases where foreign natural and legal persons want to obtain the ownership right to property not classified as agricultural or forestry land. Obtaining such a permit is subject to state or local government interests not being impaired by the acquisition of the ownership right by the foreigner.

148. There can be other restrictions based on sectoral regulations, such as when acquiring ownership rights in historical or nature conservation areas, e.g., *see* Part I, Chapter 8 for the restrictions on acquiring arable land.

§9. Restrictive Covenants

149. Rights related to properties and their beneficiaries may be entered into the land registry:

(a) ownership rights, and, in respect of state-owned real property, the organization exercising the state's ownership rights and asset management rights, also for local government property;
(b) permanent right of use for members of housing cooperatives;
(c) land use on the basis of an agreement or court decision;
(d) usufruct and the right of use;
(e) land easement;
(f) permanent geodetic markings, land survey pilot areas, right of use for the placement of power supply equipment, cable rights, water pipe, and mining easement rights, as well as easement and rights of use in the public interest;
(g) right of pre-emption and right of repurchase, purchase and sell options;
(h) right of support and life annuity;
(i) mortgage right;
(j) right of execution.

The rights detailed in points (a)–(f) were dealt with under ownership right and rights of use, while the mortgage right in point (i) will be discussed in detail in Part V, and the execution right under point (j) in Part III, Chapters 5 and 7. The following applies to the rights as per point (g).

I. Right of Pre-emption

150. In the event of the existence of the right of pre-emption, if the owner wishes to sell the item, he shall communicate the purchase offer from a third party to the holder of the pre-emption right, and the latter is entitled to buy the item from the seller by a unilateral declaration under the conditions fixed in the purchase offer. The right of pre-emption can be exercised only in case of sales; thus, it cannot be validated concerning alienation under other titles. In case of sales mixed with the exchange, the right of pre-emption may be validated only if it is determinable that the dominant element is the sale and the element of exchange is built in the contract only for the circumvention of the right of pre-emption.

151. The right of pre-emption may be established by a contract, and it can also be prescribed by law (e.g., common property, arable land, quota, nature reserve area). If there is a right of pre-emption based on a contract and both on an act, the latter precedes the previous one. In case of a right of pre-emption in favour of more than one person based on a contract, the sequence of the holders of the right is determined by the date of establishment of the right of pre-emption, that is to say, the holder of the right of pre-emption established earlier precedes the other one established later.

152. It is only possible to resign from the right of pre-emption pursuant to a definite purchase offer. If the owner intends to sell the item, he is obliged to communicate the purchase offer apart from the fact that the holder with the right for pre-emption had already declared that he did not intend to buy the item. The offer shall be communicated to the holder with the right for pre-emption at full length. The notification of the offer comes into effect with the acknowledgement of the holder of the right. The purchase offer, having been already communicated to the holder of the rights, is irrevocable. An appropriate deadline is justified by the circumstances of the holder of the right to approve the offer. The seller is exempted from the obligation of notifying the holder of the right of pre-emption concerning the offer if it would imply extraordinary difficulties or a substantial delay on account of the location of the beneficiary's domicile or other circumstances, particularly due to the number of obligees.

The holder of the right of pre-emption is only entitled to accept or not accept the offer; that is to say, it shall not be regarded as a statement of acceptance if he intends to buy the item with elements of content being different from the offer. The holder of the right is not entitled to attach the statement of acceptance to conditions. He shall practise his right of pre-emption before the fixed deadline; the omission results in forfeiture. Subsequently, the seller is entitled to sell the item to the buyer pursuant to the offer or with conditions being more favourable for him. By the statement of acceptance of the holder of the right, the sales contract comes into being, and it is not necessary to have further declarations.

153. It is frequently practiced that the seller may sell more than one item to the buyer by one contract. If these items are strongly connected, that is to say, they serve a common practical or economic purpose, the holder of the right of pre-emption shall practise the right of pre-emption jointly concerning all of the items in the contract. If there is no strong connection between the items sold in one contract, and these do not compose an economic or functional unity, the holder of the right is entitled to practise his right of pre-emption regarding the particular items separately.

154. In case of the existence of the right of pre-emption, the sale contract concluded without the notification of the holder of the right is inoperative in respect of him. The sales contract breaching the right of pre-emption is not null and void; it is only inoperative in respect of the holder of the right. In this case, the holder of the pre-emption right shall make a statement of acceptance concerning the full length of the purchase offer. On the occasion of this, the court shall examine the severity of the statement of practising the right of pre-emption and the real existence of the intention and capacity of performance. In breach of the right of pre-emption, the holder of the right of pre-emption is not entitled to act against a buyer in good faith; he is only entitled to lay a claim against the seller. If the buyer acted in bad faith, the sales contract becomes inoperative towards the holder of the pre-emption right, and he is entitled to demand the release of the item in return for the purchase price. The right of pre-emption based on a legal regulation has the effect of substantive law; that is to say, the buyer cannot refer to the fact that he had not been aware of the right of pre-emption.

155. If more than one person has a right of pre-emption on the item, the right of pre-emption based on a legal regulation precedes the other based on a contract. In the case of the right of pre-emption based on several legal regulations, the sequence is generally determined by the legal regulation; thus, e.g., the right of pre-emption under a particular legal regulation precedes the right of pre-emption of the joint proprietor under the Civil Code. If there is a right of pre-emption based on more than one contract, the right being established earlier precedes the right established later. If several rights of pre-emption had been established at the same time, the buyer shall notify the holders of the right that they are entitled to revoke their offers within eight days. If there is more than one holder of the right still intending to practise their right of pre-emption, they acquire ownership of the item in proportion to their interest among each other, and if it cannot be determined, they acquire ownership being divided equally.

The sales contract concluded in breach of the right of pre-emption is inoperative in respect of the holders of the right. On the occasion of this, the holder of the right is entitled to enforce his claims within thirty days after gaining knowledge of the conclusion of the contract. The claims arising from inoperativeness cannot be enforced after three years following the date of conclusion of the contract.

II. Purchase Option

156. Pursuant to the right to purchase (option), the holder of the right is entitled to buy the item by a unilateral declaration whenever he intends in return for a purchase price determined in advance. Consequently, the purchase option means a unilateral entitlement for the purchase of the item.

According to the supply and demand of goods, the purchase option is regarded as a power from the person intending to sell the goods to the potential buyer that provides a possibility for the potential buyer to decide to buy the item on a posterior date for a purchase price determined in advance. The establishment of the purchase option presumes the economic purpose that while allowing the purchase option, the buyer had decided to sell the item, and his intention of sale exists with a stipulated purchase price; however, the intention of purchase of the seller is only foreseeable, not definitive. The establishment of the purchase option goes beyond the legal content of the offer of concluding the contract – although it is often called an extended offer – since, in the case of the option, the obligor establishes a contractual legal relationship with the obligee, while in case of the offer, the parties are in the pre-contractual phase, even if the recipient of the offer is entitled to establish the contract by a unilateral statement of acceptance due to the validity period.

157. The contract of establishment of a purchase option shall also be distinguished from the preliminary contract since the court may establish the contract between the parties based on the pre-contract at the request of either party. Therefore, the construction of the purchase option presumes a double legal relation, the agreement establishing the purchase option on the one hand and the sales coming into being pursuant to the purchase option on the other hand. Under the agreement establishing the purchase option, the obligor is responsible for the prevention of the frustration or the derogation of the purchase right; thus, it is his obligation to maintain a behaviour whereby he can continue an activity by which the holder of the purchase option is able to practise his right during the duration of the option. The agreement providing the purchase option – pursuant to the free agreement of the parties – may result in an obligation of option fee payment with the condition that the gratuitous establishment is not considered null and void. Accordingly, the unilateral power provided for the holder of the purchase right may be gratuitous, and it may even be beneficial for the obligor according to the balance of powers.

158. The second phase of the legal construction of the option can be reached by exercising the purchase right when the sale is established between the parties. This second contract is based on the first, and although it may seem to be a contract that can be reconsidered independently, the rights and obligations deriving from it constitute an organic consequence of the agreement providing the purchase option. The agreement establishing the purchase option and the sales contract deriving from the exercise of the option are connected strongly since they are privities, each building on the other that cannot be considered and treated separately.

The purchase option's illegitimacy and its purpose of circumventing a legal regulation are closely related to the fact that in case of stipulating a purchase option for security purposes, the parties intend to deviate from the rules of pledge and especially the rules of satisfaction of the creditors' claims from the pledge.

III. Right to Sell

159. The right to sell is the inverse of the purchase option, so in this case, a unilateral right is established for the owner to sell the item to the buyer for a purchase price determined in advance within a fixed period. The rules of purchase option shall be applied *mutatis mutandis* to the right to sell.

IV. Repurchase Right

160. The repurchase right is an option (purchase right) providing an entitlement for the seller to unilaterally repurchase the item being the subject matter of the sale during a period determined earlier pursuant to a sales contract already having been concluded. Otherwise, the rules of the purchase option shall be applied.

The repurchase right may be exercised for the purchase price determined in the original sales contract; however, there is a possibility for the parties to agree on a different purchase price. If the parties have not determined the purchase price concerning the exercise of the repurchase right, the rebuyer shall pay a purchase price equal to the market value of the item on the date of practising the repurchase price.

V. Common Rules

161. It is a common rule concerning the right of pre-emption, the repurchase right, the purchase option and the right to sell that the contract establishing the right shall be executed in writing. There is a rule concerning every right that it becomes effective in respect of third parties only if it is registered in a public registry.

It is also common in each case that the right based on a legal regulation precedes the other one based on a contract. Furthermore, each right terminates if the item ceases for the sake of a cause that is not imputable to the obligor.

VI. Maintenance Agreement

162. Under a maintenance agreement, the person subject to providing maintenance must ensure care to the person entitled to maintenance and ensure adequate living conditions, while the beneficiary undertakes to provide compensation. Such contracts may only be concluded in writing. The maintenance countervalue is generally the property of the dependent, whose ownership right is obtained by the provider directly after concluding the contract; in terms of the property, the right of the dependent to maintenance can be registered in the land registry.

163. A life annuity contract differs from a maintenance agreement in that the provider of the life annuity is obliged to send the other party a cash sum or other fungible thing at certain regular intervals. In all other respects, the rules for maintenance agreements must be applied for life annuity contracts. Of course, there is nothing to stop a property owner from undertaking a different contractual obligation, but apart from the cases outlined above, these cannot be registered in the land registry. This means that there is no absolute effect, and they can only be enforced with regard to the contracting parties. If there is legal succession in terms of the owner undertaking this obligation, the obligation does not necessarily pass on to the legal successor.

Chapter 5. Security Interests (*See Also* Parts II, IV, and V)

164. Liens are considered security interests with regard to real properties and are detailed in Part V. Furthermore, purchase options and repurchase options are applied in practice for security purposes, and these issues are discussed in Part IV, Chapter 2.

Chapter 6. Joint Ownership

§1. Joint Ownership of Immovable Property

I. In General

165. Joint property is when the ownership rights of a thing are split, at predefined ratios, between multiple people. In the event of doubt, the ownership shares of the joint owners shall be equal. In the case of joint property, the single ownership right is attributed in various shares to more than one person. The proportion of the share determines the degree of the joint owners' rights and the proportion of their share in relation to the other joint owners. The size of the share can be used to determine the proportion of use as well as the degree of responsibility for costs emerging from the thing. The proportion of the share in relation to the other owners is used in exercising voting rights. In the event of doubt, the ownership shares of the joint owners shall be equal in the eyes of the law.

The legal relationship of the joint owners can be separated based on internal and external legal relationships. The joint owners' internal legal relationships pertain to possession and use, collecting proceeds and utilization, as well as expenses relating to the thing (preserving condition, maintenance, and expenses beyond prudent management) and liability for damage. External legal relationships extend to disposal rights over the whole thing and protection of ownership.

166. Joint properties have special versions such as documented joint ownership, joint ownership on boundary markers, shared courtyards, joint ownership of jointly acquired property, joint ownership of occupants in a shared household, agrarian joint ownership, corporate property, and apartment building property.

167. Every joint owner has the right to possess and use the property; however, this right cannot be practised by any joint owner to the detriment of the other owners' rights and the material legal interests associated with the thing.

A. *Joint Owners' Rights and Obligations*

1. Right to Use and Possess

168. In the internal legal relationship of the joint owners, they all have the right to possess and use the entire thing. The use of and possession of the thing is limited by consideration for the other joint owners' legal interests; that is, exercising these rights cannot be detrimental to the material legal interests of the other owners in association with the thing. In the case of joint property, the proportion of collecting proceeds cannot be changed by one of the owners not exercising their rights to possession or use, while none of the owners is legally obliged to use the other owners' share against their will or to use or pay for the use of the other owner's share of the thing when they do not require it. For example, the use of a shared property for parking does not permanently detract land from the jointly used area. But a construction built above the car, which stays in place even when the car is not there, results in a situation that permanently detracts land from the area and turns it into an object of exclusive use.[77]

169. When dealing with the use of joint property, proportion of ownership is just one, but not the only criterion. The degree of use can differ from the share of ownership if this is justified by the location of the building, geographical conditions, and differences between parts of the building. If the joint owners use their joint real property divided naturally among themselves, in the event of this joint property being terminated – with the exception of adverse possession – the shares of ownership in the land registry must be taken as a basis, not the proportion of use. A joint owner does not have the responsibility to take possession of or exclusively use another joint owner's ownership share against their will or if they do not need it.[78]

170. In the case of joint property, the use of the property beyond the owner's share requires a proportionate payment to be made to the other joint owners. When calculating the extra usage fee, the use value of the property established in the original terms of use, with the fittings and in the condition prevailing at that time, should be taken as the basis.[79] To determine the usage fee, it is not sufficient to compare the sales value of the whole property and the part used separately, as well as the area of flats and other premises with the ownership proportions. The conditions of use and profitability for living spaces, additional buildings, and land not built on must be clarified before any informed opinion can be expressed on the usage fee.

171. A peculiarity of joint property is that the exercising of the joint owners' rights is only limited by having to consider the rights and interests of the other owners; therefore, it motivates the joint owners to agree with one another on issues and conclude a contract accordingly. Such a contract, determining possession and use, is not regulated by the law of obligations but as an atypical contract specified under ownership rights in the Civil Code. The content of the contract can be freely dictated by the joint owners; the Civil Code does not specify any mandatory content. There is also no regulation as to the form of the contract, so it can be determined in writing, by word, or even by implied conduct by the joint owners. The method of use of the jointly owned real property cannot result in easement.

In the contract, the joint owners do not necessarily have to agree on the questions that the Civil Code specifically regulates. For example, expenses not exceeding the scope of prudent management, in which case the joint owners can decide with a simple majority vote based on their proportion of ownership. The Civil Code places decisions over use, possession, and utilization in the same category, so even if there is no contract, the joint owners can vote verbally too. This – with due consideration of the possibilities for settlements – creates a forced agreement for joint owners with smaller shares, in respect of which they may only contest as provided for in the Civil

77. BDT 2003/901.
78. BH 1999/170.
79. BH 1991/393.

Code. However, the contract between the joint owners – if successors have been named – is directly applicable for successors too, which means it has an in rem impact.

The content of the contract can cover a broader range of ownership rights, such as subjects which the owners can decide on with a simple majority. In the contract, the joint owners can decide to jointly transfer the entire jointly owned thing, enable it for use or usufruct, allocate it as collateral, or encumber it. Decisions in these matters require the agreement of every joint owner, as do decisions on expenses exceeding the scope of prudent management, so full agreement among the owners cannot be substituted by a vote, or more precisely, a successful agreement on this topic entails a civil law contract among the parties.

172. It is not possible to make a one-sided alteration to the contract-based use of the property. If the joint owners agree on the use and possession of the jointly owned thing, this agreement cannot be changed unilaterally or arbitrarily. If, however, the conditions taken into account at the time of the regulation have changed so significantly that the originally prudent arrangement now violates the requirements of rational management or the lawful rights of one of the joint owners, then any of the joint owners can request that the previous agreement be changed. If the joint owners divided the real property with the intention of creating permanently separate uses, then they are also separately obliged to collect the proceeds and bear expenses individually and are not entitled to additional usage fees from one another.

Regulating possession and use does not mean terminating the joint property. If the circumstances change significantly, a new agreement can be reached. Therefore, a joint owner using more than their share of the property cannot be made to pay a lump sum amount as final compensation.

173. In the internal legal relationship between the members, expenses exceeding those of prudent management require unanimous agreement. The reason for this is that while investments over and above preservation expenses and improving the condition of the thing may be useful, the original condition of the thing would be maintained without them. Such expenses can be to the financial detriment of the joint owners, who may not all want to pay them. The rule requires a unanimous decision from the joint owners not to authorize the work exceeding prudent management but to bear the joint burden of the expenses incurred. For expenses exceeding the scope of prudent management, the Civil Code requires the joint owners to vote unanimously but does not exclude the possibility of substituting legal declarations. For example, in theory, a legal declaration can be substituted in the case of construction work requiring a unanimous decision, but only, provided the conditions apply, if the joint owner benefiting from the construction accepts the expenses and if the object of the joint property is not modified during the construction.

All other decisions require a majority vote by the joint owners, but the joint owners can decide to follow different rules. In questions regarding the possession and use of jointly owned property, the majority vote of joint owners may be made verbally too. For example, a majority vote by joint owners can decide to enable tenants to connect to and use the jointly owned television system.

174. The provisions of the Civil Code on joint property pertaining to the legal relationship between joint owners of a joint property business share are only effective if they do not contradict the specific regulations of corporate law. Therefore, the joint owner affected by a members' meeting resolution should be disregarded in a vote by the joint owners of the joint business share. However, this interest of said joint owner does not in itself exclude the entire group of owners from the decision-making process.

175. If the regulation materially violates rational management or smaller legal interests, the minority can appeal the decision in court. The appeal does not suspend the execution of the decision; the court can suspend the decision if necessary. This regulation should be used if the joint owners disagree on whether the planned work is necessary for preservation and maintenance. In the absence of a decision, the court may rule on matters relating to possession, use, or utilization at the request of any of the joint owners in accordance with their ownership shares, their rights and lawful interests in the thing, and according to the requirements of prudent management.

The rules for contesting a majority decision in court are the same as previously stated. The Civil Code provides two legal grounds for appeal in court with regard to joint property. A decision materially violating rational management and minority rights can justify an appeal in court. In both cases, it can be crucial in terms of the decision whether or not the planned works constitute preservation. An appeal in court does not suspend the execution of the decision, but the court may opt for suspension based on the circumstances of the case.

176. Furthermore, the court has the authority to regulate the use, possession, or utilization method of the jointly owned property. In this case, the court ruling functions as an agreement between the parties. If the joint owners do not agree on possession and use (utilization method) of the jointly owned property, the court can regulate the possession and use (utilization method) according to the ownership shares, the rights, and legal interests of the joint owners in the property, and the requirements of rational management. The court has to proceed with great care when settling such cases of use. Primarily, it has to examine whether it is justifiable to change the current method of use. In this instance, the ownership ratios of the joint owners are very significant, but in the case of real property, other factors can also play a large role, such as the personal circumstances of the joint owners, the number of people living in the building (apartment), as well as the reasonable division of the premises most likely to avoid conflicts.

A disagreement between joint owners on possession and use – even if it only regards a specific part of the property – must be judged based on ownership shares, the legal interests and rights of the owners to the thing, and the requirements of rational management. So, there is no opportunity for the court to ignore these comprehensive settlement aspects and offer a temporary solution.

The joint owners can request that the court change the possession and method of use of the joint property if the conditions underlying the previous use have changed significantly.

The use of jointly owned, naturally divided, and unusable property can be regulated by the court by giving one joint owner exclusive use or by dividing the right of use between the joint owners. The natural result of such a regulation is that the joint owner, given no or limited use by the Court, cannot exercise his ownership rights regarding the possession and use while the other joint owner(s) is/are using the property.

2. Ruling on Proceeds

177. The proceeds of the property are divided among the joint owners according to their ownership shares; they are responsible for expenses on the same proportional basis, any obligations from the joint ownership, and any damages that may occur.

The joint owners are entitled to the proceeds from the property according to their ownership share, are obliged to bear the expenses accordingly, and must divide the cost of any damages to the property.

With regard to the proceeds or fruits of the property, it must be considered whether they can actually be divided. In this case, the joint owners gain a separate ownership right to the proceeds according to their ownership share. If the proceeds cannot be divided (e.g., indivisible thing), then they become the joint property of the joint owners as well, generally according to their original ownership shares. If, e.g., the property of one joint owner is damaged because part of a jointly owned building collapses or falls down, the compensation claim must be resolved based on the internal legal relationship between the joint owners, as per their rules on contributing to costs.

3. Ruling on Costs

178. Protecting and maintaining the condition of the jointly owned property is in the interest of every joint owner. If this is not in the interest of one of the joint owners, their obligation to maintain the condition of the property still applies since any deterioration of the property's condition would violate the other owners' interests. As a result, any joint owner is justified to take action aimed at preservation. However, before commencing this preservation, the other joint owners have to be informed, which serves the purpose of every joint owner being able to confirm the necessity for the preservation, assess the costs, and be able to make a statement about the method of preservation. Preservation expenses are paid by the joint owners in line with their ownership shares because this constitutes a necessary expense for every joint owner.

If the joint property comprises multiple things, the rights of third parties on the things arising before the inception of joint ownership shall accrue to the ownership shares replacing those things.

179. The rights of the third parties relating to the jointly owned property relate to the ownership share of the joint owner with whom they are in a legal relationship. Based on the right of disposal, none of the joint owners is allowed to burden the entire thing. In line with this regulation, in the case of joint property on a thing comprising materials with separate owners, the burdens originally on the individual components do not extend to the whole property or its components. A burden on components is reclassified according to the Civil Code and applies only to the jointly owned property created according to the component's share of the entire thing.

180. The joint owners – if they agree – can reach decisions on the joint property with a majority vote. The vote of every joint owner is proportionate to their share of the property. A unanimous decision by joint owners is required for expenses beyond the scope of prudent management, transferring the ownership right to the entire property, encumbering the entire property or assuming obligations covering the entire property.

Every owner has the right to vote in matters regarding the joint property. An agreement is invalid for formal reasons if any owner is excluded from the vote or this right is limited. In terms of the invalid decision, it makes no difference whether the decision would have been the same if the excluded owner had been allowed to vote in line with their share.

4. Right of Disposition

181. Joint owners are permitted to dispose of their ownership share. Every ownership share can be the subject of an individual transaction, so its own right can be transferred and acquired individually, provided the acquiring party is not restricted in acquiring property.

Only all of the joint owners are allowed to dispose of a jointly owned thing. As a result, the consent of all owners is required for transferring the ownership right to the entire thing, encumbering the entire thing, or assuming obligations covering the entire thing. The Civil Code discusses this under decision-making, which applies to the internal legal relationship between joint owners but is also significant in external legal relationships. A third party can only gain ownership rights for the entire thing or other rights to the entire thing if all joint owners agree. The consent of every joint owner is required to enter into a real property contract or a rental contract for part thereof or for a flat-exchange contract by a tenant. However, the joint owners may transfer their rights of disposal to each other. That said, such a declaration must be explicit and cannot be interpreted expansively.

B. Pre-emption, Pre-rental, and Pre-leasehold Rights of Joint Owners

182. Joint owners have a third-party right of pre-emption, pre-rental, and pre-leasehold with regard to the ownership share of the other joint owner. If it is apparent to the seller that the real property has joint owners not recorded in the land registry, he must disclose his offer to those owners, too, under general rules. In the case of joint owners not recorded in the land registry, the legal consequences of neglecting to disclose any offer cannot be applied against a purchaser who proceeded with the contract in good faith. The joint owners can exercise their pre-emption, pre-rental, or pre-leasehold rights in proportion to their ownership share of the part of the property in question. If no agreement is reached between them, but there is a joint owner who – even together with another joint owner – endorses the offer for the property share in question, then the rights of pre-emption, pre-rental, and pre-leasehold shall accrue to him or them alone. If there is more than one such joint owner acting alone, the owner gets to choose, and the pre-emption, pre-rental and pre-leasehold rights accrue to the selected joint owner. The pre-emption right specified in a separate law precedes the pre-emption right of the joint owner based on this law. The joint owner can exercise his pre-emption right even in enforcement procedures.

In the event of a pre-emption right, if the owner of the thing wants to sell it, the holder of the pre-emption right must be notified of the purchase offer, and he may purchase the thing from the owner (seller) with a unilateral declaration. The holder of the pre-emption right cannot transfer this right to a third party.[80]

183. The pre-emption right may only be exercised for sales and purchases, not for alienation by other legal titles. Pre-emption rights can only be enforced for sales involving exchanges if it can be determined that the sale/purchase is the dominant part and the exchange was only included in the contract to circumvent the pre-emption right.

The owner cannot circumvent the pre-emption right, burdening their right of disposal by selling the subject of the pre-emption right together with another thing for a joint price. However, the situation is different if the joint owner wants to sell separately owned, non-residential premises (garage) in an apartment building together with the owner-occupied apartment to a third party. In this case, the joint owners cannot exercise their pre-emption right with regard to the non-residential premises.

The joint owners enjoy pre-emption rights. If the sales contract is annulled, the buyer cannot be considered a joint owner of the property until the contract is annulled, and therefore, during this time, he can exercise the pre-emption right for sales contracts concluded for other ownership shares. With a sales contract annulled before the offer is disclosed to the holder of the pre-emption right, the pre-emption right may not be exercised.

184. The purchase offer must be disclosed to the holder of the pre-emption right in writing, and the letter of acceptance must be disclosed to the seller in writing for them to be effective. The exception here is if said disclosure would be extremely difficult or subject to considerable delay due to the location of the holder of the pre-emption right or other circumstances. Such an exception – exemption from the disclosure obligation – could be the relatively large number of joint owners. A joint owner has a pre-emption right only once during a case when they are informed of

80. *See* Ferenc Petrik, *Elővásárlási jog – dologi jogviszony* (*Pre-emption Right – In Rem Legal Relationship*), 55 Magyar Jog 3 f. (2008).

the offer to buy. If they do not exercise their right to pre-empt, it ceases and will not become effective again at a later date. However, a statement from the holder of the pre-emption right – with knowledge of the seller's intent to sell – that they do not wish to buy the property does not relieve the seller from the obligation to disclose an offer received later on.

185. If it is apparent to the seller that the real property has joint owners not recorded in the land registry, he must disclose his offer to those owners, too, unless it is extremely difficult to do so. In the case of joint owners outside the land registry, the legal consequences of neglecting to state the offer to them cannot be held against a buyer who proceeded with the contract in good faith. With regard to the portion of the property the joint owner wishes to sell, the person who has a legal title under the law of obligations to acquire the portion of the jointly owned property, and has had their request for the registration of the ownership right displayed in the land registry, is entitled to the pre-emption right. However, this person can only exercise their pre-emption right if the ownership right is registered in the land registry by the generally expected deadline for accepting the contractual offer.

186. The joint owners may exercise their pre-emption right together and equally for the property (or part of the property) being sold. If no such agreement is reached between them, but there is a joint owner who – even together with another joint owner – endorses the offer for the whole property for sale (or part thereof), then the pre-emption right shall accrue to him or them alone. If there is more than one such joint owner acting alone, the seller gets to choose, and the pre-emption right accrues to the joint owner selected. After the disclosure and acceptance of the purchase offer, it is not possible for the original contracting parties to demand a higher price from the party exercising their pre-emption right with reference to previous value-enhancing investments.

If a pre-emption right exists, any sale or purchase made without notifying the holder is not in effect vis-à-vis the holder. A joint owner with a pre-emption right can only claim a right to disregard their obligation to disclose the purchase offer if his actions until then were in good faith. The actions of the holder cannot be considered in good faith if the disclosure failed due to an unregistered address change, or if they did not give an indication of their intent to buy having learnt about it from another source, and only decided to exercise their right after a long time due to the higher sales value.

187. If the holder of the pre-emption right requests that the sales contract be deemed in violation of their rights and therefore ineffective, he must also make a statement accepting the purchase offer. The court will assess the seriousness of the statement, as well as the actual willingness and ability to perform. As a result of the acceptance declaration, a sales contract is concluded between the holder of the pre-emption right and the joint owner and all related demands can be dealt with in the same case. The entire purchase offer must be disclosed to the joint owner with the pre-emption right. A deadline must be given for accepting the purchase offer that is justified under the circumstances.

188. Previous legal practice expressly ruled out the joint owner exercising his pre-emption right during an enforcement procedure, stating that alienation, in this case, disregards the will of the joint owner. The new Civil Code overwrites this because the rights of the previous owner of the auctioned property cease to exist, while this does not violate the rights of the creditor. However, the joint owners have a significant interest in who the new joint owner will be after the enforcement procedure. If the property is sold through a real estate auction, the joint owner with the pre-emption right must be notified about the auction. Similarly, joint owners have pre-emption rights in liquidation procedures. They may only exercise this right during a duly announced public sale of the real property.

189. Finally, it is worth noting that the regulations of pre-emption rights must also be applied for pre-rental and pre-leasehold too. When a joint owner signs a rental or pre-rental contract with a third party, the other joint owners have the right to sign a rental or pre-rental contract under the same conditions. The pre-leasehold right of the leaseholder is akin to the pre-emption right, so in cases not regulated by legislation, the rules of pre-emption rights must be applied for pre-leasehold rights.

C. Protection of Joint Property

190. Any joint owner can individually take action to protect joint property.[81] The action of any joint owner for the protection of the joint property is effective for the entire thing, i.e., for the entire ownership right of the whole thing. Consequently, any joint owner can lawfully take action against the wrongful possessor of a flat in a jointly owned real property. Regardless of their ownership share, any joint owner can individually launch legal action for the cessation of wrongful use of the flat or to empty the flat.[82] Furthermore, the joint owner can independently request protection of possession from the possessor of neighbouring real property.[83]

D. Termination of Joint Property

1. Conditions of the Termination

191. No one can be forced to own joint property or to use or possess the thing jointly with others. As a result, the termination of joint property can be demanded by any joint owner at any time; this right cannot be waived.

The termination of joint property can be demanded by any joint owner but only by a joint owner. The joint owner cannot exercise this right if it is in violation of the other joint owners' rights. A contract in which the owners exclude certain methods of termination does not constitute a waiver of the owners' rights to terminate joint property, and therefore, such a contract is not invalid.

81. BH 1990/378.
82. BH 1979/416.
83. BH 1990/335.

192. A court is obliged to terminate joint property at the request of a joint owner; the only limitation to this in the Civil Code is if the termination comes at an inopportune time.

Besides, the judicial practice has to consider other aspects too over and above the Civil Code rules on joint property. Such an aspect is the opportunity to abuse one's rights. The court cannot terminate the joint property if it is found that rights are being abused or exercising the rights seriously violates the interests of the other joint owners.

The right to terminate a joint property cannot be exercised abusively in a way that seriously violates the interests of the other joint owners. The cases in which termination of joint property violates the rights or statutory interests of the other joint owners are too many to list. Such include when someone acquires a portion of the jointly owned property and shortly after files a suit to terminate the jointly owned property against a financially weaker, joint-owner resident who is not prepared for the change.[84]

193. A further obstruction to the termination of joint property can be the long-term shared use of the real property, which entails additional rights under the law of obligations; furthermore, the collateral function of the property share, which means the rights of other beneficiaries recorded in the land registry but who are not joint owners could be violated if the joint property is terminated. Additionally, the termination of joint property of divorced couples should be avoided when the resident former spouse is unable to possess the other half of the property as per the divorce suit agreement; there is no opportunity to auction the property while it is resided in, and, weighing up the fair interests of both parties, the resident cannot be compelled to move out.

194. When terminating joint property, a solution serving a balance of interests should always be sought. As a result of terminating joint property, none of the joint owners should gain an unfair and unjustified material advantage to the detriment of another.

2. Methods of the Termination

195. The termination of joint property can happen through natural division, by one of the joint owners taking on the shares of the other joint owners, by selling it to a third party, and turning the joint property into an apartment building. The court decides on the most appropriate method for the termination of the joint property in light of the circumstances; the only method it may not choose is one which one of the joint owners has protested against.

196. The objects of a joint property should first be divided naturally.

A prerequisite for married couples to terminate joint property on real property is settling the disagreements on disputed use. This is because only the resident or

84. BH 1986/414.

authorized user can be compelled to redeem it. The settlement of use also means that the resident joint owner (rightful user) can only be compelled to leave the property if they are willing to or have been provided with an appropriate alternative property. Deviating from this rule is only legally possible if additional facts come to light regarding one of the former spouses, which would justify the termination of their legal relationship with the other tenant and the establishment of bad faith in the case of rented properties.

If conditions for the natural division of the jointly owned property apply, deviating from this method of termination is only justified in exceptional cases. Judicial practice dictates that when terminating joint property, it should primarily be sought to separate properties naturally that are physically separable, provided that applying this method of division does not cause significant loss of value or obstruct intended use. For these conditions to be met, care must be taken to satisfy all the needs that must be satisfied for the shared parts of the property and the now independent properties to be suitable for their intended use. Regulating the method of use for the jointly owned property is different from terminating the joint property via natural division. Then again, if settling the use of joint property happens by terminating the joint property with the intent that such is permanent, the termination request may only deviate from this in cases involving a serious violation of interests.[85]

197. With the natural division of joint property, the division must occur according to the shares of the joint owners, except when it is otherwise justified by financial or practical reasons; in these cases, financial compensation must be provided. When presiding over an application for the natural termination of joint property, the Court must examine the layout of the property and strive to create a unity of interests. The spatial equality of divided real properties does not in itself constitute equality of value.

The value at the time of the natural termination of joint property is determined by the state of the real property at that time. A predicted rise in value due to future circumstances does not change the value of the property at the time of the judgment on termination.[86] The circumstances of the joint owners, the sales value of the properties created through division and their usability all mean that the properties can be given to one or more joint owners.

198. If the joint property cannot be terminated through natural division, the court must strive for one of the joint owners to acquire the share of the other joint owner. The joint owner in possession of the residential property can be ordered by the court without any obligation to acquire the property, depending on their financial circumstances. A contract for the termination of joint property through redemption cannot be considered valid until a redemption price is determined.

The termination of the joint property can only occur if the property of a joint owner is given to another joint owner and the purchase price is determined at the same time.

85. BH 225/2007, EBH 1502/2006.
86. BH 269/2010.

199. The termination of joint property in a populated building, when the compensation of a joint owner resident is received by a non-resident joint owner, can only be ordered if the non-resident joint owner agrees. The joint owner with a right to partial use of a flat must be granted as many rights during the termination of joint property as the non-owner resident would receive on other grounds. As a result, they can only be compelled to move without their consent if an appropriate alternative flat is offered to them.

200. One possible method for the termination of joint property is the sale of the property. However, this cannot happen by the court ordering the joint owners to sign a sales contract. The termination of joint property through the sale of the property happens through a court-ordered auction, for which the court can stipulate the auction conditions. The Civil Code expressly states that in these cases, the court must determine the minimum purchase price.

201. The termination of joint property through an auction relates to the entire jointly owned property and not to the share of one of the joint owners. In the case of a termination of joint property by auction, if the auction sale does not take place, the joint owners maintain their rights relating to their joint property. The fact that a resident joint owner protests and is not willing to move out does not mean it is no longer possible to terminate the joint property via an auction.

202. There is no legal regulation stipulating that in the event of a termination of joint property, the court can only order that a joint owner losing their ownership right has to move out if the joint owner agrees to this. On the contrary, the termination of joint property also terminates the former joint owner's right of use – based on his ownership right – which means they become a wrongful possessor and are obliged to hand over possession of their property to the auction buyer.

203. Transforming joint property into an apartment building can only be done based on an individual application. Transformation into an apartment building does not take priority over other methods of terminating joint ownership. Transforming a joint property into an apartment property does not constitute a method of terminating joint property in the strict sense. It is certainly not one of the most common methods. If the partial existence of the joint property is not desirable due to bad relations between the parties and the applicant cannot cover the costs of the transformation, then the transformation into an apartment building as a means of terminating a joint property is invalid.

In order for a court to decide on the termination of joint property or its transformation into an apartment building, the ownership shares must be clarified. In legal action for the termination of joint property, the court can order the transformation of the joint property into an apartment building at the request of any of the joint owners. In this case, the apartment building's deed of foundation is replaced by the court's decision, and its content, with due consideration of the opinions and interests of the parties, is established by the court in its ruling.

II. Co-ownership Applied to Apartment Buildings

204. An apartment building is established if a physically divided space consisting of at least two individual flats or non-residential areas, or at least one separate flat and one non-residential area, becomes the private property of the joint owners, but the areas of the building, building equipment, premises, or flat not determined as private property are jointly owned. If the parcel of land on which the building stands is not jointly owned, then the joint owners have land-use rights. The ownership share of the jointly owned property and the privately owned flat or non-residential area together constitute an independent property.

The ownership share of the joint owners that pertains to the joint property and the ownership right pertaining to the flat or the non-residential area cannot be transferred or encumbered separately. Apartment building property is subject to the rules of joint property.

A. Precursors to Regulation of Apartment Buildings

205. The 1914 draft of the Private Law Bill planned to eliminate the mass lack of housing by introducing building law and the possibility of apartment buildings, i.e., it explicitly rejected the idea of natural division.[87] Nine years later, on 23 November 1923, the Minister of Justice submitted a drastically different bill on apartment building properties. The bill argued that the purpose of the law was to stimulate the construction of buildings and to create a cooperative legal framework for people with less capital to undertake building projects.

The first apartment building law was Act XII of 1924 on apartment building property, which came into effect on 20 May 1924. Minister of Justice Decree 30000/1925 on the planning of apartment building properties was created on 2 July 1925 based on the authority of section 12 of the Act. In the case of a building or parts of buildings on a piece of land, Act XII of 1924 qualified an apartment building as being the exclusive property of the joint owners and the individual parts as jointly owned. The apartment building did not gain legal personality, and the building representative was qualified to represent it.

Act XII of 1924 regulated the foundation and functioning of apartment buildings and the internal legal relationship of joint owners in a mere twelve paragraphs. It is worth noting that the law specifies an official deed or legally notarized deed was required to establish an apartment building; furthermore, official approval on the building plan from the organization responsible for approving construction and an official certificate verifying the building may be lived in. Legislation required that the deed of foundation regulate numerous organizational aspects, such as maintenance of the building, its use, its repair in the case of damage, shared expenses, burden of expenses, the voting rights of joint owners, the election of a building

87. *See* s. 582(2) of the Private Law Bill of 1914.

representative, their powers, and security for shared responsibilities. To ensure compliance with shared responsibilities, the building representative was authorized to register a mortgage on the (exclusive) property without the consent of the other joint owners.

206. Following the Second World War, new regulations pertaining to apartment buildings were introduced in order to restore buildings, and then on 6 December 1948, as a precursor to nationalization, the possibility of establishing apartment buildings was suspended.[88]

The decree of the Minister of Building Affairs was a significant breakthrough,[89] which intended to help the construction of buildings using private funds through construction communities with government support. This triggered a construction boom in Hungary. Furthermore, other decrees allowed the sale of state flats to tenants,[90] which meant their transformation into apartment buildings.

207. In 1977, new laws were passed.[91] Compared to the previous regulation, the mandatory renovation fund was a novel feature, along with the opportunity to elect a management committee instead of a building representative and to have an audit committee. Decree-Law 11 of 1977 regulated the matters falling under the jurisdiction of the general meeting, prescribing detailed rules for the operation of the general meeting (convening, decision-making, procedure if there is no quorum, launching legal action to have decisions rendered invalid). The new regulation also made it possible for an apartment property to be created by a court.

By the end of the 1980s, it was very difficult to access building loans; the economic effects of the regime change restricted the opportunities for constructing apartment buildings. Act CLVII of 1997, consisting of forty-five paragraphs, came into effect on 1 March 1998. The law stipulated that even one owner had the right to establish an apartment building and that this was possible even before the building was constructed. Organizational questions could be addressed not only in the deed of foundation but also in the by-laws. In practice, it was common that preemption and pre-rental rights could be stipulated only in the deed of foundation and that the building representative could register a mortgage on the private property of a joint owner who owed more than half a year's worth of common charges. The new law regulated the operation of apartment building bodies in detail and defined the concept of expenses exceeding the scope of prudent management.

208. The currently in force law came into effect on 1 January 2004 and introduced new regulations regarding numerous facets of apartment buildings.[92] Act CXXXIII of 2003 was modified in 2009;[93] the main changes were as follows:[94]

88. *See* György Matúz, *Nyolcvan éves a társasház* (*The Apartment Building Is Eighty Years Old*), 52 Magyar Jog 4 (2005).
89. ÉM Decree 2/1964 (VII. 5.).
90. Government Decree 32/1969 (IX. 30.) and ÉVM-MÉM-PM Decree (IX. 30.).
91. Decree-Law 11 of 1977 on apartment buildings and Decree-Law 12 of 1977 on the uniform regulation of housing associations came into force on 1 Jul. 1977.
92. Act CXXXIII of 2003 on apartment buildings.
93. By the Act LXXXIX of 2009.

- it introduced legal oversight by the public prosecutor;
- it required users of private property to adhere to the house regulations and tolerate entrance to the flats in extreme situations;
- it simplified the concept of work within the flats;
- it defined the powers of the general meeting;
- it regulated in detail the parts of general meeting invitations and minutes;
- it defined the statutory rules of notification with regard to the payment of common charge arrears;
- it prescribed the involvement of a professional accountant for the audit committee in apartment buildings with over fifty tenants or more than HUF 10 million in annual income;
- it clarified the definition of emergency expenses.

Act CLXXVII of 2010 intended to clarify the legislative uncertainty present in section 51/A of the Act on apartment buildings introduced by Act CXXXIII of 2009, and with regard to the required presence of a professional accountant raised the limit from HUF 10 million to HUF 20 million. It introduced a new regulation regarding whether the general meeting of the apartment building can prescribe rules for the proper use of non-residential areas or if they can ban, in these places, the organization of activities falling under the act on gambling and games of chance, sexual/ erotic services, and the sale and distribution of sexual aids.

The Civil Code continues to define only framework rules with regard to apartment buildings; detailed regulations on apartment buildings can be found in the Act.

B. Concept of Apartment Buildings

209. One of the conditions for establishing an apartment building property is a building that is physically separate and is suitable for entry as an independent property in the land registry or is already registered as real property. Its foundation requires at least two individual real properties, which can be two owner-occupied apartments, one such apartment and one non-residential area, or two separate real properties not for residential purposes. Since there is one building, there are areas and installations, which are privately owned or can only be jointly owned.

For a property that is privately owned, it is not important how other laws may define an apartment or a non-residential area. An apartment building can be established on any real property that can be registered as an individual property in the land registry. The registration also means that the property is independent and eligible for sale under civil law.[95]

210. The apartment building property does not affect the legal independence of the properties in the apartment building. The owner of a privately owned property

94. Ld. ehhez József Rakvács, *Társasházi törvény* (*Act on Apartments*) 5 ff. (HVG-ORAC 1998).
95. Gábor Kiss, *A társasházi jog kézikönyve* (*Manual of the Apartments Law*) 23 (Novotni Kiadó 2011).

is free to dispose of, alienate, or encumber their property. However, when exercising other ownership rights, the apartment building law allows the tenants to regulate and limit the use and utilization of the property, in accordance with the legal interests of the joint owners, through the by-laws and the opportunity to convene general meetings. However, the deed of foundation can allow for the creation of pre-emption and pre-rental rights for a privately owned dwelling or premises. However, this can only be done in the deed of foundation and only for the benefit of every joint owner. Taxes and levies on a privately owned property are naturally the responsibility of the joint owner.

Private ownership can relate to part of a building or area that does not physically constitute part of the building; its ownership should be clarified in the deed of foundation. If there is no such provision, then judicial practice generally places this part of the building under joint ownership.

211. During the codification of the new Civil Code, the possibility arose for legislation on apartment buildings to be included in the new Civil Code. The reason for continuing to regulate apartment buildings in a separate law is mainly that this legislation contains numerous technical standards that change, which would have made its incorporation into the Civil Code unlikely.[96]

C. Demarcation of the Legal Framework of Apartment Buildings

212. Apartment buildings differ from joint property since, in the case of joint property, the joint owners possess intangible shares of the whole property, and every joint owner has the right to exercise their ownership rights over the entire property, but only to the degree of their ownership share. In the case of apartment buildings, the regulations on joint property still apply since the individual parts of the apartment building, especially shared spaces, are the joint property of the tenants.

By contrast, qualified joint ownership is closer to apartment buildings, in which the joint owners enter into a contract for the use of specific parts of the property. Such a contract between parties creates a law of obligations relationship, which does not constitute rights or obligations with regard to third parties. For example, the contract between joint owners means that a joint owner cannot individually encumber an area that is used exclusively by him, only the area he owns, which is an intangible share of the entire ownership right.

213. In the case of superficies, the ownership right for the land and the house built upon it are separate, and the superficiary is allowed to use the land in exchange for a superficies fee. Superficies law still exists in the private law of certain countries, such as Switzerland, Italy, and Spain.[97] In the case of superficies law, the owner of the land and the superficies right can be separated, based on which we talk about ownership rights and rights over the property of someone else.

96. Vékás, *Szakértői Javaslat supra,* 654.
97. Földi and Hamza, *supra,* 375.

214. Floor law (*partibus divis*) differs from superficies in that the floor owner also owns part of the land. In the case of a property possessed by a legal person (public company, cooperative), the ownership right held by the members or shareholders of the legal person provides an indirect opportunity to exercise ownership rights over the real property. Apartment building associations work in a similar way, as well as time-sharing contracts, which divide the use of the property into periods of time.

D. Different Legal Relationships in Regulations of Apartment Buildings

215. From an ownership right perspective, apartment buildings are Janus-faced since they partly appear uniformly in the land registry on the master sheet and partly as the individual apartment building dwellings and non-residential areas on separate sheets. Furthermore, the legal framework of apartment buildings gives rise to three different legal relationships in the law: one based on ownership right – including joint property – one based on the law of obligations, and one based on organizational relations. Beyond this, substantive law regulations determine the ways of enforcing claims and demands.

1. Exercising Ownership Rights

216. Ownership rights are fundamentally important with regard to apartment buildings, as is seen in private property and joint property. With regard to areas considered private property, the use and renovation of such areas generally impact jointly owned areas too. The fundamental question is when does the use of a private property area injure the interests of the joint owners in the apartment building? A general meeting resolution of an apartment building is invalid if it requires the use of a privately owned dwelling being used as a non-residential area or the approval of such to be accepted by the other joint owners (e.g., renting the apartment out for a film shoot).[98] Furthermore, protection of possession and neighbour rights are also in effect. The general meeting of an apartment building has the right to forbid the use of business premises in the apartment building, which differs from the activities specified in its business licence, e.g., a pizzeria that operates as a full-scale restaurant.[99] The current legal regulation specifies one general prohibition, according to which joint owners may not exercise their rights with regard to their private property if this violates the other joint owners' statutory interests. Furthermore, the owner is obliged to use the property according to its intended use, and certain activities can be forbidden in the by-laws or the rules of practising such activities defined. These regulations cover not only the owners of the private property but also any of its users.

98. BH 2007/237.
99. BH 2009/184.

2. Using Utility Services

217. The use of district heating and water creates an external legal issue for apartment buildings if there are no separate utility meters for each flat. In this case, the apartment building has to make good on any debts that individual residents do not pay, meaning the burden is ultimately on those residents who pay for their utilities. Also, in this case, the sanctions imposed by the service provider for unpaid fees impact all the joint owners, meaning they can suspend the services even to apartments that have paid their utility fees. In this respect, it has happened in judicial practice that in order to divide the water utility fees according to consumption rather than ownership shares, the court modified the deed of foundation.

Another problem is whether the general meeting can exercise ownership rights with regard to the joint property of the apartment building. Rakvács said this was explicitly unconstitutional since the general meeting has no legal 4personality and, therefore, does not have the same rights as one.[100]

3. Relative Legal Capacity of Apartment Buildings

218. The legal personality of apartment buildings extends to the maintenance of the building, the acquisition of rights, and acceptance of obligations derived from the management of issues arising from joint property and exercising rights related to joint property. Partial legal capacity raises numerous taxation and accounting problems. With regard to the underlying regulation of apartment buildings, the regulations of joint property and civil law relating to companies are mostly applicable. As a result, the lack of legal personality for apartment buildings creates significant difficulties in everyday life.

219. Act CLVII of 1997 introduced the relative legal capacity of apartment buildings with the legislative intent of removing obstacles from the representation of the apartment building and everyday administration in relation to joint property, in a similar way to business organizations without legal personality. Therefore, the law permits the group of joint owners under a common name to acquire rights and assume responsibilities within the confines of managing joint property, to have legal capacity in court, to exercise ownership rights and to pay common expenses. The common name is the common name of the apartment building. Apartment buildings have been obliged to have a name since 1998; if the owners do not name it differently, this is the address of the apartment building followed by 'apartment building'.[101] The Hungarian Constitutional Court ruling on relative legal capacity states

100. József Rakvács, *A közös tulajdon bírói gyakorlatának elemzése és annak tanulságai. A társasháztulajdon* (*Analysis of the Judicial Practice of Joint Ownership and Its Experiences. The Ownership of Apartment Building*), 8 Gazdaság és Jog 45 (2000).

101. Kiss, *supra*, 30.

that 'apartment buildings according to Sec. 3(1) of the apartment building law have certain substantive and procedural law capacities, but an apartment building is not a legal person'.[102]

Pursuant to the law, an apartment building only has relative legal capacity and can only sue or be sued in matters relating to building maintenance and joint property. The special situation of relative legal capacity is that, unlike other organizations with legal capacity, an apartment building does not have a registered seat; therefore, documents addressed to the apartment building must be delivered to the building of the representative.

4. Organizational Issues

220. For apartment buildings, there is a string of law of obligation relationships between the apartment building and the owners. Such a legal relationship is formed by the house rules and the by-laws, while in terms of content, we can also include the legal relations of joint property expenses, renovations, and preservation expenses. Apartment buildings also raise organizational questions. Although an apartment building is not a legal person, in matters with non-owners, the apartment building takes action through the building representative when cases relate to the building as a whole and to joint property. As a result, the internal affairs of the apartment building are managed by the general meeting, the administrative committee, and the auditor. A building representative is a key person in the apartment building. However, the opportunity to oversee the building representative's activities or remove them is limited. With regard to the affairs of the apartment building, the building representative obtains up-to-date information on a daily basis.

For apartment buildings, the deed of foundation is designed to lay the foundations for the legal relations between joint owners. The provisions of the deed of foundation may not be deviated from, e.g., the convening of a general meeting, which is valid if the invitation to the joint owners is sent or posted at least eight days before the date of the general meeting. Alongside the deed of foundation, the provisions of the by-laws must be followed. If they contain contradictory, imprecise, or convoluted regulations, they are not able to ensure the smooth operation of the apartment building, and thus, the general meeting resolution accepting the by-laws is invalid.

5. Enforcing Claims, Minority Rights

221. Seeking legal remedies through the court is possible by filing a suit for the invalidity of a resolution made by the apartment building's general meeting if the regulation is in violation of the law, the deed of foundation, or the by-laws, or significantly violates smaller rightful interests.[103] The Supreme Court identified that 'the needs and claims of joint owners can be enforced by convening a general meeting

102. Decision No. 3/2006 (II. 8.) of the Constitutional Court.

103. Article 42 of the Act on Apartment Buildings. EBH 2008/1795.

as per Sec. 35(2) of the Apartment Building Act, or by challenging the adopted resolution. The presiding courts correctly referred to the Supreme Court's previous legal ruling in a civil law suit, which clearly stated that the court does not have the authority to get involved in the internal affairs of an apartment building; the general rules of court action are stated exclusively in Sec. 42(1) of the Apartment Building Act'.[104]

222. Lawful minority interests are violated if the payment of expenses changes in a way that is detrimental to them. For example, doorman and security costs do not qualify as common charges; therefore, dividing these costs according to the rules on common charges is in violation of lawful minority rights.[105] However, it is not in violation of the law and fair minority interests if an apartment building general meeting states that the joint owners do not accept the costs of one joint owner interested in renovating a jointly owned section of the property.[106] We have to note that the construction authority cannot examine the validity of an apartment building general meeting resolution.

With regard to these two interest groups – the members of which may differ – the payment of justified costs is what counts. With regard to maintenance costs of buildings, parts of buildings, equipment and installations in joint property, section 9 of Act II of 1924 provided an alternative to paying costs based on ownership shares by offering the possibility to pay in proportion to the owner's interest. In practice, this can mean, e.g., that the ground floor tenant does not pay, or pays significantly less, for lift and stairwell expenses. Nowadays, when managing residential buildings that are physically divided in terms of use but which constitute an apartment building, this solution is clearly the best to avoid conflicts. The current regulations on apartment buildings would allow for such internal rules, but in lieu of this, regardless of some dwellings being private property, if a business owner does not use a utility (e.g., heating), they are still obliged to pay the proportionate cost.[107]

6. Questions of Responsibility

223. The apartment building community, as a relatively independent legal entity, is primarily responsible for the obligations of the community vis-à-vis third parties. Consequently, the apartment building is responsible for the contractual obligations which the apartment building makes. The apartment building itself is the subject of the utility services related to the operation of the apartment building. The needs and claims stemming from these contracts cannot be enforced directly against the joint owners. The same is true for contracts made regarding maintenance, renovation, etc., or even for the costs incurred by necessary preservation work. The payment of fees for absolutely necessary preservation work on the apartment building can be claimed from the apartment building, but the joint owners can only be made to pay

104. BH 2010/325.
105. BH 2007/300.
106. BH 2010/18.
107. BH 2010/253; EBH 2009/2061.

for the obligations of the apartment building proportionately to their ownership share, and only if the payment cannot be extracted from the apartment building.[108]

224. According to the main rule, joint owners can be held directly accountable for the obligations of the apartment building in proportion to their ownership share or to the degree specified in the by-laws. In respect of third parties (i.e., with direct obligations of the apartment building), the rules of simple deficiency guarantees apply to the joint owners in terms of their duty to pay.

225. In the case of rules on neighbour rights, the responsibility of the apartment building raises an interesting question. Judicial practice varies on this topic.[109] A significant number of court decisions consider the current owners of the apartment building responsible for constructions in violation of neighbour rights, regardless of whether the violation occurred under the previous owners. In other cases, the developer was found to be responsible, while there are also cases where the responsibility of the developer as well as the current owner of the flat both arose. In the case of apartment building flats, the examination of the current owner's responsibility as a respondent results in all owners being obliged to act as respondents. With densely populated apartment buildings, this method essentially makes it impossible to proceed with litigation because of the numerous successions.

There can be unnecessary disturbances under neighbour's rights between the owners of properties in an apartment building, in the case of developments, expansions (e.g., air conditioning or de-humidifier installation) to the property, which impair the living conditions of the tenants in the other flats.[110]

7. Contracts for the Use of Timeshare Properties

226. Timeshares were invented in the United States in the 1970s. The purpose was to convert expensive and little-used privately owned holiday properties into ones where the users would have the right to reside and use it while only paying for the property for as much time as they were there. They attempted to satisfy this need by emphasizing the shared use of certain holiday properties. The timeshare system was very popular in the United States and appeared in Western Europe too.

227. A time-sharing contract allows for the terms of use to be achieved through a law of obligations framework (contract for use), a law of things framework (joint property, personal easement), or via so-called indirect rights (e.g., shares in a financial

---

108. Kiss *supra*, 44.
109. Éva V. Varga, *Kit terhelhet felelősség az ingatlan szomszédjogi szabályokat sértő beépítése miatt?* (*Who Is Responsible for Building Real Estate with Breaching Neighbourhood Rights?*), 57 Magyar Jog 109 (2010).
110. Tamás Prugberger, *Az új társasházi törvény néhány jogalkalmazási problémája* (*Some Problems of Judicial Practice Concerning the New Apartment House Act*), 13 Gazdaság és Jog 11 (2005).

organization and cooperative).[111] Many different legal constructions of time-sharing were created, and the following are the most common:

- right of use based on the law of obligations, in which case a contractual legal relationship grants the purchaser the holiday property or another property for a predetermined time (e.g., ninety-nine years); the contract also allows for transfer, assignment and inheritance;
- the law of things system (*Dauerwohnrecht*), based on which the subject gains in rem protected rights to their share in the property;
- use through an intermediary organization, where an organization (public company, cooperative, association) is the owner of the property, people become shareholders or members in the organization and thus acquire the right to use it, e.g., the HAPIMAG model (Swiss legal solution) is based on a public company where the shareholders lend to the company, in exchange for which they receive a right of use to the property. In this case, the right of use contract and the sales contract for shares share the same legal fate and cannot be judged separately;
- in the asset management (fiduciary) framework, the asset manager oversees the upkeep of the property for the beneficiaries.

228. The spread of the time-sharing system brought to light certain problems that had to be managed at the legislative level. The marketing techniques used in selling the right of use to time-sharing properties were often directed at eliciting fast decisions from consumers, motivated by various presents and prizes, thereby not allowing the consumer to make a well-thought-out decision about whether they actually needed the right of use. In many cases, the necessary information was not given to potential consumers, and many promises were made only verbally while not appearing on the contract, and misleading information was often provided regarding the buy-back of the right of use. The legal construction of the right of use was often not sufficiently disclosed to the buyers, e.g., the fact they were only gaining contractual rights, not possession rights.

229. On 26 October 1994, the EU accepted Directive 94/47/EC.[112] Based on the directive, a Hungarian decree was adopted.[113] The Hungarian regulation partly takes the directive verbatim and partly goes beyond it with a good dose of administrative regulations. The EU then accepted Directive 2008/122/EC,[114] which was implemented in Hungary through another decree.[115]

---

111. Judit Fazekas, *A hazai fogyasztóvédelem jogi szabályozása* (*Regulation of the Domestic Consumer Protection*) 62 (1/2004).
112. Directive 94/47/EC of the European Parliament and the Council of 26 Oct. 1994 on the protection of purchasers in respect of certain aspects of contracts relating to the purchase of the right to use immovable properties on a timeshare basis.
113. Government Decree 20/1999 (II. 5.) on contracts for the use of timeshare properties.
114. Directive 2008/122/EC of the European Parliament and of the Council of 14 Jan. 2009 on the protection of consumers in respect of certain aspects of timeshare, long-term holiday product, resale and exchange contracts.
115. Government Decree 141/2011 (VII. 21.) on the contract for accommodation shared by time and for long-term holiday products, and about the service activity of long-term use of accommodation.

230. The contract for the right of use to a time-sharing property is a consumer contract concluded for more than one year or an indeterminate period, based on which, for a consideration, the consumer gains the right of use for one or more properties for multiple pre-determined amounts of time. Based on the contract, the company is obliged to transfer the right of use to the consumer, and the consumer is obliged to pay the consideration in exchange for the right of use. The Hungarian legal regulation uses the right of use as the basis, which is the minimum requirement in terms of the rights the contract has to give the consumer, but the contract can also include in rem, shareholder or other frameworks providing rights alongside the right of use.

The relative novelty of the time-sharing contract and its significantly different nature to classic real property contracts (sales contract, rental contract, etc.) indicates that the consumer's general right to be informed should be increased to include far more detailed information from the company selling the right. The contract has to be in writing, and one copy has to be given to the consumer. The rules regarding the language of the written notification also apply to the contract language. If the language in the country where the property is located differs from the contract language, then a certified translation of the contract in the local language has to be provided to the customer, too, except if the properties for which the right of use is being sold are in different countries. If the contract is concluded, then the written notification given to the consumer is now considered part of the contract.

Without the parties' agreement, these contents can only be changed by the seller due to significant changes in circumstances that are beyond their control. Such changes must be made known to the consumer before the contract is concluded. The contract must explicitly specify the changes the contract holds compared to the written notification.

The consumer has the right to withdraw from the contract or pre-contract within fourteen days, without any justification. This is the so-called cooling-off period, which allows the customer to think through their decision again. If the company did not fulfil their obligation to provide the consumer with detailed notification before the contract was concluded, then the consumer has three months plus fourteen days to withdraw from the contract.

In the event of a dispute, the company must prove that they delivered the pre-contract notification in written form in the required language, as well as a copy of the contract – written in the required language – and a certified translation of it in the language of the country the property is in, and that they notified the consumer in writing of the mandatory content missing from the contract, as well as the time at which they did so. If the consumer exercises their right to withdraw, the consumer can only be made to reimburse the company for the expenses associated with concluding the contract, i.e., the preparation and translation costs of the contract provided this was specified in the contract.

Consumers cannot forfeit their right specified in the decree. The decree can only be deviated from the interest of the consumer. The stipulated law that is applicable to the contract cannot result in any limitation of the consumer's rights as per the decree.

§2. Joint Ownership of Movable Property

231. The provisions in Chapter 6, §1, clearly apply to jointly owned movable property.

Chapter 7. Neighbourhood and Urban Problems

232. The right of use stemming from ownership rights is limited in private law in that the owner can only use the thing in a way that does not unnecessarily disturb others. The degree to which a neighbour is obliged to tolerate the disturbance caused by the owner's use and when it becomes unnecessary can only be determined based on specific circumstances. The definition of unnecessary disturbance is subject to the courts. If the disturbance is necessary, the tortfeasor is liable for indemnification. This general rule has been used in various cases in legal practice.

Neighbour laws cover certain specific situations that occur in everyday communal life. The common denominator of these legal standpoints is that they define specific prohibitions.

§1. Neighbour Laws

I. Earth-Support Right

233. The earth-support right is defined in terms of generally expected behaviour. Buildings can be placed in such a way that they are in close proximity to or actually touch the neighbouring land. As a result, the owner of the neighbouring parcel of land is required not to make changes to his land, which would deprive the neighbouring building of the earth supporting it. Depriving a building of this support could result in the condition of the building deteriorating; the building could buckle or become unusable. This can lead to property damage or lead to the endangerment of the lives and health of the users of the building.

The Civil Code specifies the obligations of the owners regarding earth support, regardless of what rights someone else may hold in possessing the property. The reason for this is that the owner of the building has the right whereby they can limit the rights of the possessor of the building to carry out modifications on the property, based on the legal relationship allowing possession. The building can be any kind of structure, regardless of its function.

In certain cases, it is unavoidable that the owner carries out construction work that impacts the ground support of the neighbour's building. In this case, where this support changes, the owner is obligated to strengthen the support again.

II. Use of Neighbour's Land

234. If activities for public purposes, catching animals, collecting fruit from overhanging branches, removing branches or roots, or for other important reasons are necessary, then the owner is obliged to allow entry to his property in return for indemnification. The owner may use the neighbour's land in return for indemnification if this is necessary for construction, deconstruction, modification, or maintenance work on their property.

Based on the social need for peaceful relations between neighbours, the owner is obliged to cooperate if a need to perform work relating to the neighbour's land arises. The Civil Code contains a list of examples of such work, which are situations commonly arising in everyday life. That said, the legislation extends the scope of permissible cases under the 'other important reasons' label to include other cases.

With regard to permission for entry, the Civil Code gives the owner of the neighbouring parcel of land the right, but it is argued that the necessity of the activity is a condition, so the person performing the task is entitled to enter. For example, the contractor renovating the neighbouring house that is on the border of the land parcel must also be granted this right.

Entry to the neighbouring parcel of land, or more precisely, the work done there, may cause damages. In this case, what must be examined is how necessary the damage-causing activity was in order for the person with the right of entry to achieve their purpose. If it is deemed necessary, then indemnification is required, but if it is beyond the boundaries of necessity, then the land owner can require remuneration for unlawful damage.

III. Emergency Situation

235. In the case of circumstances directly endangering the lives, bodies, or property of others and which cannot otherwise be avoided, the owner is obliged to tolerate the use and possible damage of their property for the purpose of eliminating the danger. In the case of circumstances endangering the property of others, the owner is subject to this obligation if it is foreseen that the damages caused by the dangerous circumstances will significantly exceed the damages caused by entering.

The owner can claim indemnification from people in emergency situations, from those who cause disproportional damage while eliminating the danger, as per the regulations on liability for non-contractual damages.

If the danger to multiple people's lives, bodies, or property were avoided by sacrificing certain endangered objects, the resulting damages, if their sacrifice was necessary, are the responsibility of the endangered people in proportion to their interests; this rule should also be applied to the division of costs necessary to eliminate the danger.

The rights of the owner to the thing in their possession are inferior if the lives, bodies, or property of others are in direct danger and cannot otherwise be avoided. In this case, the owner is obliged to tolerate the use of their property in order to eliminate the danger, i.e., that others can use, utilize, use up, or even cause damage to their property. If someone else's property is in danger, the principle of proportionality has to be applied; namely, in emergency situations, the owner's thing cannot suffer greater damages than would be caused to the other person's thing if it was not saved.

The damages caused by the person in an emergency situation are justified; therefore, the owner can only claim for indemnification. From a civil law perspective, all damages are illegal, except in cases where the law allows for this, and the very fact of the damage carries with it an obligation of remuneration. There is no burden to prove the illegality of the damages. However, if anyone causes an unnecessary amount of damage while trying to eliminate the danger, the owner can take action against them for non-contractual damages.

According to the Civil Code, when the lives, bodies, or property of multiple people are in danger, their obligations for indemnification and cost reimbursement are proportionate to the endangerment of their interests.

The guiding court ruling from legal practice states that if the owner's land is located on a floodplain, the owner is responsible for the risks of farming there. In the case of flood risk, justified actions by public administrations do not carry a compensation liability. If there is an emergency, the use or utilization of the thing or damages caused to it is not in violation of the law, but the owner can demand indemnification, and if the person taking action overstepped the limits for eliminating the danger, the legal action may turn out to be illegal, and the owner can demand compensation for the unjustifiably large damage caused while attempting to eliminate the danger.

IV. Use for Public Purposes

236. The owner of the real property is obliged to tolerate it if people legally authorized to temporarily use the property – to the degree needed to complete their tasks – actually use the property, gain a right of use for this, or limit the ownership right to the property. In this case, the owner of the real property is owed indemnification proportionate to the limitation. If the limitation makes the intended use of the property impossible or significantly impedes it, the owner can request the expropriation of the property.

The purpose of public use is to oblige the owner to show tolerance for the construction, use, and regular maintenance of infrastructure needed for utilities and utility services. Specific cases of public use scenarios can be found in relevant legislation.

237. If someone's in rem rights are limited in the interests of public use, this benefits others (too). As a result, in the case of such public use, the owner is entitled to indemnification. For example, the placement of a transformer building on someone else's property requires the power company to offer indemnification. In the event of public use, the owner is not entitled to lease fees or usage fees but is entitled to indemnification based on a complex examination of the limited use of the area in light of its function, location within the municipality and intended use.[116] Similarly, indemnification can be claimed in exchange for the limitations imposed when installing telecommunications devices. A causal relationship between the installation of telecommunication devices and the limitation of the use of the property can also be identified if cables are laid in a riverbed, but as a result, it is no longer possible to extract sand from the river.[117]

However, land-use plans do not constitute official action giving rise to individual obligations, so this does not result in specific rights and obligations for property owners and the exercising of their ownership rights. Neither does it create a right of

116. BDT 2003/900.
117. BDT 2000/280.

use; thus, there is no consequence that would prevent or limit the exercising of ownership rights and, therefore, justify the owner's request for indemnification.[118]

The rules on expropriation define when the extent of use for public purposes limits the ownership right to the thing in such a way that it is no longer in the owner's interest to maintain his ownership right. In this case, the opportunity for expropriation arises.

118. BDT 2003/825.

Chapter 8. Agrarian Problems

238. According to one of the theses of classic agricultural economics, land policy appears within agricultural policy as state intervention in the shaping of land ownership.[119] Indubitably, the fact of who and to what degree can own or possess agricultural land in a country is very significant and has both societal and economic ramifications. The purpose of the state's land policy is to limit the freedom of economic regulations and ownership rights with regard to agricultural land. Its purpose – among other things – is to ensure a livelihood for people in the agricultural areas of the country and to support the creation of sustainable and/or competitive holdings. The EU's land law regulations are directed at helping to develop the maximum and minimum size of holdings for efficient agriculture, avoid the fragmentation of farms to the detriment of efficiency, promote professional land use, and protect the amount of produce.[120]

239. Hungary is generally defined as an agricultural country. The statistics are straight forward: the entire country is 9.3 million hectares in size, of which 7.4 million hectares (or 79.6%) is agricultural land. Furthermore, it is a fact that market prices for land are increasing: before joining the EU, the average price of agricultural land was around HUF 300,000/hectare, which increased to HUF 535,000/ hectare by 2011 and HUF 779,000/hectare by 2014.[121]

§1. Acquiring Agricultural Land

240. The law does not relate to cases of land acquisition through intestate succession, expropriation, or remuneration.[122] It introduces the official authorization system, thereby placing the turnover of land under strict state supervision. It imposes formal requirements: the condition of a transaction involving ownership rights is that the contract be concluded on paper complying with the security features specified in legislation.

The ownership right to land cannot be gained by:

- a non-EU citizen;
- any state other than the Hungarian state, or any province or body thereof, etc.;
- a legal person; however, the law itself allows exceptions to this.

119. Endre Tanka, *Magyar birtokpolitika az Európai Egyesült Államokban. Földviszonyaink útja Moszkvától Brüsszelig (The Hungarian Agricultural Land Policy in the United States of America. Path of Our Land Relations From Moscow to Brussels)* 27 (Alterra 2004).

120. Levente Tattay, *A termőföldvásárlás problémái az Európai Unióban (Problems of Purchasing Agricultural Land in the European Union)*, 9 Európai Jog 36 (2009).

121. Szabolcs Bíró, *A magyar földpiac és az új földforgalmi szabályozás várható hatásai (The Hungarian Land Market and the Expected Impacts of the New Land Turnover Regulation)*, in *Az új magyar földforgalmi szabályozás az uniós jogban (The New Hungarian Land Turnover Regulation in the Law of the EU)* 141 (Ágoston Korom ed., Nemzeti Közszolgálati Egyetem 2013).

122. The rules can be found in Act CXXII of 2013 on the turnover of fields and forested agricultural land.

The category of a farmer is significant with regard to the acquisition of the land. A farmer is a domestically registered or domestic natural person, or EU citizen, who possesses an agricultural or forestry qualification as per a different law, or for lack of such qualifications, can prove that they have practised agricultural or forestry activities for the last three years. Only domestic natural persons and Member State citizens can gain ownership rights to land (in principle); if they do not qualify as farmers, they have the right to a maximum of 1 hectare (the close relations of a person transferring property to them are excluded from this regulation).

241. Although legal persons cannot acquire land, in the interest of certain public objectives (such as public employment services, social land programmes, etc.), some legal persons and the state can be exempted from this rule. Such legal persons include churches, mortgage credit institutions, and the local government under whose jurisdiction the land is located.

242. The ownership right to land can only be acquired in a limited capacity through exchange or gifting. Land can only be exchanged for land, and its ownership right can only be gifted to a close relative, the church, or the state.

The condition of acquiring ownership is that the acquiring party – in the contract or through a separate declaration – accepts that they will not give a right of use to anyone else; they will use it themselves for five years after the acquisition; they cannot use it for any other purposes, and that they satisfy their land use obligations. The acquired land can only be used for other purposes in exceptional cases listed in the law, such include a soil protection facility, irrigation ditch facilities, or the construction of a residential building, etc.

243. The law defines a maximum land and holding acquisition limit. In this respect, the same regulations apply to EU citizens as to Hungarian citizens. The acquiring person, or farmer, can acquire no more than 300 hectares (maximum land acquisition) of land, including the land they own or have the usufruct of. The farmer or the agricultural producer – including the land already owned – can own a maximum of 1,200 hectares of land (maximum holding).

244. As seen in the regulations outlined so far, the legislators strive to limit land turnover in several ways: they exclude non-Member State citizens from owning land, the acquisition of land is contingent on possessing the necessary qualifications, and it dictates the maximum amount of land that can be in a holding or owned in total. Furthermore, there are other tools that serve the same purpose (i.e., limiting land turnover): these are partly public law institutions and partly – and this is relevant to my topic – private law institutions: pre-emption rights and pre-leasehold rights.

Lajos Vékás pointed out that pre-emption rights do not limit the seller's right of disposal (since he is free to choose whether to sell the property or not), but it impairs their contractual freedoms because, in the end, they do not contract with their chosen buyer, but are obliged to do so with the holder of the pre-emption right. The legal system of pre-emption rights 'is a very powerful tool to make sure that the ownership rights of agricultural land are obtained by people who serve the interests of agricultural and land policies'.[123]

245. The Hungarian state became the number one player in the land turnover market in 2002.[124] This was when the state became qualified for pre-emption rights for the purchase or sale of agricultural land, and then the legislators raised the state to the number one position with the 2010 amendment of the land law. The legal policy justification for this was for 'the organisation managing the land fund to be able to enforce land ownership policy directives, and to be able to act as "market players" in cases where ownership rights are transferred'.

The current regulation supports this solution: the Hungarian government is at the top of the pre-emption list. After the state comes the farmer who uses the land, and within this category, the resident neighbour farmer, followed by the resident farmer, and finally, any farmer 'whose residence or centre of agricultural activity has been in a municipality for at least three years, whose administrative boundary is located no more than 20 kilometres from the administrative boundary of the land subject to the sale, via public or unobstructed private roads'. They are followed by farmers who do not use the land but who qualify as resident neighbours, then the farmers who do not use the land but qualify as residents, and finally by the farmers who do not use the land and who (based on the complicated definition mentioned above) live or work within a 20-kilometre radius of the property in question. Within the individual categories, family farmers, young farmers, and those beginning their careers in the profession enjoy priority.

246. Regarding the procedure, the owner is obliged to inform the parties of pre-emption rights of the contract within eight days of its signature. In practice, this means an accepted purchase offer is made public by the notary of the local government (by displaying it on the local government notice board). Those who are entitled have sixty days to submit a notification of acceptance or to relinquish their right to pre-empt. During the eight days after the deadline expires, the notary registers the received notifications and then sends them together with the original certificates to be approved by the agricultural administration body; if the transaction is exempt from the approval procedure, this is sent directly to the seller.

247. Acquisition of land ownership requires official approval. The agricultural administration body will examine the form and content of the contract and then contact the local land committee. The local land committee is the representative organization for the local farmers; its members are all elected. The land committee will adopt a position on the matter as to whether the sales contract can be accepted or not. The land turnover law defines what aspects are to be considered at this stage, such as 'is the sales contract conducive to circumventing the limitations of land

123. Vékás & Gárdos, *supra*, 689.
124. When the Act CXVI of 2001 on the National Land Fund came into effect.

acquisition' or 'is the countervalue proportionate to the value of the land,' etc. The decision of the land committee is made 'based on common facts and best knowledge'.

The land turnover law details the procedures of the agricultural administration body for which the administrative proceedings of law should be adhered to.[125]

248. It is worth noting two more institutions in relation to Hungarian agricultural law: wine-growers' associations and forest owner associations.

§2. Wine-Growers' Association

249. Special law shall be applied to natural and legal persons as well as economic organizations without legal personality engaged in viticulture, wine production, and wine trading.[126]

A wine-growers' association is a grouping of producers and wine-buyers in one or more municipalities of a wine-growing region created to promote their shared interests in the sale of their wine and to protect the origin, quality, and source of their products. Viticulture, wine production, and wine trade can only be practised in wine municipalities as a member of a wine-growers' association or in a non-wine municipality only if the producer or purchaser is separately registered.

250. Wine-growers' associations, as organizations engaged in viticulture and wine production, can be traced back to 1271 in Hungary. In the Middle Ages, there were numerous wine laws, generally providing county-level regulations. The major damage caused by Peronospora in 1982 and 1983 played a part in Act XXIII of 1893, which introduced detailed wine production regulations. Consequently, Act XII of 1894 on agriculture and agricultural policing made it mandatory to have wine-growers' associations. These two laws were supplemented by Act V of 1896, which defined the professional conditions for modern viticulture. The nationalization that followed the Second World War extended to wine-growing lands as well. Government Decree 3300/1949 put an end to wine-growers' associations and passed their rights and obligations to the state treasury. The property of the wine-growers' associations was given to the local organizations of the National Working Peasants and Farmers Union. After the regime change, Act CII of 1994 was accepted and reinstated the wine-growers' associations before being then replaced by Act CCXIX of 2012.[127]

---

125. Act CXL of 2004 on the general rules of administrative proceedings and services.

126. Act CCXIX of 2012 on wine-growers' associations.

127. Zsigmond Csoma, *A magyarországi hegyközségek 20. századi megszüntetése és újjászervezése* (*The Termination and Reorganisation of the Hungarian Wine-growers' Associations in Hungary*), 38 Acta Acad. Agriensis, Sectio Historiae (2010); János Ede Szilágyi, *Eredetvédelmi kérdések a borjogban* (*Questions of Protection of Origin in the Law of Wines*) (Novotni Alapítvány 2009); István Olajos, *A vidékfejlesztési jog kialakulása és története* (*The Evolution and History of the Rural Development*) (Novotni Alapítvány 2008).

251. Wine-growers' associations can be created with the participation of the settlements of the same wine region if:

(a) the size of the vineyards located in the administrative territory of the wine region reaches three hundred hectares;
(b) the vineyards are used by at least ten producers; and
(c) in the area of the wine-growers' associations, at least one winery has a wine production license.

If the area of the wine region is less than three hundred hectares, a wine-growers' association may operate in the wine region. A new wine-growers' association – including the separation and separation of mountain communities – cannot be established if its area does not reach five hundred hectares.

The members of the wine-growers' association are viticulture or wine producers, who work in the area of the wine-growers' association, as well as purchasers who buy grapes, must or wine from the members of the wine community within a calendar year. The viticulture and wine producer who carries out his activities in the operational area of the wine-growers' association is obliged to be a member of the association, regardless of his place of residence (location, headquarters). The viticulture and wine producer is a member of every wine-growers' association on whose territory he produces. A person who is not obliged to become a member of a wine-growers' association may take up a voluntary membership of an association based on the express provisions of the statutes.

252. Member producers and purchasers of the wine-growers' association are allowed to initiate the issue of a proof of origin certificate, and the product must first be released indicating the wine-growers' association. A member cannot request the issue of a proof of origin certificate if they have not met the membership fee and information requirements of the wine-growers' association by the deadline. Members of the wine-growers' association have pre-emption and pre-lease holding rights regarding parcels of land in neighbouring grape-production cadastres if they were permanent members of the wine-growers' association for twenty-four months before exercising their pre-emption right. Members of a wine-growers' association are obliged to pay a membership fee, adhere to the statutes and internal regulations, and perform their activities in line with the by-laws of the wine-growers' association.

253. The wine-growers' association defines rules in the wine-growers' association by-laws which apply to planting and production, the organization of plantations, unified plant protection procedures against grape damage, harvests, processing, and the production of the wine according to local specifications; furthermore, it can stipulate other professional requirements that are important for quality protection. Regulations regarding nature and environmental protection must also be adhered to. The by-laws must define activities that violate the wine-growers' association rules and their legal consequences. The wine-growers' association by-laws determine rules relating to the condition of the properties, roads, irrigation ditches, and plant protection, as well as to the maintenance of facilities associated with the intended use of real properties in areas categorized as a wine region and wine production areas (vineyards) based on the grape cadastre classification. These provisions must be adhered to by the users of other agricultural properties and managers of roads in the neighbourhood of the vineyards. Wine-growers' associations, which have contiguous grape plantations belonging to their operating area, form a common wine-growers' association. The wine-growers' association oversees compliance with local regulations.

The members of the wine-growers' association must be registered, and changes have to be constantly updated. The register of names – after the foundation of the wine-growers' association – must include the type of grape a member is growing, the age of their vines, the previous year's produce, and the amount of grapes and wine purchased from the area by the member in the previous year.

254. The wine-growers' association main decision-making body is the general meeting, which consists of all members. Every member has one voting right at the general meetings. The general meeting elects a select committee of members as defined in the statutes and elects a president from among them, who is also the president of the select committee. The president of the wine-growers' association is the president of the select committee. The president is also in charge of security for the area. The 'hegybíró' (literally: 'hill judge') is in charge of operative matters within the wine-growers' association. When carrying out public and official duties, he is directed by the Secretary-General of the National Council of Wine-Growers' Associations. The 'hill judge' is responsible for public administration matters, providing information from the records kept by the wine-growers' association, keeping the plantation cadastres, and recording the planting and removal of vines, etc. The legality of the operations of the wine-growers' association is monitored by an oversight committee elected by the general meeting of the members.

§3. Forest Owners' Association

255. Act XLIX of 1994 regulates forest owners' associations. The association is a legal person, an organization registered in the forestry sector by one or more owners of parcels of land for the performance of forest management activities and related tasks.

Such associations can be formed by forest owners. At least two owners are required. If there are fewer than ten owners, the association can be established by contract; if there are more than ten owners, a founding general meeting has to be held. Acceptance of the statutes requires two-thirds of the votes of those present at the founding general meeting. The registration and records of the association are kept by a local court of registration based on the registered seat.

256. The association issues a certificate to members verifying their interest in the association with regard to their share of the association's assets. The certificate has to display the proportion of the member's holdings in relation to the entire holding of the association. The interest in the association, besides granting a share of the association's assets, also expresses the member's voting rights and the degree of use (or right of use) of the forests used or owned by the association. The main rule is that association membership can only be transferred and inherited with the ownership right.

The association keeps a register of its members, which includes the first and last names of the members (company), their address (registered address), the size of holdings and the votes they have in relation to their interest in the association.

257. Membership of the forest owners' association is mandatory. Only owners of land registered in the land registry as being connected to forestry activities can be members. Membership requests of an owner or owners of land in a naturally contiguous forestry area cannot be rejected. Similarly, the membership request of an owner whose forested area is unsuitable for independent forest management may not be rejected either. If the owners decided to establish the association based on a two-thirds majority vote in proportion to their forest ownership, then if the conditions for forming an independent forest management unit do not apply, and in order to enforce the public interest of continuous forest maintenance, the minority owners are obliged to join the association and execute its resolutions. Association membership and the ownership right to the given forestry land can only be transferred together. The forestry area held by an association member can only be sold along with the association membership, but the transfer of the ownership right does not affect the obligations of the person carrying out the forest management work. If a member seeks to transfer his ownership or ownership share (excluding inheritance), the other members have a pre-emption right. In the case of joint property, the pre-emption right of the joint owner takes priority over everyone else's. If there is a forestry area used by the association that is a nature conservation area, the state's pre-emption right precedes everyone else.

258. The association's supreme body is the general meeting, which consists of all members. The general meeting can be held as needed but must convene at least once a year. The office-bearers of the association are the president, the members of the presidency, the chairman, and members of the supervisory board, or if the supervisory board does not have to be formed, the person elected to carry out its tasks; further positions can be established in the statutes. Associations with fewer than ten members only have to elect a president and vice president. In associations consisting of two members, they both fulfil the roles of president and general meeting or if authorized, the authorized member assumes this role.

Part II. Movable Property and Personal Property/Chattels

Chapter 1. General Classification

§1. Tangible Movable Property and Choses in Possession

I. Movable Property

259. Movable property is things that are not closely and continuously related to land or, from another aspect, do not get listed in the land registry. Naturally, the rules specified for real property do apply to movable property as well; we only intend to point out issues of jurisdiction and doctrine that arise in connection with certain special things.

260. Under the Civil Code, the provisions pertaining to things shall also apply to money and securities, including natural resources that can be utilized as capital goods. There are two approaches to money. In a general sense, money is the official medium of settlement that simplifies exchange, used by entities to determine the countervalue of different products and services. Money is a legal tender recognized by the state. As its core function, money can be used as a means of exchange that renders the bartering of goods unnecessary. Consequently, money first functions as a form of payment as well, i.e., it can be used to purchase goods and services. Money also functions as a medium of settlement, as it can be used to simultaneously quantify the countervalue of goods and services of the same worth. Given its settlement role, money is regarded as a store of value, barring inflation and deflation. In this context, it is not the physical appearance of money but the value it represents that is of importance. Second, individual banknotes and coins can also carry value due to the material they are made of or the date of issue, e.g., in the case of antique notes. Third, in everyday use, money refers to banknotes, coins, and bank money (e.g., current accounts or demand deposits) alike.

In a legal sense, there is a difference between cash and bank money. If a financial institution erroneously completes a transfer (credit transaction) to a contracted account holder business organization with double the correct amount, it is not enforcement of the owner's claim but unjust enrichment that can be cited as the legal grounds for recovery. This being a pecuniary claim, its limitation period is governed by the rules applicable to pecuniary claims (damages). It must also be noted that from a legal standpoint, money is a currency recognized by the state.

Money substitutes facilitating the exchange of goods that can only be used in a specific location or circle (vouchers, certificates, etc.) obviously do not constitute money.

261. Securities typically represent a right of some sort; therefore, the value they carry is primarily manifested not in their physical appearance but in the underlying subjective rights. As objects that can be taken possession of – just like money – securities must be subject to the rules applicable to things, as opposed to the rights and claims they represent. Rather than mere pieces of paper, securities are deeds (or dematerialized securities) with the special feature of being of value in themselves by representing or manifesting a right or a claim.

Allow us to point out here that shares in a limited liability company comprise a set of intangible rights, which can be transferred and are eligible for sale. Under the Civil Code, however, said interest does not constitute a thing, and therefore, the warranty rules concerning non-conformity in the assumed object of service cannot be applied.

262. Natural resources that can be utilized as capital goods refer to formations with or without a physical representation that can be put under man's command and control. These typically include energy, which can be electric, thermal, or gas, depending on the way it is generated. Natural resources that can be utilized as capital goods (electricity, solar energy, wind, water, energy sources of mineral origin) are also subject to the provisions pertaining to things as appropriate.

263. The body or body part of a live person is not a thing, and the provisions pertaining to things do not apply – these are protected under moral rights. If any body part or a part of the body (e.g., hair, teeth, or blood) is physically separated from a person, the disconnected part ceases to be protected under moral rights and can be taken possession of, and is considered a thing. This, however, does not imply that separation causes the person to freely dispose of the part(s) as the owner, for this is subject to limitations under both public law and the law of obligations, the latter including the prohibition of immoral contracts as a general clause. How a separated body part or organ is judged depends on its nature. Hair removed from a person's body at the hairdresser can be considered an object of ownership – a thing eligible for sale that can be taken possession of. Human organs, however, are subject to sophisticated regulations and whether they are eligible for sale is a sensitive issue. As regards the eligibility for sale, regulations on blood fall in between these two extremes.

Implants are artificial structures placed inside a person's body (e.g., hip replacement, gold tooth filling). Once placed inside the body, implants become parts thereof and as such are protected under moral rights, irrespective of their past or current owners and also regardless of the fact that the transplantation itself does not cause ownership rights over the implant to be transferred to the patient. Transplantation in itself is considered neither a transfer of ownership nor a means of acquiring ownership. As the moral rights derived from the personal integrity and sanctity of a person outweigh the ownership rights over the implant, the owner of the implant is not entitled to make an ownership claim. Ownership claims may only be enforced if the implant no longer forms part of the person's body. In this regard, organ transplants fall into the same category as implants, irrespective of whether they were lawfully removed from another person's body.

Medical aids such as glasses, hearing aids, crutches, and walkers do not become part of the human body and, therefore, are not protected under moral rights. These qualify as things, and pertaining ownership claims can be enforced.

264. As per the Civil Code, the provisions pertaining to things also apply to animals in accordance with the statutory provisions laying down derogations consistent with their natural characteristics. These primarily include animal welfare laws that limit the rights of owners and specify their obligations of ownership.

Trends first noted in German and Austrian law resulted in significant changes in the in rem rights of animals. In 1988, the ABGB was amended,[128] which stated that animals are not things and must be protected under a separate law. The provisions pertaining to things (ABGB) shall apply to animals insofar as no other legislation provides otherwise.[129] While this regulation does not define the legal status of animals, in accordance with a number of international agreements, it provides them with protection by making them subject to special legislation.[130] It can be regarded both as a declaration and a statutory regulation and also as an admonition to society at large.[131] This distances animals from things and makes them subject to special regulation – which most of all ensures their protection – while also leading to an intermediary situation compared to their previous status, for animals are no longer considered objects under law, but legal personality is not conferred upon them either. In Austrian regulations, based on the ABGB of subsidiary application, the previously effective ownership rights over animals are limited under separate legislation without being categorized otherwise under civil law. Changes in Germany's animal regulations followed a similar path. While animals under German law had also been considered common things, the amendment of the BGB stated that animals were not things.[132] Nevertheless, given the absence of a separate law on animal protection, general provisions pertaining to things continue to apply. When it comes to substitutability, legal literature describes animals as irreplaceable things and no contract may stipulate otherwise.[133] As regards the category of *res consumptibiles,* only animals intended for the production of meat can be considered, whereas divisibility has them grouped according to depreciation.[134] As a result, animals under German law are generally recognized as indivisible things. This holds

128. Article 285a based on the Act on the Legal Status of Animals (Bundesgesetz über die Rechtsstellung von Tieren. BG 10. 3. 1988. BGBl 179.).
129. Article 285a of the ABGB.
130. Monika Gimpel-Hinteregger, *Das Tier als Sache und Ersatz der Heilungskosten für ein verletztes Tier,* 11 Österreichische Juristen-Zeitung 65 (1989).
131. Rainer Lippold, *Über Tiere und andere Sachen – § 285a ABGB als Beispiel zeitgenössischer Gesetzgebungskunst,* 11 Österreichische Juristen-Zeitung 336 (1989).
132. Article 90a that was introduced in the BGB in 1990.
133. As per Art. 91 of the BGB. *See also* Birgit Brüninghaus, *Die Stellung des Tieres im Bürgerlichen Gesetzbuch* 38 (Duncker & Humblot 1993).
134. Article 92 of the BGB.

true for swarms of bees as well, for individual bees have zero economic significance. Hungary's Civil Code also points out that while animals are recognized as things, legal practice must also take into account the provisions of Act XXVIII of 1998 on the Protection and Humane Treatment of Animals.

II. Protection of Possession

265. One of the main reasons behind ensuring the protection of possessors is that, in most cases, they are the same as the owners; at least, possession is acquired by those with an appropriate legal basis. Therefore, the protection of the possessor typically entails the protection of the owner or lawful possessor as well, whose protection contributes to upholding public order.

The right to possession – or more precisely, the right to possession as a subjective right under the Civil Code – entails protection of possession, to which the possessor is entitled against anyone, with the exception of the person from whom the possession was acquired by unlawful arbitrary action. The protection of possession can be applied twofold. First as a restraint or abstinence, a mandate of third parties interfering with possession, and second, in the deprivation of possession. In both cases, it is a prerequisite that the act be carried out without a legal basis. It is not considered trespassing when a person fails to return a possession transferred unto him under an agreement.

266. As regards the protection of possession between possessor and secondary possessor, whether the latter is entitled to the protection of possession against the former depends on his legal title. A similar situation applies to joint possession. When protecting joint possession from third parties, each possessor is entitled to act on their own, which also affects other possessors' state of possession. Following the withdrawal of a courtesy permit, the courtesy user of a flat is no longer entitled to the protection of possession that is provided to former tenants until execution of the eviction order. In such cases, the notary's resolution based on actual possessory status must be amended, and the submission for the protection of possession must be rejected.

For the protection of possession, possessors are entitled to act arbitrarily or to bring an action in rem or a possessory action before a municipal notary.

A. Typical Forms of Trespassing in the Case Law

267. One of the most typical forms of trespassing is when it occurs between neighbours. This includes trespassing in relation to livestock farming, of which the following case decisions are prime examples of judicial practice. In a trespass lawsuit filed for livestock farming, it must be assessed whether any conduct is performed that can qualify as trespassing with a harmful impact on the environment, taking the interests of all stakeholders into account and in view of the type of environment at hand. In this regard, it is also important to know whether the party complaining about trespassing has moved to a location where – precisely due to the type of environment – animal husbandry is not prohibited. The extreme sensitivity of select individuals must not result in a neighbour being forced to cease farming activities that have been approved and controlled by competent authorities.[135] When keeping pets as a hobby, the animals' natural living conditions must be provided without causing any permanent and unnecessary disturbance to the life and customs of the neighbourhood. In trespass lawsuits filed for violation of neighbourhood rules, the legal principle of protecting acquired rights must also be taken into account.[136] In a residential area populated with detached family homes, where it is permitted and customary to keep animals, chicken farming in itself is not objectionable. However, it cannot spread to an extent where it causes unnecessary disturbance to the owners of neighbouring real property.[137]

As regards neighbours, evaluating the phenomena that have to do with physical proximity is yet another sensitive issue. The emission of odour (stench) does not qualify as a form of air pollution; action can be taken against it in a proceeding for the termination of trespass.[138] In trespass lawsuits brought for loud music, when establishing the facts of the case, the court must determine what technical solutions can be used to eliminate noise that owners are not required to tolerate.[139]

In the context of trespass and neighbourhood rights, building and construction represent another major category of cases. When the owner of a flat in an apartment building performs renovation works in his flat that limits the lower-floor neighbours in their undisturbed use of their respective home(s), the dispute can be resolved by the joint application of neighbourhood and trespass rules.[140]

Trespassing can also be assumed in connection with other activities, including the following cases. The means of protection of possession that can be applied against noise due to a business activity depends on how conflicting interests are weighed against each other.[141] By appropriately balancing these interests, unnecessary disturbances can be eliminated. The storage of chemicals in the proximity of a flat – if it interferes with the intended use of the flat or damages the health of its residents – generally qualifies as trespassing. The possessor is entitled to the protection even if said stored chemicals do not typically present a health hazard but are detrimental given his medical condition.[142] When an owner leases his real property with the limitation that possessors of the neighbouring property can come and go at their leisure, the latter shall be entitled to the protection of possession against a lessee preventing their entrance.[143] Trees add both to the aesthetics and environmental quality of built areas. Their ability to absorb dust and purify the air has a major role in improving a neighbourhood. The planting of trees and the preservation of existing

135. BH 1982/91.
136. BH 2012/260.
137. BH 1989/148; *see also* BH 2002/92.
138. KGD 1992/365.
139. BH 1992/100; *see also* BH 1993/735.
140. BH 2005/50; *see also* BH 1998/425 and BH 1997/581.
141. BH 2002/179.
142. BH 1986/324; *see also* BH 1994/405.
143. BH 1985/345.

foliage represent a common environmental interest. Therefore, neighbourhood disputes usually cannot be resolved with felling orders. However, payment obligations for possible damage due to shading can be warranted.[144] If, in connection with the property lines between adjacent parcels, there is a margin of error for land surveys, this fact in itself does not entitle anyone to move their fencing towards the neighbour's parcel. Such an act of trespassing may not be offset by the fact that the fencing line continued to remain within the margin of error. When an action is brought for map corrections, the court shall assess not only possession according to the new map but also the actual boundaries and shall render its decision on the dimension (size) of the area affected by the trespassing accordingly.[145]

268. Court resolutions made in the following cases are also worth noting. The fact a dispute arises between a person leasing agricultural land under a leasehold contract from a lessor who lawfully exercises the lessor's rights does not in itself establish a basis for the legality of claims by external third parties for the protection of possession.[146] Exercising the right to assembly does not constitute trespassing unless it unnecessarily interferes with the fundamental rights of others and fails to meet the condition of necessity and proportionality.[147] It is not considered trespassing when a person fails to return a possession transferred unto him under an agreement.[148]

Parties also often resort to protection of possession in cases of trespassing concerning property leases or tenure status. A lessor's protection of possession against a former lessee, now without a legal title, of a unit for non-residential purposes.[149] Until their right of tenancy is settled during a divorce action, each spouse retains his or her right of tenancy and is thus entitled to the protection of possession.[150] A person using a home in good faith but without a legal title is also entitled to the protection of possession.[151] The unauthorized videotaping of activities carried out in a neighbouring residential building, when done to prove an infringement, may be construed as trespassing even if rights relating to personality are not violated.[152] Parties entitled to the joint possession, or use, of public premises are also entitled to the protection of possession against one another.[153]

In case of trespassing, possessors may also be entitled to compensation claims in addition to the protection of possession. Damage is not caused jointly when the tortfeasors trespass separately and independently of one another.[154]

144. BH 1985/58.
145. BH 1984/223.
146. BDT 2001/520.
147. BH 2011/132.
148. BH 2007/186.
149. BH 2001/525; *see also* BH 1994/185.
150. BH 1992/634.
151. BH 1983/357.
152. EBH 2001/519.
153. BH 1993/28.
154. BH 2000/397; *see also* BH 1999/202.

B. Protection of Possession by Arbitrary Action

269. As a general principle, the arbitrary enforcement of rights is prohibited by law. Yet, there are certain situations where enforcement by the state would lead to delays causing the injured parties more harm than being able to protect their interests on their own would have. In such exceptional cases, the law provides for arbitrary action, which can also be applied for the protection of possession. Under the adaptation of the principle *vim vi repellere licere* in Roman law into modern legislation concerning the protection of possession, possessors are entitled to repel trespassing acts on their own.

Protection of possession by arbitrary action is subject to two conditions. It can only be resorted to when the trespassing is carried out as an unlawful arbitrary action and only to the extent necessary for the protection of possession, also taking the principle of proportionality into account.

270. Protection of possession by arbitrary action can take the form of self-defence or self-help. Self-defence implies that the possessor is able to avert the unlawful trespassing conduct before it is concluded (e.g., the possessor is unwilling to let her bag be yanked off her arm and physically confronts the thief). Self-help refers to the possessor's capacity to restore the lawful situation after possession is appropriated or trespassing is carried out (recognizing her stolen bag, the previous possessor takes it back from the thief). However, arbitrary action aimed at recovery of possession is only permitted in a limited number of well-founded cases and under the condition that the use of any other means of protection would be in vain.

The Civil Code does not define expressis verbis the possible means of arbitrary action for the protection of possession that may be applied if trespassing is imminent. Given the absence of legal regulation concerning the protection of possession by preventive action, there is no concrete statutory mandate for averting unlawful action when it is foreseeable (e.g., there is a likelihood that the neighbour's crumbling chimney will fall onto one's house).

271. It must be noted that protection of possession by unlawful arbitrary action typically coincides with the criminal offence of private justice that is regulated under the Criminal Code. It constitutes private justice when, for instance, possessors engage in arbitrary action aimed at the recovery of their lost possessions beyond the extent necessary, thus causing their use of force to become a means of retribution for trespassing.[155] If, in the course of a civil action for trespassing, the defendant arbitrarily demolishes a garage encroaching on his land and thus causes major damage, it shall constitute vandalism that cannot be considered a lawful arbitrary act.[156] Means of last resort cannot be cited when a resident vandalizes the lock mechanism on the front gate of an apartment building so as to facilitate entry for the physician and gas fitter he has called to his home.[157]

155. EBH 2012/.
156. BH 2004/132.
157. BH 1997/323.

Nevertheless, the protection of possession by arbitrary action that is proportionate to the protection is permitted and does not constitute a criminal offence. If a defendant acted arbitrarily against the plaintiff to recover his lost possessions – because quick and effective official means of protection of possession were unlikely to be available – but discontinued the use of force that was proportionate to the trespassing immediately once possession was recovered, the defendant may be acquitted not on the grounds of justifiable defence but, given that the act is not considered unlawful, due to the absence of a criminal offence.[158] Likewise, it is not construed as private justice where the use of force or threat constitutes an authorized means of enforcement of a claim. Therefore, a criminal offence cannot be established when, to the extent necessary for protecting his possession, a possessor arbitrarily averts attacks against his possession or acts arbitrarily in the interest of protecting an already lost possession, provided that the time lost through the use of other means of protection would frustrate protection of the possession.[159] Similar deliberations led to the decision in a case where the defendant, having used force and threat to thwart the unlawful harvest by a cooperative on land in his legitimate possession, was acquitted of private justice.[160]

C. *Protection of Possession in Notarial Proceedings*

272. Notarial proceedings conducted within the framework of administrative procedures represent one of the official means of enforcement for the protection of possession. It is primarily due to the short lead time and location-specific knowledge that protection of possession actions are assigned to the competence of municipal notaries. Given their position, municipal notaries tend to be the ones most aware of local conditions and customs and can therefore use their unique knowledge in adjudicating the possession disputes at hand. Furthermore, by applying the rules pertaining to administrative proceedings, notarial proceedings are theoretically concluded faster than if brought in court. Under administrative proceedings, a party suffering trespassing has until one year from said trespass to turn to a notary and bring the protection of possession action to eliminate the infringement. In notarial proceedings, the provisions of the Civil Code shall prevail,[161] with matters not regulated therein falling under the laws of administrative proceedings.[162] A party having suffered trespassing may initiate proceedings by request, with an obligation to notify the other party of the proceedings. The requesting party is also required to enclose with its application all relevant evidence it has collected in the matter, based on which the notary may decide to either uphold the application and enforce the resolution or, if the documents enclosed fail to demonstrate trespassing, reject it.

158. BH 2012/1.
159. BH 2000/338.
160. BH 1996/351.
161. Pursuant to Government Decree No. 17/2005. (II. 16.) on proceedings for the protection of possession in the competence of the notary and its s. 18.
162. *See* Act CXL of 2004 on the General Rules of Administrative Proceedings and Services.

The proceeding notary examines whether the party applying for protection of possession is entitled to possession or whether it is required to tolerate trespassing. In this regard, applications are only rejected if it is established beyond reasonable doubt that the applicant is not entitled to possession and must tolerate trespassing. As their primary objective, notarial proceedings are intended to ensure the protection of the person entitled to possession against an individual engaging in unlawful arbitrary conduct. As a consequence, notarial proceedings typically provide protection of an interim nature.

273. Protection of possession can be justified in two cases: to the benefit of a party having been unlawfully deprived of possession for the restoration of the original state and to prohibit breach of possession. Additionally, notaries may also evaluate the damage caused by, as well as the benefits of, trespassing.

To ensure that the state of possession is efficiently protected, notary resolutions must be implemented within three days at the latest. Bringing an action has no delaying effect on execution unless the notary has also made a resolution on damage and benefits and said action is brought either against this resolution or in connection with possession. In other cases, the court is entitled to suspend execution, but only if, based on available documents, an amendment to the notary resolution is likely.

D. Possessory Action

274. Upon the possessor's request, the court proceeding in possessory action may order the trespasser to restore the original state of possession that also includes the termination of infringement. This can entail the return of possession or the cessation of other unlawful conditions. Furthermore, the court order may call for the discontinuance or prohibition of restraint.

In a possessory action, the court makes its decision by weighing the parties' rights to possession against one another. What needs to be examined is whether one of the parties is more entitled to possession. Naturally, this is an element to consider primarily in lawsuits brought for the restoration of the original state of possession. In an action in rem, the rights to possession can be assessed only between the contestants, with the only decision being whether one party had a right to possession instead of the other and whether one was more entitled. The parties' relationship with third parties, as well as agreements concluded between non-litigating persons concerning the object of a possession dispute, cannot be examined.

Under the Civil Code, the entitlement of the party disturbed in possession is presumed. This rule is primarily intended to ensure priority to a state of possession previously established based on acquired rights over the conduct that has changed it.

275. Possessory action may be instituted immediately after trespassing has occurred or if the notary's protection of possession action was unsuccessful. If action is brought against the notary's resolution adopted in relation to the protection of possession, the court does not overrule the legitimacy of the notary's conduct and resolution; the decision focuses on the civil dispute. When settling relations under civil law, the notary is not bound by a statutory obligation to adjudicate applications for claims or, in particular, for the restoration of the original state, and the absence of a pertaining resolution may not be used as grounds for establishing liability for damages.[163]

E. The Context of the Notarial and Judicial Proceedings

276. Protection of possession in notarial proceedings and a possessory action do not necessarily succeed one another. The two procedures are essentially alternatives to one another, i.e., it depends on the decision of the harmed possessor whether to initiate notarial proceedings or bring a possessory action to court. The relation between the two proceedings is governed by temporality: notarial proceedings may only be initiated within one year following the trespassing, whereas a trespass action has no such limitation in time. In this context, it must be noted that no appeal may be lodged against resolutions made based on notarial proceedings and that, according to the Civil Code, possessory action opened following a notary resolution does not constitute action against an administrative decision. Consequently, possessors and trespassers in possessory actions are recognized, respectively, as plaintiffs and defendants, and litigation is carried out based on the material and procedural rules applicable to the judicial enforcement of civil claims.

§2. Intangible Movable Property and Choses in Action

277. In Hungarian private law, transferrable intangible property rights that do not qualify as things can primarily be found in the realm of the law of obligations, corporate law, and intellectual property. These include shares in business organizations (business shares, dematerialized securities), claims made by natural persons and certain cases of intellectual property.

I. Business Share in Limited Liability Company

278. A limited liability company is a company in which the shareholders' liability for the company's debt is restricted to the amount of their capital contribution. The minimum share capital for a limited liability company is HUF 3 million and consists of the shareholders' capital contribution, which must be at least HUF 100,000. The shareholders' relative business share defined in proportion to their capital contribution represents their share in the company. Shares are recorded in a record of the shareholders, referred to as the list of shareholders. The business share can secure different ownership rights, and the company may also acquire its own shares.[164]

Each shareholder's share of the company, referred to as its share, is partially eligible for sale and associated with intangible and shareholder rights. Each shareholder is entitled to take part in and vote at the company's general meeting and is

163. BDT 2009/2025.

164. The rules in details, *see* Tekla Papp, *Law of Business Enterprises*, in *Business Law* 245 ff. (István Sándor ed., Patrocinium 2016).

also entitled to make written decisions outside the general meeting. In addition, shareholders are also entitled to propose items on the general meeting's agenda. Every shareholder is entitled to receive a portion of the company's earnings in the form of a dividend or advanced dividend, constituting an intangible property right. Furthermore, if the company is dissolved, every shareholder is entitled to a liquidation ratio, i.e., to receiving a portion of the remaining assets after paying off the company's creditors.

Shares can be freely transferred among shareholders subject to a written contract; meanwhile, in the event of an intention to dispose of a share to an external third party, the shareholder, the company, and any third party appointed by the general meeting have a pre-emption right. The transfer of shares may be governed by stricter rules in the articles of association. The Supreme Court's ad hoc decision established that a share cannot be regarded as a thing within the meaning of the Civil Code; however, the rules of a sales contract must be applied to a share transfer contract in the event of the transfer of a business share.[165]

II. Dematerialized Share in Corporations

279. Shares can be issued both in certificated or dematerialized (book-entry) form. Certificated shares can be transferred using the complete or empty endorsement found on the back or appended to the share. The shares of a publicly traded company limited by shares can only be issued in dematerialized form. A book-entry security is a registered security that does not have a serial number, and the shareholder's name and data allowing clear identification are listed in the security account. A book-entry security is a series of symbols digitally representing the set of data containing the security's substantive accessories, all of its accessories defined in legislation, the total face value of the entire series issued and the number of securities issued in the manner defined in the Capital Market Act[166] and relevant other legislation, generated, recorded, transferred, and registered electronically. The central securities depository, KELER,[167] is required and entitled to generate all book-entry securities issued in Hungary and traded publicly or privately and to credit and handle (amend, delete) them on central securities accounts.[168]

Book-entry shares are transferred by being credited to or debited from a securities account. For book-entry shares – until proven otherwise – the owner of the share is the holder of the account where the share is kept on record.[169] If a company's statutes restrict the transfer of shares or bind it to the company's consent, these restrictions

165. BH 1994/202.
166. Article 7 of the Act CXX of 2001 on the capital market.
167. KELER Central Depository Ltd. is the sole central securities depository and a specialized bank in Hungary. It was established in 1993, and it is owned by the Central Bank of Hungary and the Budapest Stock Exchange.
168. For detailed analysis, *see* Klára Gellén, *Értékpapírjog* (*Law of Securities*) 117 ff. (Pólay Elemér Alapítvány 2009).
169. In connection with ownership and corporate governance issues, *see* particularly András Kecskés & Vendel Halász, *Stock Corporations: A Guide to Initial Public Offerings, Corporate Governance and Hostile Takeovers* 348 ff. (HVG-ORAC, LexisNexis 2013).

apply vis-à-vis third parties if the restriction and its contents are shown on the share or among the securities account data in the case of book-entry shares.

III. Intellectual Property Rights

280. The Civil Code defines general rules governing intellectual property rights, declaring that intellectual property is protected by the Civil Code. These rights are considered absolute (in rem) rights, however, not as property rights but as personal (moral) rights.[170] However, the Civil Code does not define detailed rules on intellectual property; these detailed rules are governed by specific other legislation. Intellectual property is divided into two main domains: copyrights and industrial property rights.

A. Copyright

281. The Act LXXVI of 1999 on Copyright provides protection for copyrights.[171] Copyright is held by the creator of a work. A work refers to a literary, scientific, or artistic creation. The creator has legal protection of his individual original work created through intellectual activity, irrespective of its qualitative, quantitative, or aesthetic attributes or the assessment of its standard. The author obtains copyright upon creating the work; there is no requirement for registration.

Copyright consists partially of personal and partially of intangible property rights.[172] Personal (moral) rights include the right to decide on the publication of the work, displaying the creator's name and association with the work and protection of the work's integrity. The author may not transfer his personal rights, such rights may not be otherwise devolved, and the author cannot waive such rights. The reproduction, dissemination, public presentation right, the right to communicate the work to the public and redraft the work constitute property rights. Copyrights are protected during the creator's lifetime and for seventy years following his death. The author may grant permission based on his property rights for using the work, and property rights may also be inherited. The right to use a work can be obtained under an exploitation contract. The author's permission is necessary to use the work's unique title. The author also has an exclusive right to commercially exploit any typical and original character appearing in the work and to authorize such exploitation (*merchandising*).

The Copyright Act also defines special provisions for certain genres. These include computer program creations (software), databases, works ordered for the purpose of

170. *See also* Éva Jakab, *Konzepte des Eigentums im Wandel der Zeit*, in *Geistiges Eigentum und Urheberrecht aus der historischen Perspektive* 45 ff. (Éva Jakab ed., Pólay Elemér Alapítvány 2013).

171. Act LXXVI of 1999 on Copyright.

172. For detailed introduction, *see* Anikó Grad-Gyenge, *Szerzői jog és iparjogvédelem a magyar magánjogban* (*Copyright and Industrial Property in the Hungarian Private Law*), 7 ff. (Patrocinium 2014).

advertising, films, and other audiovisual works, creations of fine art, photography, architecture, applied art, industrial design and designs of engineering structures.

282. In the event of copyright infringement, the author can have recourse to civil law remedies, claiming:

- the establishment of infringement by the court;
- that the infringement and acts directly threatening with infringement be ceased and the infringer be enjoined from any further infringement;
- that the infringer makes amends for his action by a statement or in some other appropriate manner, and, if necessary, that such amends should be given appropriate publicity by and at the expense of the infringer;
- that the infringer provides information on parties taking part in the production, distribution or performance of goods or services affected by the infringement, as well as on business relationships established for the infringing acts;
- the recovery of the enrichment achieved via the infringement;
- the injurious state of affairs be terminated, the antecedent state of affairs be restored, the seizure of materials and devices used exclusively or primarily for the infringement as well as the seizure of goods be resulted from the infringement or the delivery thereof to a particular person, or the recall or definitive removal thereof from commercial circulation, or the destruction thereof.

In the event of copyright infringement, the author may also claim damages under the rules of civil liability or relief. The author may seek the remedy stemming from the infringement of copyright against a person whose services are being used in connection with the copyright infringement.

B. *Industrial Property*

283. Industrial property rights may apply to patents, utility models, designs, or semiconductor topographies. The conditions and acquisitions of all protection are regulated by specific other legislation. For these, obtaining protection requires a lengthy process, and protection does not emerge automatically with creation.

1. Patents

284. The Patent Act governs the protection of technical creations.[173] Under the Act, patents may be granted for any inventions in any field of technology that are new, involve an inventive step, and are susceptible to industrial application.[174] The

---

173. Act XXXIII of 1995 on the Protection of Inventions by Patents.
174. For detailed discussion, *see* Grad-Gyenge, *supra*, 18 ff.; Levente Tattay, György Pintz & Anett Pogácsás, *Szellemi alkotások joga* (*Law of Intellectual Property*) 35 ff. (Szent István Társulat 2011); Gábor Faludi, *Szerzői jog, iparvédelem és a ptk. koncepciója* (*Copyright, Protection of Inventions and the Concept of the Civil Code*), 5 Polgári jogi kodifikáció 3 ff. (2003).

following are not regarded as inventions: discoveries, scientific theories and mathematical methods, aesthetic creations, schemes, rules and methods for performing intellectual acts, playing games, or doing business, programs for computers, and presentations of information.

Under the Act, the person who has created an invention shall be deemed to be the inventor. An invention is only subject to comprehensive protection if it is protected by patent protection. Patent protection begins with the publication of the patent application to the Hungarian Intellectual Property Office, but the patent dates from the date of the application. Patent protection may apply for up to twenty years. Rights derived from an invention and from patent protection, with the exception of moral rights, may be transferred, assigned, and pledged. The patentee may grant permission to exploit an invention under an exploitation contract (patent licensing agreement), and the person exploiting the invention is required to pay royalties.

285. Where the subject matter of a patent application or a patent has been taken unlawfully from the invention of another person, it qualifies as an infringement of invention. In such a scenario, the injured party or his successor in title may claim a statement to the effect that he is entitled wholly or partly to the patent and may claim damages under the rules of civil liability. By contrast, an infringement of a patent is when somebody unlawfully exploits a patented invention. The patentee may have recourse to the following civil remedies:

- the establishment of patent infringement by the court;
- he may request an injunction that the infringer cease his infringement or any acts directly threatening this;
- he may demand that the infringer give information on the identity of persons involved in the production and distribution of the infringing goods or the provision of infringing services and of their channels of distribution;
- he may demand satisfaction from the infringer by way of a declaration or by other appropriate means; if necessary, the declaration shall be made public by the infringer or at his expense;
- he may require surrender of the enrichment obtained by the infringement of the patent;
- he may request the seizure, the transfer to a specific person, the recall, and the definitive removal from the channels of commerce or destruction of the infringing products, as well as of the means and materials exclusively or principally used for infringement;
- the patentee may also claim damages under the rules of civil liability.

2. Protection of Utility Models

286. Any solution relating to the configuration or construction of an article or to the arrangement of parts thereof which is new, involves an inventive step and is susceptible to industrial application may be granted utility model protection.[175] Utility model protection may not be granted, in particular for the aesthetic design of an article and plant varieties. A ministerial decree governs the filing of utility model protection.[176] Utility model protection applies for a term of ten years from the date of filing.

3. Trademarks

287. Trademark protection may be granted for any signs capable of being represented graphically provided that these are capable of distinguishing goods or services from those of other undertakings.[177] Signs which may be granted trademark protection are, in particular:

- words, a combination of words, including personal names and slogans;
- letters, numerals;
- figures, pictures;
- two- or three-dimensional forms, including the shape of goods or of their packaging;
- colours, a combination of colours, light signals, holograms;
- sound signals; and
- combination of signs defined above.

Trademark protection shall have a term of ten years and may be renewed for a further period of ten years.

4. Geographical Indications

288. Geographical indications and appellations of origin which are used in the course of trade to identify the geographical origin of a product shall be granted protection as geographical indications.[178] Geographical indication means the geographical name of a region, locality or, in exceptional cases, a country which serves to designate a product originating therein, the specific quality, reputation, or other characteristics of which are due essentially to that geographical origin and the production, processing or preparation of which takes place in the defined geographical area. Appellation of origin means the geographical name of a region, locality, or, in exceptional cases, a country which serves to designate a product originating therein, the specific quality, reputation or other characteristics of which are due exclusively or essentially to the geographical environment, with its inherent natural and human

175. Act XXXVIII of 1991 on the Protection of Utility Models.
176. Decree 18/2004. (IV. 28.) of the Minister for Justice on the formal detailed rules of filing utility model protection.
177. Act XI of 1997 on the Protection of Trade Marks and Geographical Indications.
178. Geographical indications are also regulated in the act on the Protection of Trade Marks and Geographical Indications.

factors, and the production, processing, and preparation of which take place in the defined geographical area. Protection of the geographical indication shall begin with registration and shall be effective retroactively from the date of filing of the application for an unlimited time.

5. Designs

289. Design protection may be granted for any designs which are new and have individual character.[179] Design means the appearance of the whole or a part of a product resulting from the features of, in particular, the lines, contours, colours, shape, texture, or materials of the product itself or its ornamentation. These may be any industrial or handicraft items. Design protection has a term of five years and may be renewed for a further period of five years, four times at the most.

6. Plant Varieties

290. Plant varieties are protected by plant variety rights.[180] Final plant variety rights have a term of thirty years in the case of grapes and trees and twenty-five years for other plant varieties from the time they are granted.

7. Topographies of Microelectronic Semiconductor Products

291. Topography means the three-dimensional disposition, however, expressed, of the elements, at least one of which is an active element, and of some or all of the interconnections of a microelectronic semiconductor product, or such a three-dimensional disposition prepared for a semiconductor product intended for manufacture.[181] The protection of integrated circuits has a term of ten years.

8. Know-How

292. Know-how was not defined statutorily for a long time. The expression 'know-how' is not used in the Civil Code, but its equivalent translation is. Under the effect of Hungarian legislation, commercial secrecy also applies to technical, economic, and other practical knowledge of value held in a form enabling identification, including accumulated skills and experience and any combination thereof if acquired, used, disclosed, or published in violation of the principle of good faith

179. Act XLVIII of 2001 on the Legal Protection of Designs.
180. Chapter XIII of Act XXXIII of 1995.
181. Act XXXIX of 1991 on the legal protection of topographies of microelectronic semiconductor products.

and fairness.[182] This protection shall not apply if a person obtains the know-how or any knowledge which essentially has the same attributes by means of development independent of the proprietor or by way of testing or analysing a lawfully acquired product or lawfully received service. The protection of know-how is provided under the law of business secrets.[183]

9. Goodwill

293. The term goodwill, as used in economic and commercial terminology, has no generally accepted Hungarian equivalent (commonly referred to as 'good reputation of the undertaking', or alternatively consumer experiences, assessments, prestige, etc.). A company's goodwill may stem from many different sources: the technical standard of its operations, the standard of its output, attractive product design, etc. This represents a significant economic value and embodies a substantial competitive advantage; however, Hungarian private law does not protect these values in the form of goodwill. The business methods, corporate strategies, internal organizational and marketing or advertising solutions that give rise to and bolster goodwill must also be factored in. In many cases, these can be classified as knowledge and experience, representing intangible assets that are regarded as know-how and are protected as such.

§3. Funds (Capital; Investment Fund)

294. Investment funds play a significant role in the global financial system, and their exceptional ability to incorporate capital can have a positive impact on the competitiveness of entire industries. As early as the 1980s, a certain level of legal harmonization that took place in the European Economic Area had already boosted competitiveness, which was a precursor of today's almost fully interoperable establishment where regulatory arbitrage is kept to a minimum. Handling billions of forints and/or euros in assets, fund management companies are subject to a multitude of legal regulations and operate under strict supervision. Therefore, before a fund's first investment unit can be subscribed, a multi-stage authorization procedure must be conducted.

As for the legal background, Undertakings for Collective Investment in Transferable Securities (UCITS) is of particular importance.[184] Given its legal nature, the transposition of the directive is not mandatory; it can be implemented by the Member States in their national law with similar content, as was the case with Hungary's.[185]

---

182. *See* in details Márta Görög, *A know-how jogi védelmének alapvető kérdései* (*Fundamental Questions of Legal Protection of the Know-How*) particularly 65 ff. (HVG-ORAC 2012).
183. Act LIV of 2018 on protection of the business secret.
184. Amended by the Directive 2014/91/EU of the European Parliament and of the Council of 23 Jul. 2014.
185. Act XVI of 2014 on the collective investment forms and their operators, as well as on the modification of particular financial acts.

While the Civil Code provides important provisions, particularly concerning the foundation of business associations, other administrative statutory laws must also be applied.[186]

295. As a first step in the foundation procedure, a business association is to be established, which can only take the form of a company limited by shares. Its registered capital must be at least EUR 125,000. For real estate funds, a minimum initial investment of EUR 300,000 is required. Fund managers engaging in operations defined in the UCITS are subject to licensing.

296. Once established as a business association and licensed by the Central Bank, a fund manager can commence its activities. According to their form of operation, investment funds can be either private or public; they can be accessible to professional or retail clients; their terms can be open or closed-ended; and the primary type of underlying assets can also be defined. For public funds, the minimum initial capital is set at HUF 200 million for securities funds and HUF 1 billion for real estate funds, whereas, for private funds, the respective amounts are set at HUF 100 million and 500 million. The registered capital of private equity funds can only comprise cash contributions. For private equity funds, at least 10% of their registered capital, but no less than HUF 250 million, must be paid up whenever investment units are subscribed, ensuring that the amounts payable by persons subscribing certificates of the same series are identical.

Following the unit subscription deadline, unless subscribed, the amounts invested must be refunded to respective investors within seven days. If subscribed, the fund manager must ensure registration with the Central Bank without delay. If the subscription is successful and the appropriate exhibits are submitted to the Central Bank, the fund can be registered. Registration results in the formation of a separate legal entity, the statutory representative of which is the fund manager that proceeds on behalf of the investment fund. Investment units must be entered into the clearing house within thirty days of registration.

297. That is when actual fund management can commence, which is subject to a detailed set of regulations both from an organizational aspect (e.g., compliance of regulatory capital, rules on custodians) and also in terms of how the managed fund is invested (e.g., listing and registration of contracts, drafting the investment policy).

§4. Chattels Personal and Chattels Real (*See Also* Part I)

298. In connection with the chattels personal, *see* Part II, Chapter 1, §2; regarding chattels real, *see* Part I, Chapters 1–2.

186. Act CXXXIX of 2013 on the Central Bank that prevails in authorization procedures and, for the lesser details, the lower-level Government Decree No. 79/2014. (III. 14.).

Chapter 2. Legal Interests

299. The ownership of movable property also extends to their use and possession, the collection of relevant proceeds, and the right of disposal. In connection with these rights, the provisions under Chapter 2 of Part I must be applied.

Chapter 3. Equitable Interests

300. Given that equitable relief is not recognized under Hungarian law, no equitable interests apply to movable property either.

Chapter 4. Security Interests (*See Also* Parts I, IV, and V)

301. Similarly to real property, the lien on movable property is construed as a security interest (also refer to Part V). Furthermore, the issue of fiduciary securities also arises, which is discussed in detail under Chapter 2 of Part IV.

Part III. Acquisition of Property Rights

302. There are several systems in terms of the modalities of acquiring ownership rights based on their relationship to the grounds of the transaction. According to the stipulations of certain private law codes, for instance, the French Code civil,[187] the Belgian Civil Code,[188] and the Italian Codice civile,[189] the conclusion of legal transactions forming legal titles for the acquisition of ownership is accepted for the transfer of ownership right (consensual versus conventional system).

The traditional system builds on the customs of Roman law and makes a distinction between the modalities of acquiring ownership (*modi acquirendi dominii*) and the legal grounds thereof (*causa acquirendi dominii*) and requires both for the legally valid transfer of ownership rights.[190] The German, Swiss, and former Dutch Civil Codes are based on this principle,[191] which requires an additional legal act beyond the legal titles, such as taking movable property into possession or the registration of real property in an official public registry.[192] In terms of the latter legal systems, we must also make a further distinction, as German law is qualified by an abstract system according to which the validity of a right in rem contract must be evaluated individually and is independent of the validity of the legal transaction forming the legal grounds.[193] By contrast, the Austrian, Swiss, and Dutch legal systems, similar to the Hungarian one, are characterized by a causal system under which if the contractual legal relationship forming the basis of the transfer of ownership right is invalid, then the legal act aimed at transferring ownership right must also be considered invalid. Accordingly, rulings on the requirements aimed at prohibiting the transfer of ownership rights are also subject to different regulations. Under French law, the restraint on alienation also applies with regard to third parties, while in German law, the right of alienation cannot be excluded or restricted and only applies to the law of obligations.[194]

---

187. Articles 711 and 1138 of the French Code civil.
188. Articles 711 and 1138 of the Belgian Civil Code.
189. Article 1376 of the Italian Codice civile.
190. Földi and Hamza, *supra* 317. L.P.W. van Vliet, *Transfer of Movables in German, French, English, and Dutch Law* 23 ff. (Ars Aequi Libri 2000).
191. *See* Art. 929 of the BGB, Art. 714 of the ZGB and Arts 667 and 671 of the former Dutch Civil Code.
192. Földi and Hamza, *supra* 317 ff.
193. Vliet, *supra* 32.
194. Article 399 of the BGB.

303. In Hungarian law, we can distinguish between the modalities of acquiring ownership based on whether we are talking about movable or real property and whether the modality of acquisition is original or derivative.

The original modalities of acquiring movable property are through an official ruling or official auction, adverse possession, appropriation of *bona vacantia*, and finding property. The original modalities of acquiring real property were through an official ruling or official auction, adverse possession or appropriation. The derivative modalities of acquiring movable property are: transfer, the appropriation of goods, crops and yields, game, fish, and other farmed aquatic animals, manufacturing, unification and succession. The derivative modalities of acquiring real property are transfer, accretion, annexation, incorporating construction, building on land owned by someone else, and succession.

Chapter 1. Transfer of Property by Contract Inter Vivos

304. Hungarian private law adheres to the traditional system in terms of the transfer of ownership right; as a result, the transfer of ownership consists of two phases. The transfer requires an adequate contract or other legal titles alongside the transfer of the tangible property or registration in the land registry in the case of real property. To acquire the ownership right of movable property, a contract or other legal grounds for the transfer and the related transfer of possession of the property are necessary. To acquire the ownership right of real property, a contract or other legal grounds for the transfer and the related registration in the land registry are necessary.

The legal titles suitable for acquiring ownership can be discovered based on the subject matter of the various contracts or legal transactions. The contracts and other legal transactions in which the transfer of ownership can be found among the parties' scope of services have adequate legal grounds. Legal grounds suitable for the transfer of ownership may include sales contracts and their various types and subtypes, exchange contracts, donation contracts, maintenance and life annuity contracts, etc. The contract only represents an adequate legal title for the buyer; however, the adequate modality of ownership transfer is also necessary for acquiring the thing's ownership right.

305. It is important to emphasize that, as a main rule, ownership can only be acquired from the owner (referred to as the principle of *nemo plus iuris*). An exception from this is a buyer acquiring movable property in good faith from commerce in exchange for consideration and transfer in exchange for money or a bearer instrument.

Judicial practice is consistent in the matter of considering sales contracts valid despite the fact that the seller is not yet the owner of the indirect asset forming the object of the transaction at the time of contract conclusion. In these cases, the contract is not aimed at an impossible service, nor is it in breach of any law, as the seller may acquire the ownership right of the indirect asset forming the object of the transaction before the fulfilment date stated in the contract. If this fails to materialize, the seller has committed a breach of contract. Of course, in cases where the transfer of the thing forming the indirect object of the sales contract is impossible, to begin with (e.g., property that is not eligible for sale or subject to a restraint on alienation and encumbrance), the sales contract is qualified as null and void due to the breach of law or the impossible service.

306. The seller has the option of retaining its ownership right in writing at the time of contract conclusion until payment of the full purchase price at the latest. In the case of real property, the maintenance of ownership right must be noted in the land registry, while in the case of movable property, it must be noted in the credit collateral or other official public registry. The seller is protected by the maintenance of ownership right, which ensures that the buyer cannot dispose of the thing until he has paid the full purchase price. As a result, in the event of a breach of contract by the buyer, the seller has the option of restoring the original state, and no third party can prevent this by obtaining rights to the thing. An exception is if one fails to make an entry in the registry. In the event of a failure to make an entry, the person making the acquisition from the buyer in good faith and in exchange for consideration obtains ownership rights, and a lien is also established by the buyer to the benefit of a third party. At the same time, if the seller transfers his ownership right to a third party during the maintenance of the right, he is committing a breach of contract, and the buyer thus becomes eligible to claim indemnification from the seller.

When a sales contract is concluded with a retain of ownership right, the right of use and for reaping the benefits of the thing after the buyer has taken possession of the property is transferred to the buyer, along with the obligation to bear costs incurred by using the property. In the event of a real property purchase and sale, during the maintenance of the ownership right, all burdens and risks related to the thing taken into possession are transferred to the buyer.

The seller's condition for maintaining ownership right is, therefore, independent of the other validity requirements of the contract's formalities, only valid in writing. It is important to stress that the ownership right cannot be maintained in the period following payment of the full purchase price.

307. Within the scope of the rules of transfer, the Hungarian Civil Code makes a distinction between the transfer of movable and real property. Under the narrower interpretation, the legal transaction involving movable property materializes in a real act, namely the physical handover of the property. This interpretation is significantly broadened by the simplified modalities applicable when transferring possession of the thing, as described under the section on the transfer of possession. Accordingly, the physical handover of the transferable thing is not a prerequisite, and relinquishing power over the thing suffices for the transfer.

An entry in the land registry replaces the transfer of possession of the property when transferring the ownership right of real property. The Real Estate Registration Act defines detailed rules on the formal and substantive elements that must be included in a document in order to register ownership rights.

In the case of certain movable property, there is an official public registry pertaining to either the ownership right or keeper status. In these cases, however, changes in ownership materialize even without entry into the registry. For instance, when transferring a vehicle, the keeper having acquired ownership of the vehicle has an obligation to conclude a third-party motorist liability insurance policy even if the transfer is not recorded in the registration certificate.[195]

An example of the relationship between the legal grounds and the modality of ownership transfer is when a contract is concluded for something that the seller does not actually own. In such cases, the sales contract (which represents the legal grounds) can still be valid, and the transfer of ownership is to be evaluated within the scope of the seller's contractual performance obligation.[196]

The Civil Code regulates the contracts which provide title for the transfer of ownership. Among these contracts, the most important ones are the following.

---

195. EBH 2007/1688.
196. EBH 2003/867 and EBH 1999/96.

§1. Sales Contract

308. Under the sales contract, the seller undertakes to transfer ownership of some item to the buyer, and the buyer undertakes to take possession of the item and pays the purchase price. If the subject matter of the sales contract is a real estate property, the seller shall also transfer possession of it. The provisions relating to the sale of items shall also apply to contracts for the transfer of a right or claim.[197]

There shall be four important elements of content, namely: (i) the parties, (ii) the subject matter of the purchase, (iii) the determination of the purchase price, and (iv) legal title (sale), that is to say, the intention of the transfer of ownership.

309. Concerning the subjects of the sale, we only call attention to the fact that the parties shall be identifiable by the contract.

310. The direct subject matter of the sale is human activity, the transfer and the acceptance of the item, as well as the payment of the purchase price. The indirect subject matter of the sales contract can primarily be an item. In the literature, the transfer of rights and claims by the title of sale has caused controversy; however, the new Civil Code made it possible by applying the provisions relating to the sale of items to the transfer of rights and claims. In case of an indirect subject matter, the limitations of legal rules and contracts, the marketability of the item and the restraint on alienation and encumbrance shall be considered. The case of composite items shall be remarked concerning the subject matter of the sales contract. The legal consideration of components (parts) is always equivalent to those of the main item since the use under normal conditions is not possible without it (e.g., a motor car with three tyres or without an engine). The accessories (e.g., snow chain or light fixtures in a real estate) only facilitate the use under normal conditions, and their legal consideration is equivalent to those of the main item only in case of doubt; however, unless there is a different agreement, it is included in the transfer of title. In several cases, the delimitation of the two is difficult (e.g., a first-aid package in a motor car or a built-in wardrobe in a real estate). The subject matter of the sale can be a future item as well. In this case, it is important to delimitation the future sale (*emptio spei*, e.g., gambling contracts authorized by the state) and the sale of an expected item (*emptio rei speratae*, in which case the coming into being of the subject matter of the sale is a precedent condition).

---

197. From the literature, *see* particularly Gyula Eörsi, *A tulajdonátszállás kérdéséről* (*About the Question of Transfer of Title*) (Légrády testvérek 1947); István Gárdos, *Fiduciárius biztosítékok az új Polgári Törvénykönyvben* (*Fiduciary Collaterals in the New Civil Code*), 16 Gazdaság és Jog (2008); István Gárdos & Péter Gárdos, *Az engedményezés és a vételi jog biztosítéki célú alkalmazása* (*The Application of Assignment and Purchase Option as Collateral*), 12 Gazdaság és Jog (2004); István Gárdos & Péter Gárdos, *Ismét a fiduciárius biztosítékokról* (*About the Fiduciary Collaterals Again*), 13 Gazdaság és Jog (2005); István Kemenes, *A biztosítéki célú vételi jog egyes jogalkalmazási kérdései* (*Certain Questions of Legal Practice Concerning the Purchase Option for Collateral Purposes*), 2 BDT (2009); Gábor Kiss & István Sándor, *A szerződések érvénytelensége* (*Invalidity of the Contracts*) (HVG-ORAC 2014); András Kisfaludi, *Az adásvételi szerződés* (*The Sales Contract*) (Közgazdasági és Jogi Kiadó 2003); László Leszkoven, *A biztosítéki célú vételi jog néhány kérdéséről* (*About Some Questions of the Purchase Option for Collateral Purposes*), 12 Gazdaság és Jog (2004).

311. The parties shall express their purpose of transfer of title. Without it, the contract cannot be considered a sales contract; however, a contract by another title may be established (e.g., lease).

312. The parties shall agree on the purchase price that can only be a payment instrument accepted by the state. The purchase price shall be determined by money, and if the consideration is not money, there may be an exchange contract. When determining the purchase price, there may be a difference between the currencies of the purchase price and the payment of it; moreover, rules decreasing the exchange rate risks can be constituted for the delayed payment. In this regard, there is a limitation concerning the products with official prices (e.g., tobacco products) and in case of gross disparity in the values exchanged (*laesio enormis*). It is acceptable if the parties refer to the market rates as long as the latter are determinable, and it is also acceptable if they stipulate the mechanism of the procedure (e.g., expert estimation) on the basis of which the factual amount of the purchase price can be determined by money. If the parties agree on market rates, the average price of the market in the location and on the date of the performance shall be paid. There is a possibility of determining the purchase price of the subject matter of the sale by weight, and in this case, the purchase price shall be calculated by the net weight. In the case of official prices, the purchase price may be stipulated by legislation.

I. The Formality of the Sales Contract

313. As a general rule, there are no special models concerning the formalities of the sales contract in the Civil Code. There may be formalities stipulated by other laws or by the parties:

- other laws may prescribe that the sales contract shall be executed in writing in order to be valid (e.g., in case of sales contract of real estate);
- it is possible that the written form is not a condition of validity; however, it is necessary for the registration of the ownership of the buyer into a certain registry (e.g., sales contract of a car);
- the parties can also stipulate themselves the written form of the contract.

Typically, the sales contract may be established orally, in writing, by implicit conduct (by a real act), or by a judicial decision (e.g., in case of preliminary contract or obligation to contract). Certain elements of the content of the sales contract may be influenced by the fact that the contract is concluded through auction or tender. It shall be emphasized that in case of a legal regulation prescribing certain formalities for the establishment of a valid contract, the preliminary contract is valid only with these formalities.

II. The Obligations of the Parties While Performing the Sales Contract

314. The main obligations of the seller:

- Transfer of title of the item (making the necessary declarations for this).
- Transfer of possession of the item to the buyer concerning real estate property (which may be realized by alleviated manners of transfer of possession as *traditio longa manu, traditio brevi manu, consitutum possessorium, traditio symbolica, cessio vindicationis* stb.).

The accessory obligations of the seller:

- Obligation to give information about the subject of the sale, which cannot be replaced by the incidental knowledge of the buyer from other sources. In case of false information, it shall be examined whether the buyer's purpose to buy would have existed if the information had been appropriate, since, in the case of the lack of this purpose, the invalidity of the contract may occur. If the purpose of buying would have existed even in the case of false information, the legal consequences of breach of contract may apply.
- The set-up being required for the usage under normal conditions is also the obligation of the seller since the buyer may not necessarily know the characteristics of the subject matter of the sale, and he may not have the necessary knowledge to operate it.
- The transfer of the necessary documents for usage under normal conditions, such as prospectuses, instructions for use, guarantee certificates, etc., is also the obligation of the seller, as well as the transfer of the invoice or receipt.

315. The main obligations of the buyer:

- payment of the purchase price (that may be realized in cash or by bank transfer, in the latter case, we consider the credit on account of the seller as the performance);
- reception (and examination) of the item.

The accessory obligations of the buyer:

- giving transaction receipt;
- bearing the costs concerning the contract (e.g., cost of labour of the notary or attorney);
- payment of the fee of the procedure for registration of the title (an administrative fee of real estate registry).

III. Legal Effects of the Sales Contract

316. The sales contract only means an appropriate title to the buyer; however, there shall be an adequate manner of transfer of title for the acquisition of the ownership of the item. Therefore, the Hungarian Civil Code follows the system of traditions, in which case the manner of transfer of title of ownership and the title of transfer of title of ownership shall exist at the same time in order to transfer the title.

We shall emphasize that as a general rule, the title may be transferred only to an owner (principle of *nemo plus iuris* or *nemo dat quod non habet).* The case of the buyer acquiring tangible items for consideration in good faith in commerce (compare with the case of the purchase of a stolen motor car from a trader or another person),[198] or in case of transfer of money or transferable shares, is an exception to this rule.[199]

The judicial practice is consistent as the sales contract is not invalid because the buyer is not the owner of the item being the indirect subject matter of the sale on the date of the conclusion of the contract. In this instance, the service is not impossible, and the contract is not unlawful since, until the date of the performance, the seller may acquire the title of the item being the indirect subject matter of the sale. If this is not realized, the seller breaches the contract. Naturally, if the transfer of title of the item being the indirect subject matter of the sale is already excluded (e.g., non-marketable items or items under the prohibition of alienation or encumbrance), the sales contract is considered null and void for being unlawful or having an impossible performance.

While concluding the contract, the seller has the possibility to retain his title of ownership in writing at the latest until the purchase price is paid fully. In the case of real estate property, the retention of title shall be recorded in the real estate register, while in the case of movable property, it shall be registered in the collateral registry or into another pubic registry.

317. The retention of title protects the seller since, through this, the buyer cannot dispose of the item until he pays the purchase price in full. Consequently, in case of breach of contract by the buyer, the seller has the possibility of restoration that cannot be invalidated by a third person acquiring entitlement regarding the item. The failure to register in the registry is an exception to this since, in the absence of registration, a third person acquiring from the buyer for consideration in good faith shall acquire the ownership and the lien established by the buyer on the item for a third party shall also come into existence. Nevertheless, if the buyer transfers the title of the item to a third party during the retention of title, he breaches the contract; thus, the seller may lodge claims against him to recover the damages.

In case of concluding a sales contract with retention of title, the right of use and enjoyment is transferred to the buyer; while transferring the possession of the item to him, he has to bear the costs related to the use of the item. Concerning the sales of a real estate property, the encumbrances and the risk related to the item in possession of the buyer are also transferred to the buyer during the effect of the retention of title.

---

198. Section 5:39(2) of the Civil Code.
199. Civil Code Art. 5:40.

The stipulation of retention of title by the buyer is valid only in writing regardless of other validity necessities of the contract's formalities. It shall be highlighted that the retention of title cannot be maintained after paying the purchase price in full.

IV. Warranty of Title

318. The warranty of title of the seller provides the buyer with the acquisition of the title of ownership of the item pursuant to the definition of the sale. If the acquisition of ownership is not realized, the buyer shall request the seller to eliminate the hindrance within a prescribed time limit, or he may require another adequate guarantee from the seller. In the event of non-compliance within the said time limit, the buyer shall be entitled to withdraw from the contract and claim damages. If the seller has acted in good faith, the buyer shall be entitled to require only the damages incurred by the conclusion of the contract.

If the ownership of the buyer is hindered by a right of a third party, or the value thereof is reduced by such hindrance, the buyer may request disencumbrance within a prescribed time limit. In the event of non-compliance within the deadline prescribed, the buyer may carry out the disencumbrance from the purchase price available or at the seller's expense. If disencumbrance is not possible or if it would cause unreasonable expenses, the buyer shall be entitled to withdraw from the contract and claim compensation or to have the consideration proportionally reduced in exchange for freeing the encumbrance. The buyer shall be entitled to these rights even if the deadline set for disencumbrance has elapsed without any result and the buyer does not wish the disencumbrance of the item.

The buyer shall not be entitled to these rights if he knew or should have known at the time the contract concluded that unrestricted ownership could not be acquired unless the seller had guaranteed the acquisition of unrestricted ownership by the buyer.

Therefore, the claim of warranty exists regardless of the good or bad faith of the seller without any particular deadlines.

V. The Termination of the Sales Contract

319. Concerning sales contracts, the termination with ex tunc effect; that is to say, by withdrawal or by a mutual agreement with retroactive effect, may have legitimacy. The parties are entitled to withdrawal if the other party seriously breaches the contract (e.g., the lack of payment of the purchase price, the omission of the transfer of title) or if the parties themselves stipulate this right in the event of other circumstances.

Both the withdrawal and the mutual agreement of the parties terminate the contract retroactively to the date of the conclusion of the contract; that is to say, there is restitution of original status. The latter involves the return of the services already performed; furthermore, the parties shall settle accounts with one another regarding the damages that occurred in the meantime.

VI. Special Rules Concerning Consumer Sales Contracts

320. The Civil Code prescribes special rules for two cases concerning consumer sales contracts. It shall be remarked that in the general part of contract law, there are further rules in favour of the consumer regarding consumer sale as a consumer contract; however, these rules are presented in the general part of contract law and are related to the law of consumer protection.

The risks shall pass to the buyer if the seller hands over the item in his own carriage to the buyer or to a third party named by the buyer or if the carrier hired by the buyer was recommended by the seller. If the carrier hired by the buyer was not recommended by the seller, risks shall pass at the time of handing over the item to the carrier.

The other case is the late performance of the seller. As a general rule, the seller shall perform to the buyer within thirty days after the conclusion of the contract. The buyer is entitled to withdraw if:

- the seller does not perform even after an extended time limit;
- the seller refuses to perform;
- the late performance results in the lapse of interest of the buyer.

§2. Special Types of Sales Contract

321. Related to special modes of the sale contract, the transfer of title in return for the purchase price – that is to say, the sales transaction exists – however, there are special rules concerning the establishment or performance of the contract. Consequently, the rules of the sales contract are the background rules of the special modes of the sales contract.

I. Purchase upon Delivery Subject to Inspection

322. The speciality of this type of sale is that the buyer is entitled to inspect the subject matter of the sale only after the conclusion of the contract, and under the contract, he may have a unilateral option to demand or not to demand the entry into force of the contract. Pursuant to the contract, it depends on the unilateral decision of the buyer whether he keeps the goods and pays the purchase price or returns the goods, and by this, he does not have an obligation to pay the purchase price. The buyer is not obliged to explain his decision. The coming into being of the contract is conditional upon the buyer's intention to buy the item according to the visual inspection. If the buyer fails to declare his intention, the contract shall not enter into effect.

II. Purchase upon Delivery Subject to Testing

323. In case of purchase upon delivery, the purchase comes into existence by the sole decision of the buyer. In this case, he has more entitlements considering that he is allowed not only to inspect the subject matter of the sale but to take its possession and test it under normal conditions. If the buyer does not intend to keep the item, he is obliged to return it to the seller. If the buyer returns the item and does not intend to maintain the effect of the contract, he shall not pay for the use under normal conditions during the testing (of course, he is obliged to refund the cost of further use and the possible damages). However, the seller is not responsible for the defects occurring during the testing period. If the item has a defect that is recognized or could have been recognized by the buyer during the testing, the seller is released from the consequences of lack of conformity.

It is not a purchase upon delivery subject to testing if the buyer stipulated the characteristics of the subject matter of the sale in the contract, then he realizes after the conclusion of the contract that the goods transferred to him are not appropriate. In this case, there is a lack of conformity with all of its legal consequences, and in the event of an adequate explanation, the buyer is entitled to ultimately withdraw from the contract.

Regarding the contracts between parties being in different locations, there may be a case similar to the purchase upon delivery subject to testing, since generally, the buyer may be able to come to know the goods after the delivery of the product.[200] Concerning its legal construction, this case is similar to the purchase upon delivery subject to testing; however, the Government Decree shall be applied only for consumer contracts. Furthermore, in this case, the contract comes into effect by transferring the product, and the buyer has an obligation to pay the purchase price.

III. Purchase by Sample

324. The parties have the opportunity to define the quality of the goods in the contract by reference to a sample, and the obligation of the seller is to perform with a product being equivalent to the sample. It is basically possible in the case of replaceable items that can be determined by quality and quantity. It shall be remarked that if the defect was recognizable in the sample, the seller shall not be responsible for the lack of conformity. According to the judicial practice, the sale from a catalogue belongs to this case; however, it is controverted in the literature.

IV. Hire Purchase

325. In case of a hire purchase, the buyer is not obliged to pay the purchase price in full to the seller on the date of the conclusion of the contract or of the transfer of the title since he can compensate it in several instalments pursuant to a scheduling defined by the parties. There is a risk for the seller concerning the performance of the contract, and in the event of the buyer's failure to make the instalment payments when due, the seller has the possibility to terminate the payment facilities, or

200. In the event of this, the prescriptions of the Government Decree No. 45/2014. (II. 26.) shall be taken into consideration. Concerning the sales under the effect of the Government Decree, the s. 20(2) provides the buyer the possibility to withdraw without explanation within fourteen working days.

according to his option, he is entitled to withdraw from the contract. In the event of the first failure, the right of the latter can be exercised by the seller only if the buyer has been informed thereof in advance and sufficient time has been allowed for performance. However, the hire purchase does not automatically involve the retention of title that can be taken into consideration pursuant to a particular agreement. Therefore, it is possible – and it frequently happens in practice – that the buyer of the hire purchase sells the item in commerce for consideration to another buyer in good faith, and then the seller intends to withdraw from the contract after the failure of the payment, but he cannot regain the item.

If the seller withdraws from the contract due to the failure to pay the purchase price, the parties shall restore the original condition existing on the date of concluding the contract. Consequently, the seller shall repay the buyer the instalments of payment already acquired, and the buyer shall return the item to the seller. The restitution of the original condition is complete if the buyer pays remuneration for the use of the item and if he refunds the cost of damages that occurred while using the item under abnormal conditions.

V. Special Rules of Sales Contract of a Real Estate Property

326. The sales contract of a real estate property shall be executed in writing, or otherwise, it is null and void. Therefore, the contract of a real estate property has different legal effects: in case of a sales contract of a real estate property having been concluded orally, the contract comes into being; however, it is null and void. A sales contract of real estate having been written in a simple private document comes into being validly; however, it is inappropriate for the registration of the title to the real estate registry. It is necessary for the validity of the contract that the statement of purpose aiming at the transfer of title of the real estate property shall be marked out, then the document shall contain the designation of the real estate and the consideration, or if it is gratuitous, it shall be recognizable. Furthermore, the parties shall sign the document that can be realized in a way that each party signs a document with the same content separately. If a sales contract of real estate written in a public document or in a document countersigned by an attorney or a legal counsel comes into being validly and meets the requirements of the Act on real estate registry and the Decree of the Ministry of Agriculture and Rural Development No. 109/1999. (XII. 29.), then the ownership of the buyer can be registered to the real estate registry. The submission of a contract having the required formalities (e.g., signature on every page) and conditions of content (e.g., the existence of a definitive and irrevocable contributory statement concerning the registration of the ownership) pursuant to the Act on real estate registry is necessary for this.

VI. Forward Sales Contract

327. Pursuant to forward transaction for the sale of items defined by type and quantity, the seller undertakes an obligation to transmit items defined in the contract in the future, while the buyer shall receive them and pay the purchase price.

By the forward transaction for the sale of items defined by type and quantity, the seller undertakes to transfer items not necessarily at his disposal at the time of the conclusion of the contract (*emptio rei futurae*). The parties may stipulate that they attach the quality and the method of examination of the quality and quantity and the order of objection regarding quality and quantity to a standard, a technical condition, eventually to a usage, a sample regulation, a sample, or a detailed description.

Concerning the forward transaction for the sale of items defined by type and quantity, the parties may define the maximum extent of deviation of quantity considered appropriate to the contract. Obviously, in these cases, the price is also adjusted to the quantity performed in reality. If the item transmitted by the seller does not attain the minimum quantity having been stipulated by the parties, then the quantity having been originally stipulated shall be considered while applying the legal consequences of the breach of contract.

The buyer is entitled to withdraw from the contract at any time without explanation; however, in this case, he is obliged to reimburse the damages caused at the expense of the seller.

VII. Sales Contract for the Supply of Own Produced Agricultural Goods

328. Under this contract, the seller (manufacturer) undertakes an obligation for the transfer of title and possession in the future of agricultural goods, products defined by quantity that he produced himself or animals defined by quantity raised or fed by himself, and the seller is obliged to take the possession of the items and pay the consideration of value. Therefore, regarding its subject matter, this contract may refer to crop production or breeding and fattening animals.

The parties may define the contractual quantity by a unit of measure being adapted to the speciality of the agricultural goods, by the full produce of a defined territory, by the full yield of a defined animal or by the proportion of them. The quality and the method of examination of the quality and quantity and the order of objection regarding quality and quantity can be defined by a reference to a standard or another prescription, a usage known by both parties, a sample regulation or by a detailed description.

Due to the speciality of the contract's subject matter, the seller is entitled to perform before the deadline stipulated in the contract if he provides enough time to the seller for preparation concerning the reception. It is also a speciality of the contract that the seller is entitled to perform 10% below the quantity stipulated even without the previous agreement of the parties.

Under this contract, the seller (manufacturer) undertakes an obligation for the future supply of agricultural goods and products defined by quantity that he produced himself, or animals defined by quantity raised or sustained by himself (i.e., to say, transfer the title and the possession to the seller), and the seller is obliged to take the possession of the items and pay the given value. Alterations from sales contract:

- the date of the performance of the manufacturer is later than the date of the conclusion of the contract;

- the subject matters of the contract are agricultural goods or animals produced or raised by the manufacturer himself; thus, the contract has an indirect subject matter;
- the buyer has an obligation to accept the performance, even if the seller performs 10% below the quantity stipulated in the contract;
- the seller is entitled to perform before the stipulated date in the contract.

In case of sales contracts for the supply of agricultural goods and animals produced, raised, or fed by himself, there is a possibility for the buyer to provide services to the seller in order to facilitate the performance and to give information concerning these services.

The seller is not entitled to refuse the repayment of the services having been given by the buyer for accounting or as a deposit on the basis that these services could not be covered by the result of the production.

§3. Other Types of Title-Transfer Contracts

I. Contract for Works

329. According to Roman law, the main difference between the contract for works and the contract for production of items in the future was decided based on who owns the material. Nowadays, the difference is principally based on the intensity of the customer's/buyer's right to instruct, that is to say, the scope of his influence concerning the partial processes of the activity of the manufacturer. There may be a transfer of title also in case of contract for works if the entrepreneur uses his own materials to obtain the result. However, regarding the contract for works, the main performance refers to the attainment of the result, not to the transfer of title.[201]

II. Exchange Contract

330. In the case of exchange contract, the main aspect of delimitation is that the obligation of paying money concerning the buyer is replaced by the obligation of transfer of title and possession of another item; that is to say, the exchange contract is a sales contract where there are buyers on both sides.

III. Contract of Gift

331. The contract of gift differs from the sales contract in the aspect that the donee benefits from a gratuity; that is to say, he has no obligation to pay a purchase price or any other countervalue. Consequently, in the case of a contract of gift, the liability of the donor for indemnity is less serious than the liability of the seller, and in certain cases, the donor is entitled to revoke the gratuity.

201. Ádám Boóc, *The Works Contract*, in *Business Law* 361 ff. (István Sándor ed., Patrocinium 2016).

In the case of a contract of gift, the donor is entitled to claim back the gift without terminating the contract in the event of specific circumstances. The recovery of the gift is possible for the following reasons: the jeopardization of the livelihood of the donor, the serious infringement of the donee, or a relative living together with him, and failed or false assumption.

§4. Acquisition of Ownership from a Party Other than the Owner

332. Ownership right can be acquired from the owner of the tangible property through transfer. At the same time, the party making the acquisition in good faith and in exchange for consideration in the context of trade acquires the movable property's ownership right by way of the transfer even if the transferring party was not the owner. Acquisition in the context of commerce involves the buyer purchasing from a seller and concluding the sales contract in its own name in the context of its lawfully conducted professional business operations. Following the acquisition of ownership right in trade, the third party's rights encumbering the property that were created prior to the transfer and with regard to which the party acquiring ownership right exhibited good faith cease to exist.

The rules of '*nemo plus iuris*', familiar with Roman law, apply universally in Hungarian private law, according to which nobody can transfer more rights to another party than they hold. The safety of commerce competes with this private law principle. In the interest of the latter, the Civil Code offers the opportunity to breach the principle of *nemo plus iuris*, albeit only in a narrow application. Acquiring from a party other than the owner is governed by specifically defined rules. This rule can only be applied to movable property, which resolves the uncertainties surrounding the regulation offered by the old Civil Code.

333. The Civil Code rule is restricted to acquisition in the context of trade, so the cases prevailing under the former regulation, where the owner entrusted the property to the seller, and the ownership right can also be acquired from the latter, have been removed from the Civil Code. In an effort to simplify the interpretation of trade, legislators have defined it by imposing a condition vis-à-vis the seller. The seller must be engaged in professional business activity, and the contract must be concluded in this context. As a result, it does not matter whether the seller is a natural person or legal entity, nor where the contract is concluded. At the same time, it remains essential that the seller conclude the specific contract lawfully and in possession of adequate licences for engaging in the activity. The requirement that the seller must conclude the contract in his own name rather than acting as a representative is also linked to this. Property sold in the context of trade is when an authorized natural person or legal entity concludes a legal transaction with the other party in the capacity of seller, commission agent, lessor, etc., and the other party thus acquires ownership right in a derivative manner. According to the statutory assumption, the buyer can only regard the trader as the owner if the latter concludes the legal transaction in its own name.[202] It does not qualify as a sale in the context of trade if a company otherwise engaged in vehicle sales sells a vehicle to allow the buyer to repay its outstanding debt owed to the seller by offsetting the vehicle's value against the purchase price.[203] It does not qualify as acquisition in the context of trade if the buyer concludes a sales contract with a private individual not engaged in the trade of vehicles on the auto market, even if the contract is concluded with the participation of the dealer.[204] The buyer, acting in good faith, acquires the vehicle's ownership right from a professional auto dealer even if the seller was not the vehicle's owner.[205] The exceptional rule of acquiring ownership from a party other than the owner that enables the acquisition of ownership in the context of trade cannot be interpreted broadly.[206] Accordingly, a case where the undertaking engaged in trade purchases property from a private individual for the purpose of selling it in the context of its business operations is not included in this definition of purchasing.[207] If the seller is not listed as the seller in its own name in the contract, it does not qualify as a sale in the context of trade.[208]

334. The condition for the buyer is to act in good faith. Good faith in this context refers to the person not knowing or not having been able to know with due care that the seller is not the owner or is not authorized to transfer the thing's ownership right. The presence of good faith can generally be assessed in the specific circumstances of the transaction by using the objective benchmark of generally expected conduct in the given situation. Based on judicial practice, the buyer has an obligation to provide evidence of his good faith. Judicial practice is uniform with regard to the fact that in the event of acquisition from a party other than the owner, the contracting party is not regarded as acting in good faith if the transfer's ownership right is questionable. The buyer does not acquire an ownership right of the vehicles sold in the context of trade if he knows or should know that the trader is not the owner of the vehicle.[209]

335. The Civil Code restricts the options to acquire property from a party other than the owner to acquisition based on a sales contract. Earlier legal practice includes a decision in a similar case where it was stated that if the seller pays its rent due to the buyer partly in cash and partly by transferring the ownership right to his car, i.e., in kind, this does not qualify as a sale in the context of trade.[210] In other words, the rules governing contract conclusion with a party other than the owner can theoretically not be applied to contracts combined with a sale. At the same time, it remains to be seen to what extent this narrowing of the interpretation can be

202. EBH 1999/13; BH 1997/119.
203. BDT 1999/49.
204. BH 1996/418.
205. BH 1996/48.
206. BH 1980/239.
207. BDT 1999/49.
208. EBH 2000/303.
209. BH 1996/419.
210. BH 2010/40.

applied in scenarios where the buyer offers an older item of property to be offset against the purchase price of the new item of property, and the offset amount is only a fraction of the purchase price.

336. The conclusion of the sales contract is also closely linked with the fact that the buyer can only acquire an ownership right for a consideration. The text of the legislation does not provide guidance on whether consideration needs to be proportionate to the value of the property. In our opinion, the absence of adequate or proportionate consideration should nevertheless be examined in specific cases. Although the Civil Code does not impose this specific requirement on the contents of the transaction, it can be taken into consideration in terms of the generally expected behaviour in the context of good faith. The buyer's good faith may be damaged if the purchase price is much lower than even the discounted purchase price generally prevailing in trade.

If the sale materializes under the aforementioned conditions, the buyer obtains the ownership right to the thing free of any encumbrances. In this context, however, two restrictions apply: the rule only governs encumbrances that arose prior to the transfer; and only applies to encumbrances in respect of which the buyer acted in good faith.

§5. Acquisition of Ownership of Money and Securities

337. If money or securities are transferred to a party according to the rules of transferring securities, the party becomes the owner even if the transferor was not the owner.

Over and above the cases of acquisition by an acquiring party acting in good faith and providing consideration in the context of trade, the Civil Code also allows for exceptions from the principle of *nemo plus iuris* based on the attributes of the thing. A novelty introduced in the Civil Code is the absence of restriction on bearer instruments. Money is a means of payment; the person having possession of a banknote or coin is the lawful owner from the perspective of others. It is true that, in this case, the safety of trade is prioritized, as having to prove that one is holding money in a lawful manner would significantly hinder the conclusion of legal transactions.

The rules of the Civil Code pertain to legal tender but not to unique or historic banknotes, which are not used as legal tender.

A similar situation applies to securities. The transfer of securities is governed by special rules addressing securities. In the context of the transfer of securities, while complying with these fundamentally formal rules, the person acquiring the security becomes the owner.

Chapter 2. Transfer of Property by Death

338. Succession materializes upon the death of the testator, with the latter's legacy acquired by the heirs. Succession is the legal succession in the event of death, with a beneficiary designated in every case; in other words, the testator's legacy is transferred to a new owner in every instance.

Succession is closely linked to ownership in terms of its content. Succession represents an extension of ownership following one's death and represents a right for the owner to pass on the assets that he owned during his lifetime after his death. Article XIII(1) of Hungary's Fundamental Law grants everyone the right to ownership and succession. From the testator's perspective, succession is, in fact, an extension of the right of disposal over the contents of the estate, regulates the fate of the estate left without an owner and represents a continuation of the testator's property law personality in respect of the heirs. The range of assets that can be inherited is defined by the rules of ownership of a specific society, and the rules of succession also depend on this framework, which defines the rules governing the transfer of assets after the death of the owner and the beneficiaries thereof.

339. The Civil Code defines the essential elements of succession as a legal institution in the following manner: 'a deceased person's entire estate is passed on to his heirs'. Succession is a concept only and exclusively tied to a person; we can only talk about succession in relation to a person as the subject. When addressing other subjects and legal entities, we refer to legal succession, the rules of which are governed by specific provisions defining the subjects' legal situation. Whether succession is also legal succession dogmatically speaking is another question, representing a narrower interpretation of the concept, meaning legal succession only with respect to a natural person and linked to the end of human life.

The legal effects of succession materialize with the death of a person. The criteria of the onset of death pose an essentially medical rather than a legal question; however, the time of death may have significance in terms of the succession (Hungarian law does not make an assumption on the order of death in the event of commorientes). Death is considered to be equal to the pronouncement of death and the judge's establishment of the fact of death. Regarding the definition, succession materializes upon the testator's death without any further legal action or accepting declaration by the heir, by the power of law (*ipso jure* succession). This simultaneously means that the testator's estate is not left ownerless, as an estate without a claimant does not exist in Hungarian law. Stemming from the *ipso jure* succession system, the order on the transfer of legacy issued by the notary public is not constitutive and only serves to officially certify the succession.

§1. The Legacy

340. The legacy is essentially the testator's estate. Given that an estate is conceptually the set of rights and obligations of a subject, legacy in this context has a narrower sense than total estate. This is because the rights and obligations explicitly tied to the testator as an individual forming part of his estate ceased to exist with the testator's death (e.g., maintenance obligations and rights, personal easements (usufruct, use), engagement contracts, etc.).

The potential transfer of the testator's civil law type, non-property rights and obligations (linked to him as an individual) are governed not by succession law but by the other rules of private law (e.g., intellectual property).

Only the testator's private law estate, private law rights and obligations are included in the estate transferred through succession, while the public law (public administrative) elements are not; the latter ceased to exist with the death of the right holder or the obligor, or if they persist in certain regards, their further fate is governed not by succession law but by other legislation (e.g., social security).

341. The matter of the *legal relationship of succession* represents a dogmatic problem in terms of the scheme of succession law, namely whether succession itself can be regarded as a legal relationship and, if so, who the parties involved are. The difficulty lies in the fact that succession is triggered by the death of a single person, the testator, so it cannot be interpreted as a legal relationship between the testator and the heir because the legal effects materialize from the very fact of the termination of legal subjectivity. Representative of legal sciences attempted to remove the concept of legal relationship from the scope of succession by defining succession as a *single-person legal situation* (similar to ownership right). However, according to the generally accepted position, the legal relationship of succession is a unique phase of the ownership right relationship and other civil law legal relationships depending upon ownership right that arises upon the testator's death and upon the assumption by the testator's legal successors of the former's position.

§2. The Inheritance

342. In the broader sense, succession means that the deceased person's estate or a portion thereof is transferred to a different person after the former's death; in other words, it represents the share of the legacy applicable in the event of death *on any legal grounds*. In the narrower sense, succession means the *universal* succession of the deceased person's estate, including both rights and obligations. The various forms of *singular legal succession* are thus not included in the narrow interpretation of succession, such as succession or the right to the reserved portion. Only the person to whom the entire legacy is transferred can be regarded as the heir; furthermore, anyone who has amassed estate during their lifetime, i.e., has an estate, will also have a universal legal successor, i.e., an heir (necessary universal legal succession).

On this basis, an heir is someone who acquires an entire legacy alone, as well as someone who inherits a specific portion of a legacy along with others. If the testator has more than one heir on the basis of either the law or his disposition of property upon death, they are regarded as co-heirs in terms of their mutual relationship.

343. The rules of inheritance defined in the Civil Code are familiar with succession through a disposition of property upon death or based on law. The key characteristic of the relationship between succession under a disposition of property upon death and intestate succession is that intestate succession can only occur if the testator did not dispose of his legacy in a disposition of property upon death. The circumstance also embodies the obligation to respect the testator's intent. These two forms of succession may prevail simultaneously, parallel to one another; if the testator only disposed of a portion of his estate in his disposition of property upon death, the rules of intestate succession will govern the remaining portion of his estate.

Disposition of property upon death is the umbrella term for the legal transactions tied to the onset of death, i.e., the suspensory condition. Dispositions of property upon death include not only wills but also agreements as to succession and gifting upon death. Any legal transaction that contains a declaration of intent to achieve a specific legal effect in the event of death is considered a disposition of property upon death. All legal transactions containing provisions applicable in the event of death are considered dispositions of property upon death, which is significant because the rules of disposition of property upon death, in particular those governing formal requirements, apply.

A disposition of property upon death is essentially a legal transaction bound to a condition, which is that the beneficiary of the disposition must survive the testator. The condition is not merely the onset of death (as is the case for life insurance) but also the beneficiary's survival beyond the party making the declaration.

Succession on the basis of a disposition of property upon death is the primary form of succession, as intestate succession only comes into play when and if there is no disposition or if it is invalid or ineffective. If the disposition is valid and effective but does not apply to the testator's entire estate, then the rules of intestate succession apply to the remaining portion of the estate.

§3. Intestate Succession

344. The legal heirs are primarily the testator's children, each entitled to an equal portion of the inheritance.[211] The children of the child or more distant relatives debarred from succession inherit in lieu of the latter in equal parts.

If the testator does not have any descendants, the spouse and the testator's parents will inherit jointly. However, in the event of descendants, assets that were transferred to the testator from an ascendant (or from a collateral relative) through inheritance or free handover will be inherited by the collateral relatives on the branch of origin of the assets.

---

211. Detailed introduction can be found in Orsolya Szeibert, *A törvényes örökösöknek minősülő hozzátartozók és rokonok köre, tekintettel a polgári jogi kodifikációra* (*The Group of the Relatives and Cognates Qualified as Intestate Heirs, Regarding the Civil Law Codification*), in *Az új Ptk. öröklési jogi szabályai, tapasztalatok és kihívások* (*The Inheritancy Rules of the New Civil Code, Experiences and Challenges*) 119 ff. (Ágnes Juhász ed., Novotni Alapítvány 2015); Lajos Vékás, *Magyar polgári jog, öröklési jog* (*Hungarian Private Law, Law of Succession*) 32 ff. (Eötvös József könyvkiadó 2014); Ferenc Fábián, *Előadásvázlatok az öröklési jog köréből* (*Lecture Notes in the Law of Succession*) 70 ff. (Patrocinium 2014).

The testator's surviving spouse inherits usufruct of the dwelling shared with the testator (as well as of the lineal estate) if there are descendent heirs and is also entitled to one child's share of the remainder of the legacy.

In the absence of descendants or a spouse, the testator's parents each inherit an equal portion. In lieu of a parent thus debarred from the inheritance, his or her descendants inherit just like the child's descendants. If a parent debarred from succession does not have any descendants, only the other parent or his or her descendants will inherit. If there are neither parents nor descendants of the parents, the testator's grandparents inherit in equal proportion. The descendants of a grandparent debarred from succession inherit, and the other set of grandparents inherit in lieu of a grandparent deceased without any descendants. If a set of grandparents has been debarred and they have no descendants, the entire legacy will be inherited by the other set of grandparents or their descendants. If there is no grandparent or descendants of grandparents, then the testator's great-grandparents or their descendants will inherit.

If neither the testator's grandparents nor a collateral relative of the great-grandparents is eligible for inheriting (there are none or have been debarred from the inheritance), the testator's more distant ascendants will be the legal heirs, each entitled to an equal portion.

The Civil Code pronounces the state as the beneficiary of intestate succession as a last resort if there are no other heirs. So if the rules of intestate succession must be applied in the absence of a disposition of property upon death, and the testator has no heirs according to the rules of intestate succession, the state becomes the testator's legal heir. This is why we can say that if somebody had an estate during his lifetime, then he will have an heir after his death. The state does not have the right to reject an inheritance in its capacity as the legal heir, so the state is the final heir by necessity in this context. The state may also inherit in the wake of a disposition of property upon death; in this capacity, the prohibition of rejecting the inheritance no longer applies; in other words, as an heir under a will, the state may reject the inheritance in accordance with the general rules.

The MNV Zrt. is competent in all cases involving legacies where the state inherits in any form, and this body exercises rights related to the status of heirs and bears all burdens related to the legacy. Decree 45/2002. (XII. 25.) of the Minister of Finance on the representation of the Hungarian State in the event of inheritance by the state and the exercising of other rights conferred upon the state.

§4. The Reserved Portion

345. The reserved portion of an estate plays an important role alongside succession under a will and intestate succession. The reserved portion is the portion of the testator's estate that is bequeathed to the testator's relatives or spouse despite the testator's express intent. The reserved portion is generally applied when the testator has made a disposition of property upon death and has bequeathed less to the beneficiary in the deposition than the portion due to the beneficiary based on the reserved portion. Exceptionally, the reserved portion may also be applied if the testator did not write a will, and legal heirs are thus entitled to the legacy. It is possible that the testator has decreased the future legacy by means of free handover to such an extent that the legal heir entitled to a reserved portion of the estate only receives a portion smaller than the reserved portion. In this case, the legal heir entitled to a reserved portion may lodge a claim against the beneficiary of the free handover for the supplementation of the reserved portion despite the application of the rules of intestate succession to the legacy.

346. The testator's descendants and spouse are the parties primarily entitled to the reserved portion of the estate. The testator's parents are only entitled to the reserved portion if the testator has no descendants, i.e., they would be the legal heirs in the absence of a disposition of property upon death. The descendants' claim for the reserved portion may apply up to any degree of descendence in accordance with the principle of substitution, meaning a descendent of even the remotest degree may claim the reserved portion. Also, in line with the rules of intestate succession, the testator's children and the descendants of children debarred are primarily entitled to the reserved portion. Adopted children are treated equally to biological children in this regard, and foetuses may also be entitled to the reserved portion on the condition of being born alive as per the general rules.

The surviving spouse's entitlement to the reserved portion varies depending on whether or not the testator has any remaining descendants. If any descendants remain, the surviving spouse inherits a child's portion along with the former. As a result, the spouse's reserved portion of the estate also applies to the child's share. If the testator has no surviving descendants, then the surviving spouse inherits together with the parents, and the former's reserved portion essentially applies to half of the legacy.

The testator's parents can claim the reserved portion if the testator has no descendants left, in which case, they are entitled to the reserved portion along with the surviving spouse. If neither the descendants nor the surviving spouses are entitled to inherit, the parents alone are entitled to the reserved portion. The parent's reserved portion also applies to the lineal estate inherited by someone else based on the testator's will.

347. The degree of the descendant's reserved portion of the estate is aligned with the child's legal share of the inheritance, i.e., one-third of the child's legal inheritance (As a result, the testator may essentially only dispose of two-thirds of his legacy and the disposition of property upon death). The reserved portion of all additional descendants – stemming from the principle of substitution – is adjusted to the reserved portion of his direct predecessor.

If the testator has no descendant but does have a spouse, the basis of the parents' reserved portion is half of the legacy. Moreover, each parent may claim *one-third of the lineal estate* passed on from his or her branch as the reserved portion. Lineal assets must be taken into account individually with regard to each parent, and both parents are only entitled to the reserved portion personally. In the event of exclusion from inheritance, he or she is not substituted by his or her descendants, and neither parent can substitute for the other in this regard.

In the absence of a spouse, the testator's legal heirs are his parents, so the extent of their reserved portion is the entire legacy, i.e., half of their legal inheritance.

In the event of intestate succession by descendants, the spouse is entitled to usufruct of the shared dwelling and the related furnishings and appliances in his or her capacity as the legal heir. In this scenario, the spouse's reserved portion will be a limited usufruct equivalent to a degree of the usufruct that meets the spouse's needs, taking into account the property inherited by him or her.

§5. Probate Proceeding

348. As the heir obtains the inheritance through the power of the law without any separate legal action, he becomes the owner of the property included in the legacy from the time of the testator's death, i.e., from the opening of succession. The sole restriction on exercising partial ownership rights is the existence of a widow's right on any of the items of property included in the legacy. If the surviving spouse is entitled to a widow's surviving spouse, he or she may take possession or retain possession of the legacy or an adequate portion thereof based on this right, so if the testator's spouse has usufruct of the item of property, it must be surrendered after usufruct has ceased.

The same rule applies to the specific legatee, who acquires an ownership right of an item of property included in the legacy according to the rules of disposition of property upon death, equally to the heir of the property. His claim for succession is an ownership claim and thus has no statute of limitations. However, the obligatory legatee and the beneficiary of the device become entitled to claim the service described in the will by the power of the law; in other words, his claim for succession is obligatory in nature and is, therefore, governed by the rules of the term of limitations. The claim for succession is made against the so-called unauthorized heir. The unauthorized heir is someone taking or holding the legacy or a portion thereof into possession on the grounds of succession without valid legal grounds. The unauthorized heir qualifies as a wrongful possessor; therefore, his legal situation depends on whether he acted in good or bad faith.

Succession proceedings are conducted before the notary public having jurisdiction based on the testator's last place of domicile. In the context of the succession proceedings, the notary public hands over the legacy to the heirs. The notary resolution in this respect may be binding if the heirs do not raise any objections to it or provisional if there is a legal dispute among the heirs. In the latter case, the heirs may contest the order on the transfer of the legacy in court, and the court has the final word in the dispute.

Chapter 3. Possession

§1. The Adverse Possession

349. A person who has had adverse possession of real property for fifteen years or any movable property for ten years as his own acquires ownership through adverse possession. Upon the acquisition of ownership of movable property by way of adverse possession, the rights of a third party on the object shall cease if such arose before the adverse user acquired possession, and in respect of which the duration of the adverse possession has expired, except when the adverse user did not act in good faith in respect of those rights. The existence of restraint on alienation and encumbrance does not preclude the acquisition of title by way of adverse possession if other conditions for adverse possession are met. An ownership share of a thing may also be acquired under the general provisions on adverse possession.

In fact, the legal justifications for adverse possession coincide with the arguments offered in support of the statute of limitations. If somebody fails to exercise their ownership right, to use the thing or to make a claim for the person using the thing to transfer or return it to them, he will no longer deserve protection. At the same time, adverse possession is precluded if the owner is not in a position to exercise his ownership rights for admissible reasons. However, there is a general social and economic need linked to the utilization of assets and to ensure that various assets do not remain without an owner. In order for somebody to use or utilize the available material assets, they must have a sound legal basis. If someone is unsure whether the use of an asset contributes to his wealth, he will not exercise the right of preserving their condition and the right of use or not exercise these rights to the degree that a rightful owner of the asset would.

Adverse possession is an original way of acquiring ownership; in other words, it is independent of the previous owner of the thing. Adverse possession ensures ownership on the basis of the law and simultaneously terminates the former owner's rights regarding the thing. Because adverse possession is a way of acquiring ownership, it does not apply to other rights, so, e.g., usufruct cannot be acquired through adverse possession.[212]

§2. Conditions for Adverse Possession

350. The Civil Code lays down conditions for adverse possession. Adverse possession requires the adverse user to treat the thing as if it were his own. This is a subjective element in adverse possession, while the other conditions are objective circumstances. When examining the conditions of adverse possession, it is essential to evaluate the possessor's subjective conscience, namely whether he considers the possession as his own. If this cannot be determined, there is no need to further examine the objective criteria of adverse possession. Possession as one's own in this

212. BDT 2000/225.

context means that the adverse user deems that the thing constitutes his own property, or at least that possession of the thing is independent of the rights of others, and possession is final. It, therefore, suffices for the adverse user to regard his possession as final and to express this in an objective manner. This must be expressed towards the world, for instance, by paying burdens associated with the ownership right, issuing the declarations linked to powers of the owner, etc.

For example, possession on the grounds of a widow's usufruct cannot be regarded as a possession as one's own and thus precludes adverse possession.[213] Ownership right cannot be acquired through adverse possession if the user fails to cite adverse possession in the event of a transformation of the plot of land resulting in a change in topographical lot number and area in the course of uninterrupted use as one's own, and if another ten years have not elapsed from this point in time until the initiation of legal proceedings. In addition, the state may not acquire ownership right on the grounds of adverse possession if the real property registered as the property of a private individual was transferred for management based on a statutory temporary utilization obligation.[214] The acknowledgement of ownership right and the undertaking of the obligation to hand over possession in and of themselves preclude possessions as one's own. Leasing as the legal grounds for possession prevents the start of adverse possession until termination of the legal relationship irrespective of the possessor's intent. The exercising of a right allowed as a favour or for a specific period shall not lead to adverse possession.[215] It is important to stress that the acquisition of ownership through adverse possession is not impeded by provisions restricting the acquisition of real property if adverse possession has already begun prior to its entry into force.

351. The second condition for adverse possession is its continuous, i.e., uninterrupted nature. This does not necessarily mean that the adverse user must maintain a physical hold of the thing throughout the period of adverse possession. If the possessor relinquishes possession of the thing on any grounds (e.g., lending arrangement, pledge, deposit, rental, leasehold) to a third party, this third party will be the secondary possessor and the adverse user the possessor; the act of adverse possession comes into play with regard to the latter. Uninterrupted possession is, therefore, not conditional on the adverse user holding possession himself. In judicial practice, a widow's usufruct on a real property under adverse possession, for instance, does not preclude possession as one's own,[216] while in other cases, possession as one's own, as one of the fundamental criteria of adverse possession precludes adverse possession by deed, which may potentially be based on a widow's usufruct.[217]

352. The third condition of adverse possession is that the possessor must have possession of the thing, and the requirement of uninterrupted possession applies.

213. BH 2006/154.
214. BDT 2010/2311.
215. BH 1979/287.
216. BDT 2007/1642.
217. BDT 2001/392.

When evaluating a claim based on the acquisition of ownership through adverse possession, the actual possession circumstances prevailing at the time of expiry of the adverse possession period are taken into account. It should be noted that joint possession may not give rise to the acquisition of exclusive ownership for either possessor due to the absence of possession as one's own.

353. The Civil Code distinguishes between movable property and real property in terms of the fourth condition – the adverse possession period. It should be noted that the adverse user's good faith is not a precondition for the acquisition of ownership through adverse possession based on the Civil Code.

§3. Adverse Possession and Encumbrances on the Thing

354. Adverse possession is an original way of acquisition, so for movable property, any encumbrances on the thing cease with adverse possession. An exception to this is if the adverse user acted in bad faith; however, bad faith only needs to be examined with regard to any third-party rights. As a result, if the adverse user knew or should have known if proceeding with due care of any third party rights pertaining to the thing, although it will acquire the ownership right over the thing, the encumbrances will remain in place.

A restraint on alienation and encumbrance cannot pose an impediment to adverse possession. A restraint on alienation and encumbrance does not preclude the lapse of the adverse possession period. This rule stems logically from the fact that the adverse user is not the earlier owner's successor, and there is no legal transaction for the purpose or on the grounds of alienation between the former owner and the adverse user, so obviously, we are not talking about alienation.

§4. Adverse Possession of an Ownership Share

355. Adverse possession may apply not only to an entire ownership right but also to a specific ownership share. If the original owner has ownership in the undivided common property and the adverse user exhibits conduct that fulfils the statutory conditions, there is no impediment to its acquisition of ownership. The acquisition of the intangible ownership share of real property through adverse possession is possible and is not conditional to a binding public administrative decision on the divisibility of the land.[218] In accordance with the exemption from the restraint on alienation and encumbrance, in this scenario, the joint owners cannot exercise their statutory pre-emption right because the original owner does not conclude a contract with the adverse user for selling the thing. At the same time, in the case of the exclusive use of a building built on a land parcel owned by somebody else, the ownership right of the building cannot be adversely possessed in a manner that separates the ownership right of the land parcel and the building.[219]

218. BH 2009/204 and BH 2011/7.
219. BH 2013/120.

The joint owner's option to exercise adverse possession in the case of joint property raises an important question in terms of the ownership share of the other joint owner. In this scenario, the conditions on adverse possession laid down in the Civil Code apply, but the presence of the statutory elements of adverse possession must be examined more closely, and also whether the conduct of the joint owner citing adverse possession can be reconciled with the joint owners' rights and with the rule on the statutory interests associated with the thing. In the event of joint property, use that is different from the ownership share may not entail the adverse possession of the additional area.

§5. Adverse Possession and the Land Registry

356. If the ownership right of real property is acquired through adverse possession, the adverse user acquires the ownership right *ipso jure* but will not be listed as the owner in the land registry. In order to have his ownership right registered in the land registry, the adverse user must certify his ownership right. The land registry can only evaluate this fact based on a deed in the context of proceedings for the registration of ownership rights. This document may be an agreement on adverse possession – a deed underlying the registration – based on which the adverse user's ownership right can be registered in the land registry. The acquisition of ownership can be established based on a statement issued by the owner listed in the land registry if the registered owner acknowledges that an agreement was reached between him and the actual possessor for the transfer of the property's ownership right. The ownership right of the actual possessor based on more than fifteen years of possession as one's own can be registered by editing the land registry if the available data does not preclude the acquisition of ownership through adverse possession.

357. If the asset's original owner does not give its consent to the registration, the adverse user may prove adverse possession through litigation claiming registration in the land registry, and the adverse possession can be subsequently registered based on the judicial ruling. It should be emphasized that the legal grounds of the acquisition of ownership are also adverse possession in this scenario as well. Adverse possession is the legal ground for the acquisition of ownership with an in rem effect, allowing the owner of property acquired in this manner to dispose validly of the property without having his ownership right listed in the land registry; he is only unable to exercise his ownership rights vis-à-vis a party who has acquired rights to the real estate in exchange for consideration, based on the land registry. This is corroborated by the ad hoc decision according to which if the acquisition of ownership through adverse possession has already materialized during the spouses' union, the surviving spouse may only claim ownership of its own half, while any additional claims may be enforced by the deceased spouse's heir.

It should be noted, however, that if the adverse user does not register his ownership right in the land registry, he cannot cite his acquisition of ownership based on adverse possession against a party acquiring ownership right in good faith and for consideration. The same holds true for the rivalry between adverse possession and acquisition of ownership based on an official ruling. For instance, in terms of arable land acquired from a compensation auction, which also qualifies as a contract for countervalue, acquisition of ownership based on adverse possession not recorded in the land registry is not permitted.[220] However, if all statutory conditions for the materialization of adverse possession are met, the actual possessor of the real property can successfully cite adverse possession against the owner registered in the land registry – as legal grounds superseding the building on land owned by someone else in good faith – if he built on the land during the period of possession.

§6. Adverse Possession by Deed

358. The new Civil Code introduced the case of adverse possession by deed. This exceptional scenario applies when the adverse user has concluded a formerly valid written contract with the owner for the acquisition of an ownership right, i.e., the legal grounds for acquiring ownership prevail, but the registration of the acquisition of ownership in the land registry is not performed or fails. A further requirement is that the adverse user must already have paid consideration for the real property to the owner. In this case, the adverse user not only has lawful possession of the real property as his own but also has the necessary legal grounds for the acquisition of ownership, and it is merely the transfer of the title that did not materialize. This offers a solution to the situation where the ownership right is claimed by reducing the time of adverse possession to five years.

The rules governing adverse possession by deed must also be applied to adverse possession underway at the time of entry into force of the Civil Code, with the condition that if the period of adverse possession necessary for adverse possession by deed has already elapsed or less than one year remains of it, the possessor acquires the property's ownership right one year after the entry into force of the Civil Code.

§7. Legal Succession in Adverse Possession

359. A new possessor shall be entitled to add to the period of his own adverse possession the time that qualified as the duration of adverse possession during the possession of his predecessor.

The Civil Code enables legal succession in the context of adverse possession. Legal succession occurs when the adverse user passes on (e.g., sells) possession or if legal succession materializes independently of the adverse user (e.g., succession).

A new possessor is only entitled to add to the period of his own adverse possession the time that qualified as the duration of adverse possession during the possession of his predecessor if his predecessor did not acquire the ownership right through adverse possession. A new possessor is entitled to add to the period of his own adverse possession the time that qualified as the duration of adverse possession during the possession of his predecessor if the two uses are identical on the basis of

220. EBH 1999/109.

an area or, in the event of use applicable to a different area, the real property is divisible or divided based on the smaller area of use. Pure use, if not associated with an objective expression of possession as one's own, may not result in adverse possession.

§8. Exclusion of Adverse Possession

360. As explained earlier, the Civil Code does not require the adverse user's good faith for it to acquire ownership. However, in cases where a person comes into possession of a thing not only in bad faith but in an explicitly unlawful way, he cannot acquire the ownership right. Such unlawful actions are clearly criminal acts, and they include violent and underhand conduct according to the Civil Code. In the case of the latter two, the person acquiring possession of the thing is not necessarily engaging in a criminal act, but his conduct is radically contrary to the conduct expected in civil legal relationships. It should be noted, however, that a third party acquiring or otherwise becoming the legal successor of a person having acquired the assets in such a manner is not precluded from adverse possession if his possession complies with the other statutory conditions.

Ownership share can be adversely possessed according to the general rules of adverse possession. However, in the case of land that constitutes a single land registry unit, the property's ownership right cannot be acquired through adverse possession if the conditions of adverse possession only prevail in respect of a portion of the land, and the land cannot be divided up. The provision stating that the property's ownership right cannot be acquired through adverse possession if the conditions of adverse possession only prevail in respect of a portion of the land and the land cannot be divided up applies to the scenario where the object of adverse possession is a territorially defined portion of the real property. It does, therefore, not impede the adverse possession of a specific ownership right by the joint owner. So, in summary, adverse possession in the case of joint property may apply to a specific ownership share; however, adverse possession does not give rise to joint property.

§9. Suspension of the Duration of Adverse Possession

361. If an owner is not in the position to exercise his ownership rights for an excusable reason, adverse possession shall not take place for one year from the termination of the impediment, even if the duration of adverse possession has elapsed or there is less than one year left.

There is no guarantee rule on the owner's side that prevents the adverse possession of its thing if the owner is not in a position to exercise ownership right for an excusable reason. Among the reasons warranting the application of the rule of adverse possession, we mentioned that the owner's negligence or neglect provides the basis for adverse possession.

However, after the reason or circumstance restricting the owner's proprietary rights has been resolved, the owner is expected to exercise his ownership rights. The legislation provides a one-year window for this; after the lapse of this period, the legal effects of adverse possession materialize, or adverse possession continues.

§10. Discontinuance of Adverse Possession

362. Adverse possession is considered discontinued if the owner brings action to enforce his claim for having the thing surrendered, the owner exercises his ownership rights in connection with the thing, or the possessor loses the property against his will and fails to reacquire it within one year, or does not file for court action within one year to have the thing returned by its new possessor. If adverse possession is discontinued, the duration of adverse possession that has elapsed up to that date may not be taken into consideration, and the period of adverse possession begins again following the termination of the reason for discontinuance.

Exercising the owner's rights results in the discontinuance of adverse possession. The exercising of two characteristic proprietary rights applies in this specific context: a claim for the surrendering of the asset enforced through judicial avenues and the exercising of ownership rights. A claim for the surrender of the asset through judicial ways is made in the form of legal ownership action. The exercising of proprietary rights over the thing may theoretically include the exercising of any right. According to judicial practice, the encumbrance of a property with a mortgage is an activity in the context of the owner's right of disposal that results in the discontinuance of adverse possession.[221]

363. At the same time, the following cases do not entail the discontinuance of adverse possession. The transfer of ownership based on legislation or an official ruling does not qualify as the exercising of the owner's right of disposal and does not entail the discontinuance of adverse possession.[222] From the perspective of the discontinuance or continuation of adverse possession, a statement or action made to resolve any unregulated situations prevailing internally among the joint owners, if made while leaving the joint owner's ownership right intact, does not qualify as the exercising of the right of disposal.[223]

Analogously to the rules of the discontinuance of the statute of limitations, the time elapsed until the discontinuance of adverse possession cannot be taken into account when calculating the adverse possession period; in other words, adverse possession is reset once the interrupting circumstance resolves.

221. BH 1997/20.
222. BDT 2012/2611.
223. BH 1996/251.

Chapter 4. Accession

364. Hungarian private law regulates various modalities of acquisition under unification and processing, including processing, conversion, unification, mixing, annexation, transformation, incorporation construction, or building on the land of another.

§1. Processing and Conversion

I. The Concept of Processing

365. Processing and conversion are classified under processing (*specificatio*) and refer to two cases featuring different terminologies. In both cases, the situation consists of the processor creating a new object in good faith with the input of his own labour but from material that constitutes someone else's property.

According to the general understanding of the concepts, processing and conversion essentially consist of creating a new thing compared to the original thing, for example, if somebody makes clothing from textiles or jewellery from gold bullion. Processing and conversion only take place if the nature of the original thing changes to such an extent that restoring it to its original state is not possible or would entail significant harm. The new thing essentially preserves the material of the original thing. This material-based approach prevails within the Sabinian school of Roman law, which argues that material remains unchanged after processing, and so the owner of the original thing has the ownership right of the new thing. By contrast, the Proculean approach raises the issue that the thing does not remain identical in the wake of processing, and an entirely new thing is created (*nova species*), which thus terminates the original owner's ownership right of the original thing.[224] Hungarian law subscribes to this second approach, taking into account Justinian modifications in certain regards. As a result, processing or conversion in the course of which the original thing remains the same thing under general understanding does not raise the issue of acquisition of ownership.

366. From the perspective of the acquisition of ownership, processing, or conversion clearly only has relevance if the thing undergoing processing or conversion to create a new thing is owned by someone else. It should be noted in this regard that the processor must act in good faith, meaning that he should process the foreign material as if it were his own, proceed with due care and consider himself an entity with adequate legal grounds granted by the owner. Obviously, if the processor knows that the thing is somebody else's property, he cannot acquire the ownership right through processing. For instance, a tailor does not acquire ownership of the suit made from material supplied by the client, as he lacks adequate legal grounds for such acquisition.

224. *See* Földi & Hamza, *supra* 343.

367. The Civil Code defines a clear set of rules governing the acquisition of ownership by the processing or converting party. A person who manufactures a new thing for himself in good faith by processing or converting another person's thing shall reimburse the value of the thing or surrender ownership of the new thing in return for reimbursement of the value of his work, whichever is chosen by the owner of such thing. If the value of the work significantly exceeds the value of the processed or converted thing, the owner of the thing may demand compensation for the value of the thing. If the person performing the processing or conversion has acted in bad faith, the right to choose shall accrue to the owner of the material. If the owner of the material opts to acquire ownership of the new thing, he shall pay compensation only up to the extent of his actual gains. If ownership of the new thing is acquired by the person performing the processing operation, the rights of any third party on the thing shall cease. If title to the new thing belongs to the owner of the material, any right on the material shall apply to the new thing as well.

II. Processing and Conversion in Good Faith

368. If the processor acted in good faith, the original owner of the object has the right to decide whether to opt for the object's ownership right and reimburse the processor's labour or to allow the processor to gain the ownership right in exchange for compensation for the object's value. The Civil Code's regulatory logic is thus based on the processor automatically acquiring ownership right of the newly manufactured object, and the object's original owner only has a corrective right regarding the resulting property law situation. In both cases, the Civil Code stipulates a settlement obligation. If the thing's original owner continues to claim its ownership right, he is required to provide consideration for the value of the processor's labour input. This means the total value of the processor's labour rather than the objective value gain stemming from processing. However, it should also be factored in that if the thing's original value was greater when exercising his right to choose, the original owner may claim the reimbursement of the original thing's value rather than his ownership right.

One exception to the main rule is when the value of the processor's labour input significantly exceeds the value of the original thing. In this case, the original thing's owner is not entitled to a right to choose, and the processor acquires the ownership right of the processed or converted thing, while the original owner may claim the reimbursement of the thing's value. When talking about significantly higher value, what matters is not how the thing's objective commercial value has changed but rather the value of the labour actually invested by the processor. The Civil Code leaves it to judicial practice to define when the case of significantly higher value applies.

III. Processing and Conversion in Bad Faith

369. If the processing or conversion is in bad faith, only the material's owner has the right to choose, irrespective of the value of the processing or conversion work or whether the value of the new thing exceeds the value of the original thing. In this context, it is important to emphasize that ownership right of the material remains with the material owner in the event of processing or conversion in bad faith, as the processor's or converter's good faith necessary for acquiring ownership is lacking. The material's owner right to choose applies in this scenario, similar to the rule governing processing and conversion in good faith. If the material's owner opts to pass on the ownership right of the new thing arising as a result of processing or conversion to the processor or converter, he may claim reimbursement of the material's value. It should be noted that in this scenario, because the material's owner is still entitled to the ownership right of the thing, the material's owner is, in fact, exercising his statutory sell option. If the material's owner claims the new thing's ownership right, he is only required to compensate the processor or converter for the enrichment, contrary to processing or conversion in good faith. In this case, it is not the processor's or converter's labour that is taken into account as the basis of settlement but the difference in the thing's commercial value before and after conversion. In some cases, processing or conversion decreases the thing's value compared to the material's value; in our view, a compensation claim may be enforceable vis-à-vis the processor or converter on the grounds of non-contractual liability.

IV. Third-Party Rights

370. Based on the premise that processing gives rise to a new thing, in other words, the processor or converter acquires the ownership right of the thing through an original mode of acquisition, the legislator declares any third-party rights on the thing as terminated if the processor or converter acquires the ownership right. In the event that the material's owner becomes the owner of the new thing, third-party rights may still apply to the thing.

It should be noted that from a dogmatic perspective, the regulation reduces two legal facts with the legal grounds of processing based on the right to choose. The Civil Code presumes good faith as a conceptual criterion for processing or conversion, so if the processor acted in bad faith, he did not acquire the ownership right of the new thing on the basis of processing. In this case, the material's owner may decide to waive his claim for the ownership right of the new thing; in other words, the processor's acquisition of ownership is established based on the material owner's legal declaration.

§2. Unification and Mixing

371. If the objects of several persons are unified or mixed in a way that the separation of such objects may only be accomplished by inflicting substantial damage or at an unreasonably high cost, or if this cannot be accomplished at all, ownership of the final product shall be claimed jointly by the persons affected in proportion to the value of the objects in existence at the time when unified or mixed.

If, based on value, quality, economic function or for any other reason, either of the unified or mixed things should be considered the main component of the new thing created through unification or mixing, the owner of such thing shall have the option to either retain ownership of the thing created through unification or mixing and compensate the other owners or to surrender it to them in return for compensation. The right to choose may not be claimed by the person who himself caused the unification or mixing in bad faith. In that case, the mala fide former owner may demand compensation only up to the extent of actual gains.

372. If the thing created by unification or mixing is given into joint ownership in accordance with the relevant provisions of the Civil Code on joint ownership. The rights of third parties on the things affected by the unification or mixing shall accrue to the ownership shares replacing those things. If there is a right on one of the things, and the thing created through unification or mixing becomes the property of the person who owns the other thing, the right on the thing shall cease. Any right on the thing shall pass to the thing created through unification or mixing if it becomes the property of the same person who owned the thing on which the right existed.

373. In the context of regulating unification, the Civil Code factors three main criteria: the difference between strong and weak unification, equal and subordinate unification, and finally, the good or bad faith of the person initiating the unification.

374. The Civil Code only regards strong unification as unification or mixing. The prerequisite for strong unification is that the original things can only be separated with disproportionate damage or cost, which in fact can be qualified as strong unification in the economic sense, or they cannot be separated at all. Accordingly, weak unification is not considered a mode of acquiring property. For instance, an operator in possession of a cable television system based on an operating contract does not become the system's owner to the degree of his investment unless specifically agreed with the owner. In this case, the investment cannot give rise to joint property either; however, it does not preclude the enforcement of a claim under the rules of unjust enrichment.[225]

375. In the event of the unification of equal things, joint property is created on the thing; in the event of subordinate unification, the owner of the principal component has the right to choose whether to keep the ownership right of the thing. Subordinate unification is when a thing that is less significant economically or in value is unified with the principal thing. In this regard, the rule of *accessio cedat principali* prevails in Roman law, i.e., the subordinate thing shares the fate of the principal thing. The Civil Code diverges from this rule and grants a right of choice to the original owner of the principal component with regard to acquiring ownership (or not) of the thing resulting from the unification.

In a certain sense, this approach pushes dogmatic boundaries. The ownership right of the thing created through unification or mixing is assessed based on the owner's right to choose rather than automatically based on the fact of unification or

225. BH 2004/461.

mixing. As a main rule, joint property is created through unification or mixing. However, the Civil Code lays down specific rules on the termination of joint property: the owner of the principal component has the option to terminate joint property, ignoring any other potential claims.

376. In the matter of the principal and subordinate component, what matters is which thing is economically significant, contrary to the earlier regulation, which emphasized the thing's value.[226] The sowing of forest tree seeds on real property used for the cultivation of grass or as a pasture does not generate an ownership right for the sowing party on the grounds of processing, unification or building on the land of another.

It should be noted that the unification (mixing) of things only creates joint property with regard to movable property; the ownership right of real property cannot be acquired on these legal grounds.[227]

377. Good and bad faith are factored into the degree that a person initiating unification or mixing in good faith but not acquiring ownership right of the thing is entitled to indemnification, while a person acting in bad faith is only entitled to claim indemnification for the enrichment of the joint owners.

Based on third-party rights, burdens on the thing must logically be judged based on the rules of joint property. Any original burden on the component becoming joint property is split in proportion to the joint property during the unification. A different law applies in the event that the component subject to a burden is acquired in the context of unification or mixing by the owner of a component owned by somebody else, in which case, as the main rule, the burden ceases as per the rules of original ways of acquisition. The other rules of the Civil Code may result in an exception compared to the above scenario.

As a main rule, the legislator prescribes the creation of joint property as a result of unification or mixing, and actual acquisition of ownership only applies to subordinate unification.

§3. Sale of a Converted, Processed, Merged, or Compounded Thing

378. If ownership of a converted, processed, merged, or compounded thing is claimed by neither of the parties, it shall be sold, and the received price shall be divided among the entitled parties in accordance with their ownership share. In this case, the party who is entitled to claim compensation only up to the extent of his actual gains shall be entitled to no more than that part of the received price, which remains after the satisfaction of those entitled to full indemnification.

A practical rule applies to the ownership right situation of processed, converted, unified, or mixed things in the event that the thing thus created is not claimed by

226. BH 2009/176.
227. BDT 2013/3010.

any of the joint owners or interested parties. In this case, the thing must be sold and the purchase price must be distributed among the right holders in proportion to their ownership share.

The Civil Code does not specify the party entitled to sell the thing. Optimally, the parties will sell the thing jointly. However, the option for selling differs in the legal situation emerging in the wake of processing or conversion, in which case no joint property is created among the parties; instead, the Civil Code defines the ownership right of the thing and the rules of settlement related to manufacturing or conversion. In our opinion, in this case, the person acquiring ownership right according to the rules of processing and conversion becomes entitled to sell the thing. Meanwhile, unification and mixing give rise to joint property, so in this case, the thing can be sold according to the rules of joint property.

The Civil Code only grants entitlement to a mala fide person to claim a reimbursement in the course of settlement if the other party has gained enrichment, so the sale of the thing is primarily aimed at indemnifying persons acting in good faith while selling the good in order to reimburse a person acting in bad faith is only secondary in terms of priority.

§4. Annexation

379. The Civil Code lays down specific rules governing the unification of things owned by different parties in the course of construction. In the old Civil Code, annexation was a subtype of building on the land of another, while it is addressed as a separate case in the current Civil Code.

Annexation refers to construction added to a building owned by someone else using one's own materials. The precondition for establishing annexation is that it must significantly increase the real property's value. If annexation fails to significantly increase the real property's value, no joint property is created among the parties and settlement between the parties is governed by the rules of unjust enrichment.

380. If the conditions of annexation are met, joint property is created between the parties; however, the parties may diverge from this subject to their mutual agreement, with the option of freely disposing over settlement matters regarding the real property's increase in value. If building on the land of another (annexation) gives rise to joint property, the share respectively represented by the entire real property and the added (annexed) edifice must be examined to define individual ownership shares.

If joint property is created among the parties, their respective ownership shares must be established in proportion to the annexed portion relative to the value of the real property when the construction is completed. When defining ownership shares, it is, therefore, not the total cost of the annexation that is factored in but its added value to the real property.

381. Annexation in bad faith shall be governed by the rules of encroachment based on the rule referencing mala fide building on the land of another.

§5. Incorporating Construction

382. If a person uses another person's material for building on the land, upon which the materials used shall become permanently attached to the land, such material shall become the property of the landowner unless there is an agreement to the contrary between the owner of the material and the owner of the land. If a person uses another person's material for construction, upon which the materials used shall irretrievably become part of the building, such material shall become the property of the owner of the building, unless there is an agreement to the contrary between the owner of the material and the owner of the building.

383. The precondition for incorporating construction is to use foreign material for construction. Foreign material means that the builder has no rights over the material that will qualify it as its own. Another key condition for annexation is that the incorporated material must become a component of the plot. If the incorporated material does not become a component of the real property, this means that it can be separated from the plot without inflicting damage to it. Because, in this scenario, the plot and the incorporated material are not bound to a close extent that would warrant the acquisition of ownership as a legal consequence, the owner of the incorporated material is entitled to uninstall the incorporated material and remove it from the premises.

The Civil Code defines a similar rule for scenarios where the annexation applies not to a plot but to a building.

384. It should be noted that the Civil Code does not define any separate rules for the indemnification of the incorporated material's owner in the event of acquisition of ownership through annexation, nor does it make any distinction between builders acting in good or bad faith.

§6. Building on the Land of Another

385. Building on the land of another refers to building on someone else's land using their own materials without having obtained the necessary rights from the owner of the land. If a person builds a structure in good faith on another person's land without entitlement, ownership of the structure shall be acquired by the owner of the land; however, he shall reimburse the builder to the extent of his actual gains. The court shall be entitled to compel such builder to buy the land or a part thereof (if the land is divisible) at the request of the land's owner. The builder shall acquire ownership of the land or an adequate part thereof if the value of the building considerably exceeds the value of the land or the relevant part of the land. At the request of the landowner, the court may find that the builder has acquired ownership of the building alone; in such a case, the builder shall have the right of use on the land.

I. Materialization of Building on the Land of Another

386. Building on the land of another occurs when the builder builds using his own materials on real property that is someone else's property or joint property. Only the builder or the party commissioning construction can acquire ownership right through building on the land of another; bearing the costs of construction does not in and of itself confer this title status upon the builder.

The in rem and ownership legal consequences of building on the land of another can only be applied if the parties have failed to come to an agreement on the legal consequences of building on the land of another. In light of the subsidiary nature of the rules of building on the land of another, if a contract was concluded between the parties, their rights and obligations must be derived from the contents of this contract.

The condition for acquiring ownership by building on the land of another is that the structure must be durable in the long run, and the builder must have the necessary permits for building it.[228] The builder is not entitled to acquire the ownership right if the erected structure has only been granted a temporary permit. This scenario also calls for the clarification of the conditions defined by the authority for the structure to remain in place because the settlement between the parties may be shaped by these conditions.[229] Acquisition of ownership by building on the land of another cannot be established on the basis of a construction or occupation permit issued by the relevant administrative body of the mayor's office.[230]

II. Legal Consequences of Building on the Land of Another

387. When building on the land of another, dogmatically speaking, the plot constitutes the principal thing, and the structure has the same legal fate as the plot (*inaedificium solo cedit*). The regulation essentially gives priority to the land owner's right to choose in the event of building on the land of another. The landowner may choose to either acquire the building's ownership right while reimbursing the builder for his enrichment or alternatively, the builder will be required to purchase the land or a specific portion thereof. The Civil Code only provides guidance on settlement in the former scenario. If the owner of the land acquires the building's ownership right, then the builder is only entitled to compensation for the value added to the real property by the annexation, irrespective of the builder's investment. In the second case, the Civil Code does not provide any guidance for defining the purchase price in a scenario where the landowner requests the purchase of the plot or a portion thereof by the builder, i.e., exercises a sale option. The parties may obviously agree on the purchase price, but if this does not occur, then in our view, besides an expert valuation of the plot's market price, the purchase price can also be defined in the context of a legal battle in court. In the latter case, we believe that

228. BH 2002/355.
229. BH 1984/147.
230. BH 1999/321.

although the builder is in a position where he may purchase the plot's ownership right, he actually acquires the right in the context of a sales transaction.

If the parties decide to regulate the legal consequences of building on the land of another in a contract, they are not bound by law to any ratios of ownership acquisition that would apply in the absence of a contract. The absence of the mortgagee's consent does not render such a contract invalid.[231] When assessing a claim based on building on the land of another, the value upon completing construction is generally used as the basis. If, however, the matter is only settled long after the construction has been completed, potentially decades later, and during this time, the builder or joint owner living in the building has had exclusive use of the structure, the value of which has decreased significantly relative to that of the real property in the course of wear and tear, it may be warranted to diverge from the general principles.[232] Ownership right on land acquired by building on the land of another is created upon the completion of construction. However, this does not mean that consideration for the portion of land is defined based on the market value prevailing at the time the ownership right is created. This is because the ownership right is resolved when the ruling is passed, and thus, the consideration is calculated based on the market value prevailing at this time.[233] In the event of bona fide building on the land of another, if the value of the building substantially exceeds the value of the land or an appropriate portion thereof, then the builder acquires ownership of the building only at the request of the landowner or subject to the parties' written agreement, or if the landowner has granted its consent to such a request from the builder in the context of a lawsuit.

The legal consequences of building on the land of another cannot be applied if the parties have reached a different agreement on the regulation of ownership resulting from building on the land of another.

The sole exception from the land owner's discretionary decision right is when the value of the building substantially exceeds the value of the land or a specific portion thereof. The scenario presents two sub-scenarios. The builder either acquires ownership right of the land or the specific portion thereof or – as an exception to the exception – at the request of the landowner, the builder only acquires a land use right. The Civil Code does not provide any guidance on the consideration due to this, so in our view, the consideration must be defined based on the land's market value.

III. Building in Bad Faith on Land of Another

388. If the builder has acted in bad faith or if the owner of the land protested against the construction at a time when restoration of the original state would not have caused unreasonably great damage to the builder, the provisions on encroachment shall be applied. A builder shall be considered to have acted in bad faith if

231. BH 2007/334.
232. BH 1997/582.
233. BDT 2000/247.

before the beginning of the construction work he knew or should have known under the circumstances that such building infringes upon the owner's ownership rights.

The Civil Code defines important elements for determining whether the builder acted in bad faith. The builder's bad faith is tied to objective bad faith; the builder knew or should have known under the circumstances before the beginning of construction that such construction infringes upon the owner's ownership rights. Likewise, it is also considered to be the equivalent of bad faith if the principal owner objected in due time when restoration of the original state would not have incurred disproportionate damage. In the latter case, the builder began construction in good faith, but the continuation of construction despite the owner's objections renders the builder mala fide. If the owner of the land protested against the construction at a time when restoration of the original state would not have meant disproportionate damage to the builder, the builder shall be treated equally to a mala fide builder.[234]

The rules on encroachment shall apply to building on the land of another in bad faith.

IV. Provisions on Joint Ownership

389. According to the Civil Code, the rules governing building on the land of another also apply *mutatis mutandis* in the event of joint property. Construction involving the shared assumption of costs does not result in the acquisition of ownership on the grounds of building on the land of another in the case of jointly owned real property. Any maintenance, renovation, refurbishment, or other construction work not affecting the building's structure does not qualify as construction creating a joint property. The outcome of such works is expressed in the market value of the individual ownership shares rather than in the size of the ownership shares. If the joint owners have agreed to share the costs of construction, building on the land of another does not apply even if the final cost exceeds the budgeted cost.[235]

234. BH 2003/232.

235. EBH 2005/1303 and BH 2006/109.

Chapter 5. Appropriation

§1. Acquisition of *Bona Vacantia*

390. Ownership of vacant movable property shall be considered acquired by any person who takes possession of the object to acquire ownership. Movable property shall be considered vacant if it was never previously owned by any person or it was abandoned by its owner with intent to relinquish ownership.

The rules governing the acquisition of *bona vacantia* only apply to movable property. *Bona vacantia* are goods over which nobody holds ownership rights (*res nullius*). One example is a thing originating from nature that has no owner or a derelict object which has been abandoned by its owner (derelictio). Ownership right can be acquired through possession with the intention of acquiring ownership of such an object.

391. Waste placed in a receptacle *located on public premises* and waste placed on public premises in the context of a *municipal clean-up* do not qualify as *vacant* movable property. The owner of these items is the public waste management service provider, which in these cases *acquires the relevant ownership rights* by the power of law.[236] Municipal waste placed in a receptacle forms the property of the waste generator until it is taken into possession by the public service provider, so this waste does not qualify as vacant movable property.

392. *Bona vacantia* only includes movable property because somebody already has ownership rights over real property, and ownership rights on your property cannot be abandoned.

§2. Acquisition of Game and Fish

393. Game, the fish living in rivers and natural lakes, and other useful aquatic animals comprise the property of the state. Game that was killed or captured or that has fallen on hunting grounds shall be owned by a party authorized to hunt, and who owns the hunting ground where the animal was killed or captured, or where it has fallen, provided that his hunting right applies to that game. In the absence of such hunting right, the game shall become the property of another authorized hunter if the land from where the game migrated is owned by that person and if he has hunting rights for the game that was killed or captured or that has fallen. The ownership of fish and other useful aquatic animals shall be acquired by the person authorized to exercise fishing rights.

394. Game, the fish living in rivers and natural lakes, and other useful aquatic animals comprise the property of the state according to the Civil Code and are therefore not *bona vacantia*. The acquisition of ownership over the game is possible

236. Section 43(1) and (2) of Act CLXXXV of 2012 on Waste.

based on the hunting right.[237] On the basis of the Hunting Act,[238] the owner of the land qualifying as a hunting area holds the hunting right – as a right or concession – as an integral part of the land ownership right. An independent hunting right applies if the hunting area is owned by a single person, including the Hungarian state. A joint hunting right applies if the hunting area is owned by several persons, including the Hungarian state, in which case the owners of the hunting area share the hunting right.

Other people may also be entitled to hunt besides the owners. These include the leaseholder of a hunting right, the opportunity to hunt at the invitation of the hunting right holder (guest hunting), and if the hunting right holder allows the hunting of a specific species and number of games on the basis of an agreement (contract hunting).

395. The ownership right of game is governed by the hunting right based on a territorial principle. The hunting right holder on whose hunting area the game is killed, captured, or dies acquires the ownership right of the game. The Hunting Act specifies the property right situation of the game based on this fundamental rule.[239] Game killed or captured in the hunting area and its trophy, shed antlers, the lawfully collected eggs of wild birds, and the carcasses of dead game constitute the right holder's property. Injured game migrated from a different hunting area becomes the property of the right holder of the location where the game was injured – subject to the consent of the hunting right holder – if, subject to the consent of the hunting right holder, the game is killed or found dead in the context of a subsequent search. The carcasses of game killed on non-hunting territory and shed antlers are the property of the right holder from whose hunting area the game originates. In the event of doubt, the right holder of the hunting area closest to the place of discovery shall be regarded as the owner. Game held lawfully in a wildlife park or hunting farm established on a hunting area – unless agreed otherwise with the operator of the wildlife park or hunting farm – constitutes the property of the right holder. Game held lawfully on a game farm established in a non-hunting area – unless agreed otherwise – constitutes the property of the game farm's operator. The firing of the first fatal shoot qualifies as the killing of red deer, fallow deer, mouflon, wild boar, and deer. For other games, the firing of a shot resulting in the immobilization of another game or its capture using a predatory bird qualifies as killing. The taking into possession of a live game by rendering it immobile qualifies as the capturing of game.

396. The fishery right holder may provide permission to capture fish on the territory of the fishery.[240] In the aqueous areas of fisheries, the capturing of fish and activities conducted for this purpose may be carried out in possession of a commercial and ecological licence, a fishing licence in the case of selective fishing, a state-issued angling ticket in the case of recreational fishing, or a state-issued fishing

237. *See* Act LV of 1996 on the Protection of Game, Game Management and Hunting (hereinafter: 'Hunting Act') and its implementing decree, Decree 79/2004 (V. 4.) of the Ministry of Agriculture and Rural Development govern the hunting right.
238. Section 3(1) of the Hunting Act.
239. Section 9 of the Hunting Act.
240. Pursuant to Art. 37 of Act II of 2013 on Fisheries Management and the Protection of Fish.

ticket or touristic fishing ticket. A catch log shall be kept on all fishing and angling activities. A person licensed to catch fish acquires ownership of the fish and other useful aquatic animals upon capturing them.

§3. FOUND PROPERTY

397. Finding is an original way of acquisition where the owner has lost possession of the object for reasons beyond his control, and the finder's efforts to return the object have failed. The legal fate of a lost thing and that of a thing abandoned for the purpose of abandoning the ownership right is, therefore, different. If the owner terminates this possession of the thing by abandoning his ownership right, the thing will be deemed ownerless. By contrast, in the event of loss, the owner only loses possession of the thing, but his intention does not extend to abandoning his ownership right. In this regard, it is the owner's intention that defines the legal fate of the thing; however, this intention is not necessarily expressed to the world at large, so the person finding the thing may not be able to decide whether the item is a vacant object or lost item still owned by someone. To reach a definitive decision on the matter, the law prescribes detailed rules governing attempts to return the thing, and if the thing cannot be returned to the owner based on these attempts, the law makes the assumption that the owner's intention also extends to abandoning his ownership right, meaning that the finder acquires the ownership right over the ownerless thing.

I. Conditions of the Finding

398. A person who finds a thing that is presumably owned by somebody else and takes possession thereof shall be considered to have acquired that thing if he claims ownership thereof, provided that he has done everything within his power in order to return the thing to its rightful owner, and the owner or any other person authorized to collect it has not come forward to take possession of the thing within one year, or within three months in the case of live animals, of the day on which it was found. If the thing is found by several persons collectively, the rights and obligations of the finder shall accrue to the co-finders equally and collectively. Co-finder shall also mean the person who had been the first to discover the object and had endeavoured to take possession thereof; however, another person managed to take possession before him.

399. There are several conditions for the finder to acquire ownership, which must be met at the same time. The finder must have the intention to acquire ownership; in other words, possession of the object in and of itself does not entail the acquisition of the ownership right. In addition, the finder must do everything in his power to return the thing to its rightful owner. A further condition is that the owner must not claim the thing within one year or three months in the case of a live animal.

If the thing is found by several persons collectively, the rights and obligations of the finder shall accrue to the co-finders equally and collectively. Participation in finding is not necessarily linked to taking possession of the thing; for instance, if somebody notices a lost thing and notifies another person to pick it up, he has participated in finding the thing.

400. The finder shall deliver the thing he has found to the person who lost it, to its owner or any other person authorized to collect it, or to the notary with jurisdiction by reference to the place where it was found, within eight days from the date of the find. If delivered to the competent notary, the finder shall declare whether he wishes to lay claim to ownership of the thing.

If the person having an entitlement to collect the thing can be identified, the notary shall give the thing to its rightful holder without delay. If the person entitled to collect the thing cannot be identified, the notary shall retain possession of the thing for a period of three months from the date of receipt. If the entitled person fails to come forward during that time, the thing shall be released to the finder if he filed a claim for it at the time of delivery.

The notary shall make out a certificate on the finder's claim. If the person entitled to collect the submitted thing can be identified, the notary shall immediately hand over the thing to the authorized person. If the person entitled to collect a thing cannot be determined, the notary shall retain possession of it for a period of three months from the date of submission. If the entitled person fails to come forward during that time, the thing classified among the usual things subject to personal ownership shall be released to the finder if he filed a claim for it at the time of submission.

401. The finder shall be entitled to use the thing without causing any physical harm to the thing; however, he shall not be entitled to alienate it or encumber it and may not allow others to use it, as his use during this period is temporary, and he only has a contingent right of use granted for a provisional period. If the entitled person does not contact the notary or the finder within one year from the time of the finding, the finder acquires the ownership right of the surrendered thing. Any third-party rights on the thing cease upon acquisition of the ownership right, as finding is an original method of acquiring ownership.

402. If the entitled person fails to claim the thing within three months of the handover and the finder did not claim ownership right of the thing when submitting it, the notary shall sell the thing. The provisions on the sale of the things seized during administrative enforcement procedures shall also apply to the sale of found things.

If the rightful owner comes forward before the time of sale, the things shall be released to him, or if he comes forward after the sale, the sum received shall be paid to him. However, the entitled person shall forfeit his right to the thing or to the sum received upon the sale if he fails to come forward within one year of the date when the thing was found.

If the entitled person fails to claim the thing within three months of depositing it at the notary and the finder did not claim ownership right of the thing at the time of finding it, the notary shall sell the thing.

II. Finding in Public Place

403. Instead of the general rules governing found property, special rules apply for things found in publicly accessible buildings and areas or on the vehicles of a public transportation company. This different regulation is warranted by the fact that keeping records or using other recording tools that allow the identification of the person having lost the thing is possible in such places or an employee or person discharging activities at the location who may have information on the identity of the person having lost the thing may be found.

The finder shall relinquish possession of things found in publicly accessible buildings and areas or on the vehicles of a public transportation company to an employee of the operator of such buildings or means of transportation without delay. The finder may not lay claim to such things. If the person entitled to collect the thing can be identified, the operator shall notify such person and shall give the thing to its rightful holder without delay if he comes forward. If the person entitled to collect the thing cannot be identified, the operator shall retain possession of the thing for a period of three months from the date of receipt, or, if lacking facilities for its safekeeping, deliver it to the notary within eight days from the date of receipt If the entitled person did not come forward within three months to claim the thing, the operator or the notary shall sell the thing in question.

III. Finder's Fee

404. If the thing that has been found cannot be safeguarded – due to it being perishable or for any other reason – the notary or the operator shall provide for its sale without delay. This rule is aimed at preventing or mitigating damage.

If the entitled person comes forward before the time of sale, the thing shall be released to him, or if he comes forward after the sale, the sum received shall be paid to him. The entitled person forfeits his right to the thing or to the sum received upon sale if he fails to come forward within one year of the date when the thing was found. This rule is based on the premise that the ownership right of the person having lost the thing only ceases one year from the time of the loss. As a result, if such person presents himself to the temporary possessor within one year, the object must be surrendered to him, or the price received for the object must be restituted to him.

405. If a thing that has been found is of substantial value and its finder does not acquire ownership thereof, he shall be entitled to a reasonable finder's fee on condition that he has done everything within his power to have the thing returned to its owner. Co-finders shall be entitled to an equal share of the finder's fee. The finder may refuse to give up the thing that has been found until his claim for cost reimbursement and for the finder's fee is satisfied. The finder shall also have those rights if he has released the found thing to the authorities. The authority shall be allowed, with the finder's consent, to deliver the thing to the person entitled to collect it or pay him the purchase price received, except if the person entitled to collect the thing has deposited the value of the thing with the authorities. The sum deposited replaces the thing found.

To incentivize the finder, the Civil Code prescribes the payment of a reasonable finder's fee. The sum of this finder's fee is defined based on judicial practice, which also factors in the value of the thing. Consequently, the finder of a dog is generally not entitled to a finder's fee. The finder may claim the costs incurred by looking after the dog based on the rules of responsible custody.[241]

If the owner of a thing that has been found, the person who lost it or any other person authorized to collect it does not come forward within a period of one year, or three months in the case of live animals, and the finder does not acquire ownership thereof, ownership or the purchase price received for the sale of the thing shall accrue to the state. The aim of this rule is to ensure that the thing or the sum derived from its sale does not remain ownerless and its ownership status is duly resolved. Acquisition of ownership by the state in this manner materializes by the power of the law, *ipso jure*.

§4. Treasure Finds

406. If a person finds a valuable thing which has been hidden by unknown persons or the ownership of which has otherwise been forgotten, he shall be obliged to offer it to the state. If the state does not claim the thing, it shall become the property of the finder; otherwise, the finder shall be entitled to a finder's fee proportionate to the value of the thing. If the found thing is classified as protected cultural goods, its ownership may be claimed by the state.

407. Finding treasure differs from regular finding in that for the latter, the value of the found thing has no significance, whereas, for the former, the value is a precondition for realizing the statutory definition. While the ownership right of both the valuable and worthless thing can be acquired through finding, ownership right can only be acquired through finding treasure with regard to a valuable thing. However, finding protected cultural goods qualifies as the finding of treasure if all other statutory definitions are fulfilled.

The other key difference of finding treasure compared to normal finding is that the thing is hidden by unknown persons, or the ownership right of the original owner otherwise falls into oblivion. A found thing has usually been lost by its owner, but it is also possible that the owner has hidden the thing and has subsequently failed to find it.[242]

In the case of finding treasure, the wording of the law does not define any period for the original owner to reclaim the thing. Based on the two definitions of the law, the thing must have been hidden by unknown persons; in other words, in such cases, finding the thing results in the acquisition of ownership irrespective of the time of

241. BH 1988/1.

242. In case of a treasure-trove, it is not necessary to take the thing in possession, only the finding counts. Iván Siklósi, *A kincstalálás római jogi, jogtörténeti és modern jogi kérdésköre* (*Treasure Trove in Roman Law, in Legal History and in Modern Legal System*) 166 (Patrocinium 2016).

the hiding. However, the ownership right falling into oblivion presumes that the thing was hidden so long ago that the owner no longer remembers that the thing was once his property.

The key difference between found property and found trove resides in the identity of the person acquiring ownership. As the main rule, the state may claim ownership of the treasure while the person finding it is entitled to a proportionate finder's fee. However, the state may decide to reject the treasure; in this exceptional case, the finder is entitled to the ownership right. In the case of protected cultural goods, the state does not have the right to reject the goods, and the ownership right of the treasure is automatically bestowed upon the state.

408. In terms of the finder's fee, the finder of trover is entitled to a proportionate finder's fee, as opposed to a reasonable finder's fee due to the finder of an object. In our opinion, the amount of the proportionate finder's fee also depends on the value of the object, but it must be factored in that, in this scenario, the thing is not returned to the original owner. If a thing is returned to its original owner, he only gains wealth ostensibly because the thing was his to begin with, so the finder must be rewarded for his effort made to return the thing. By contrast, when finding treasure, the state acquires the ownership of a thing that was originally not its property; in other words, the state gains wealth. As a result, the finder's fee due to the finder of the treasure must be higher than in the event of a normal finding.

409. Special legislation states that cultural goods are significant and characteristic objects, visual, audio, or written monuments or other evidence of the creation or development of living or non-living nature, humanity, the Hungarian nation or the history of Hungary – with the exception of real property – and artistic creations.[243] The Act on Protection of Cultural Heritage governs the protection of archaeological heritage and the classification of archaeological excavations, and the classification as monumental heritage. Cultural goods kept in museum institutions, archives, image and audio archives functioning as public collections, and in libraries kept as 'Museum nature' documents qualify as protected cultural goods.[244] As a result, according to the above-specified statutory provision, it is not likely that found treasure is to be inherently classified as a protected cultural good, as it is not preserved in a museum institution, archive, public collection, or library. In such cases, classification as a protected cultural good must be carried out in accordance with the law, and the thing can also be temporarily classified as a protected good until the procedure is concluded.

243. The provisions of Act CXL of 1997 on the Protection of Cultural Goods, Museum Institutions, Public Library Services and Cultural Education provides guidance regarding protected cultural goods. Item (sz) of Sch. 1 to this Act. Section 7(4) of Act LXVI of 2011 on the Protection of Cultural Heritage also uses this definition.

244. Pursuant to Art. 46 of the Act on the Protection of Cultural Heritage.

Chapter 6. Expropriation

410. Ownership of real estate property may be acquired under exceptional circumstances for public use against immediate, full, and unconditional indemnification. Indemnification shall be provided by the persons who acquire ownership through expropriation.

Expropriation is partly a question of constitutional law, representing the strongest potential restriction of the fundamental right to property while also partly being one of the modes of acquiring ownership under civil law. Both in terms of chronological order and within the legislative hierarchy, the constitutional principle and guarantees must first and foremost prevail (in the Fundamental Law and the Act on Expropriation),[245] only then followed by civil law regulation.

§1. Historical Background of Expropriation

411. In Austria, the ABGB governs expropriation,[246] which may be exercised in the interest of the common goods in exchange for adequate indemnification. Legal history likes to attribute the origin of this to Hugo Grotius's theory of *dominium eminens* – disseminated in German legal territory by Christian Wolff – according to which a landowner is entitled to acquire the property of serfs if warranted by a common interest (*utilitas publica*) (the theory of *ius eminens* was probably not invented by Grotius, but was part of common legal knowledge). Under the provisions of the Codex Theresianus,[247] expropriation could take place for the purposes of general interest, and no indemnification was due in exchange; the owner had to treat the event as a kind of accident and had to bear the loss alone. In Azzoni's view, claims for compensation could be adjudged on the grounds of fairness. Martini's work derived the theory of *jus eminens* from the social contract, with the discrepancy that it could only be applied in the face of danger threatening the state or particularly large profit. However, Martini only considered expropriation appropriate if coupled with indemnification. Martini's disciple Zeiller, the leading drafter of the ABGB, completely abandoned the theory of *ius eminens* and strictly tied the state's expropriation right to the condition of full indemnification. Expropriation, an opportunity for the state to change ownership rights constituting a fundamental right of its citizens, naturally requires regulation at the constitutional law level, which supersedes the matter's regulation under the civil code.

412. Besides offering adequate statutory regulation of the former owner's interests in the event of expropriation, with most legal disputes aimed at the amount of indemnification, we must not forget the further legal fate of the expropriated thing. This is particularly important in a scenario where a third party holds some kind of right of use on the thing subject to expropriation, which may be coupled with an investment, and so the third party's rights are prejudiced to a greater extent, or the

245. *See* Act CXXIII of 2007 on expropriation.
246. Article 365 of the ABGB.
247. Codex Theresianus, Part 2 Ch. I. §VI, Nos 159 and 160.

third party suffers a greater loss than the owner. Adequately addressing these issues at the level of legislation is a difficult task. In any case, in Austrian law – similar to Hungarian law, expropriation is an original mode of acquiring ownership, through which the expropriated thing becomes the new owner's property free of any encumbrances.

413. When talking about expropriation, defining the grounds for such an exceptional measure is a fundamental question that carries theoretical relevance. The French Constitution of 24 June 1793 only allows expropriation for public benefit and in exchange for indemnification,[248] and likewise, the French Code civil only allows expropriation despite the owner's intent in the general interest (*l'utilité public*) and in exchange for fair indemnification.[249]

The German Constitution and regional expropriation laws – which remained in force under the Basic Law passed in Bonn after the Second World War – also allowed for expropriation in the public interest and coupled with fair indemnification for the owner. In Austria, a citizen is required to relinquish his ownership for the common good in exchange for fair, i.e., proportionate,[250] indemnification.[251]

Adequate compensation, in other words, proportionate indemnification, is also an important matter, in terms of which any third-party rights on the expropriated thing must not be forgotten, over and above the owner. On this subject, the general tendency is that expropriation results in unencumbered ownership right for the state, and so it terminates per se any third-party rights on the thing. This also applies to contractual rights on the thing subject to expropriation. Austrian judicial practice regulates this by extending the expropriation to the third-party rights on the thing and also treats purely contractual claims on the thing in the same way.

§2. Rules of Expropriation under the Fundamental Law

414. Expropriation represents the most radical intervention into private autonomy in the realm of private property. The Fundamental Law declares with regard to expropriation that 'property may only be expropriated exceptionally, in the public interest and in the cases and ways provided for by an Act, subject to full, unconditional, and immediate compensation'.[252] Expropriation is, therefore, primarily a question of constitutional law, representing the most radical restriction of the right to own property, and furthermore, civil law only provides guidance on the detailed rules. Both in terms of chronological order and within the legislative hierarchy, the principle and guarantees laid down in the Fundamental Law must first and foremost prevail, followed only then by civil law regulation.

248. Item 19 of the introductory provisions of the French Constitution of 24 Jun. 1793.
249. Article 545 of the French Civil Code.
250. József Szalma, *Kisajátítás – jegyzetek a horvát kisajátítási törvényről* (*Expropriation – Notes on the Croatian Expropriation Act*), 52 Jogtudományi Közlöny 396 (1997).
251. Article 365 of the ABGB.
252. Article XIII(2) of the Fundamental Law.

On the topic of property as a constitutional right, it is worth looking at the James case tried by the European Court of Human Rights, which expresses that in a democratic society, the economic and social public interest related to ownership can be interpreted in many different ways. Thus, the constitutional examination of public interest as defined by a parliamentary majority must be restricted to examining whether citing such interest was arbitrary.[253]

§3. Detailed Rules of Expropriation

415. Act CXXIII of 2007 on Expropriation defines the detailed rules of expropriation. The introduction to the Act declares that its purpose is to ensure the acquisition of real properties absolutely necessary for the realization of objectives of public interest determined by law and that expropriation may only be applied as an exceptional instrument of withdrawing ownership.

I. Entities Requesting Expropriation and Objectives Serving the Common Good

416. Expropriation may be requested by the state, the local government or a third party if such party is engaged in discharging a public interest objective or a party required by the state to proceed on its behalf and in its own name to request expropriation.

Such public interest objectives include, provided that the detailed conditions apply: national protection, the exchange of territory based on an international agreement, territorial and municipal planning, the installation of educational, health care, or social facilities in the context of mandatory state or mandatory municipal activities, infrastructure development, energy production; energy supply, mining; electronic communication services, heritage protection, natural protection, water management, public water utility services, sustainable forestry, the cultivation of protected forests, protected trees, and the cultivation of forests in the public interest, the cancellation of construction restrictions; real property usage rights restricting or terminating the intended use of the real property for public interest objectives, termination of drawbacks stemming from easements, environmental protection, sports infrastructure development, or the installation of official bodies contributing to the National Assembly's work.[254]

417. Expropriation may only occur if the public interest objective cannot be achieved by limiting ownership of the real property, or if the usage right in the public interest, the cable right or the easement right is established based on the law without reaching an agreement with the owner, or if the competent authority has not

253. Ferenc Fábián, *A tulajdon alkotmányos korlátozhatóságáról* (*About the Possible Constitutional Limitation of the Ownership*), in *Ünnepi tanulmányok Sárközy Tamás 70. születésnapjára* (*Festal Studies to Tamás Sárközy's 70th Birthday*) 75 ff. (Tamás Nótári ed., Lectum 2010).

254. Specified in Art. 4 of the Act CXXIII of 2007 on expropriation.

authorized such rights. Expropriation may also occur if the property's ownership right cannot be acquired through purchase or, in the case defined by law, through exchange. In addition, expropriation may also be warranted if the public interest objective can only be implemented on the specific real property, or if multiple real properties are suitable for implementing the public interest objective, then implementing the objective on other property would entail greater prejudice to the property; and the public benefits of the activity implemented through the expropriation significantly exceed the loss caused by withdrawing the property. When evaluating this, the expropriation authority must compare the significance of the public interest activity, in particular its impact on the area's development, the number of people served by the activity or service, the impact on employment and the real property's attributes; in the case of a heritage protection value or environmental protection value, the significance thereof and the proportionality of the withdrawal of ownership must also be examined.

The conclusion of a sales contract or exchange contract must be considered to have failed if the offer of the party requesting expropriation – made within one year preceding the submission of the expropriation request – was not accepted by the owner or other party entitled to indemnification within thirty days of receipt, or such party failed to issue a response; furthermore, the owner or other party entitled to indemnification cannot be clearly identified, or legal proceedings concerning the real property's ownership are underway and have been entered in the land registry, are pending entry or have otherwise been certified. Similarly, the conclusion of the contract shall be regarded as having failed if the place of domicile, place of residence or registered office of the owner or other party entitled to indemnification is not known or the offer of the party requesting expropriation can only be communicated to him with great difficulty or would entail a substantial delay; a large number of owners or parties entitled to indemnification does not qualify as such a circumstance.

418. The owner may also initiate the expropriation or the purchase of the real property if he acquired ownership of the real property prior to the emergence of the following restriction, and the real property's intended use is determined by a public interest objective – defined in legislation – of the local building regulation to be implemented later in time that the owner cannot be expected to implement, and such objective, or the public interest usage right or easement – once such right has been established – significantly impedes or terminates ownership and construction rights, the property's intended use.

419. A preliminary expropriation plan is necessary for expropriation.[255] If the real property listed in the expropriation plan is acquired through purchase or exchange, pre-emption and repurchase rights or the purchase option – based on legislation or a contract – cannot be exercised on the property. The expropriation may pertain to a specific part of the real property (partial expropriation). Territory intended to be built on cannot be partially expropriated if the remaining portion of

255. The rules laid down in Government Decree 178/2008 (VII. 3.) concerning the drafting, review, and validation of an expropriation plan, and regarding certain issues of compensation for expropriation.

the real property is smaller than the smallest allowed plot size, except if the plot was originally smaller than the smallest allowed plot size. On territory not intended to be built on, partial expropriation is possible if the remaining portion of the real property is smaller than the smallest allowed plot size; however, subject to the parties' agreement, the remaining portion must also be expropriated. At the owner's request, the remaining portion must be expropriated if, in the wake of the real property's partial expropriation, the remaining part of the property can no longer be used for its original purpose, the original right or activity can no longer be exercised or only at a far higher cost, and the remaining portion of the property cannot be sold cost-effectively.

420. Expropriation of the remaining portion may be requested at the latest before the completion of the expropriation hearing. The owner of the real property affected by expropriation may only dispose of the property's ownership during the expropriation procedure to the benefit of the party requesting expropriation, or subject to the consent of the party requesting appropriation, if disposing to the benefit of a different party; the owner must be notified of this in the notice on the launch of the expropriation procedure. The expropriation authority may enter a provisional prohibition on the property's alienation in the land registry for the duration of the expropriation procedure to the benefit of the party requesting the expropriation.

II. Other Permits Necessary for Expropriation

421. The expropriation of agricultural land – if the use of agricultural land is necessary to achieve the purpose of the expropriation – may occur if the land authority has authorized definitive use of the land for other purposes or has consented to different utilization.

Before expropriating real property owned by a foreign state or international organization, the position of the minister for foreign affairs and trade must be obtained.

Expropriation for mining purposes is subject to the relevant opinion of the mining supervisory authority on the justified nature of such purpose.

Real property (or portions thereof) taken into asset management for national defence purposes by the ministry led by the minister in charge of national defence may be expropriated subject to the consent of the minister for national defence or to their classification as necessary for national defence purposes.

III. Expropriation Resolution

422. Unencumbered ownership of the property materializes once the expropriation resolution comes into force. The expropriation resolution shall regulate any third-party rights to the real property and state all facts pertaining to the property.

If monetary compensation is granted, third-party rights to the real property and the facts pertaining to the property shall cease. If indemnification is granted in the form of the replacement property, the rights pertaining to the expropriated property are transferred to the replacement property. Any lease, leasehold, or usufruct rights must be transferred to the replacement property at the request of the right holder; the relevant request may be submitted until the end of the expropriation hearing. Leases on homes and non-residential premises cannot be transferred to the replacement property.

IV. Indemnification

A. General

423. The owner of the expropriated real property is entitled to full, immediate and unconditional indemnification for the withdrawal of his ownership right and the holder of any third-party rights on the real property is entitled to full, immediate and unconditional indemnification for the termination of his right, with the exception of lien and enforcement right holders. Indemnification for terminated rights must be taken into account when granting indemnification for the withdrawal of ownership of the property.

When determining the amount of indemnification, the following must be factored in: the local market value of real property suitable for comparison, or if the real property's actual market value cannot be determined – due to the absence of comparable real property or the absence of a market for such property, or due to a statutory restriction on their sale – the real property's position within the municipality, its public utility infrastructure, or in the absence thereof, the opportunity for installing public utilities, its geographic and economic attributes, or for agricultural land, the branch of agriculture, its land qualification criteria and the property's profitability.

424. As a main rule, indemnification is granted in cash. Indemnification may also be provided in the form of a replacement property subject to an agreement between the owner and the party requesting expropriation. If the value of the replacement property is greater than the indemnification due for the expropriated property, the owner must pay the difference. In warranted cases, exemption from paying this difference or an additional discount may be granted in the expropriation resolution. If the value of the replacement property is lower than the indemnification due for the expropriated property, the difference shall be paid to the owner in cash.

If the owner or user is using the home or non-residential premises located in an expropriated building, the party requesting expropriation shall supply an adequate replacement home or replacement premises. The replacement premises shall be deemed adequate if the same activities can be continued there under similar circumstances. If the right holder does not accept the adequate replacement home or replacement premise offered (as determined in an expert opinion), he shall be granted indemnification in the form of cash.

B. Reimbursement of Loss in Value

425. The loss in value stemming from expropriation must be reimbursed. In the case of real property used for agricultural purposes, the value of standing or hanging crops on land used for agricultural purposes must, in particular, be reimbursed as a loss in value if such value can be determined at the time of transfer into possession, or, if this cannot be determined, the value of the expected yield during the business year underway; in the case of forests, the value of standing trees must be reimbursed as loss in value; furthermore, in the event of the partial expropriation of real property, the loss and the remaining portion's value must be reimbursed.

The cost of any agricultural work not carried out must be deducted from the value of standing or hanging crops or the value of the expected yield during the business year underway.

C. Reimbursement of Costs

426. The cost of agricultural and forestry work completed on agricultural or forestry land and other expenditures incurred during the year underway shall be reimbursed as a cost related to the expropriation; the difference between the rent on a home (or non-residential premises) located in an expropriated building and the replacement home (or non-residential premises) shall also be reimbursed for a five-year period.

D. Payment of Indemnification

427. As a main rule, indemnification must be paid by the state or local government acquiring ownership through expropriation or the third party requesting expropriation. The indemnification shall be paid in one lump sum.

E. Collateral Expenses

428. The party required to pay indemnification for the expropriation – over and above indemnification due for the withdrawal of the real property's ownership right, the termination of rights on the real property and for loss of value and other costs stemming from the expropriation – shall also reimburse the cost of moving or the relocation of the person or organization engaged in professional business activity, the reorganization of production facilities, production downtime and revenue lost due to any suspension of the expropriation procedure, as well as any justified and certified costs incurred – within no more than ninety days of the occupation of the expropriated property – by the beneficiary of indemnification on account of addressing any drawbacks caused by the expropriation.

V. The Expropriation Procedure

429. The provisions of the Administrative Proceedings Act govern expropriation procedures as background regulations.[256] The expropriation procedure is conducted by the expropriation authority. The expropriation authority has jurisdiction based on the location of the target property. The administrative time limit for the expropriation procedure is forty-five days, which is extendable once in warranted cases by thirty days at most.

The expropriation procedure is launched upon request and is to be submitted by the party requesting expropriation. The expropriation authority then sets a hearing date and appoints a court expert to formulate an expert opinion on the expropriation and also defines a deadline for the formulation of this opinion. The expert must be summoned to the hearing. There is no need to schedule a hearing or to hold a scheduled hearing if the party requesting expropriation pens a deed confirming the agreement reached on the indemnification of expropriation and the expropriation authority regards the agreement as lawful.

The expert opinion shall be presented at the hearing, and comments made on the expropriation plan and the expert opinion in advance shall be discussed at the hearing. The expropriation authority and clients may request the expert opinion be supplemented. The owner, as the user of the property, must issue a statement no later than the hearing on the amount of time necessary for relinquishing possession of the property.

The expropriation authority makes its decision on the expropriation factoring in objectives and conditions and the various criteria. If the party requesting expropriation and the other clients reach an agreement on indemnification, the expropriation authority accepts this agreement in the resolution.

No appeal may be made against the expropriation authority's decision, which may only be contested through legal proceedings for the judicial review of the administrative decision.

256. Act CXL of 2004 on the General Rules of Administrative Proceedings and Services.

Chapter 7. Insolvency

430. Within insolvency procedures, there is a distinction between enforcement procedures, which may be instituted against both natural persons and legal entities, and liquidation procedures, which may be instituted against legal entities (business organizations).

Enforcement procedures may be initiated on the basis of an enforcement deed, i.e., a binding court resolution or notarial deed. Enforcement procedures are managed by an independent court executor under the supervision of the court. In the course of the procedure, the executor may seize the debtor's assets and sell them in the context of an auction (*see* the section on auctions).[257]

The subject of a liquidation procedure is an insolvent business organization, while liquidation procedures are aimed at satisfying creditors in a statutory manner if an insolvent debtor is wound up without leaving any successor.[258] In the course of liquidation procedures, an executor appointed by the court is entitled to sell the business organization's assets, primarily in the context of an official auction.

257. In details, *see* György Schadl, *The Concept, Importance and History of Judicial Enforcement*, in *Business Law* 699 ff. (István Sándor ed., Patrocinium 2016).

258. *See* Tamás Fézer, *Insolvency Law: Bankruptcy and Liquidation*, in *Business Law* 285 ff. (István Sándor ed., Patrocinium 2016); Péter Miskolczi Bodnár & Gábor Török, *A magyar csődjog alapjai* (*Foundations of the Hungary Bankruptcy Law*) 85 ff. (HVG-ORAC 2002); Ádám Boóc et al., *Csődjog* (*Bankruptcy Law*) 193 ff. (HVG-ORAC 2007^2); László Juhász, *Csődjog* (*Bankruptcy Law*) 101 ff. (Dialóg Campus 2003).

Chapter 8. Acquisition of Ownership by Official Procedure

431. Any person who has acquired a thing in good faith by means of official resolution or official auction shall gain ownership irrespective of who the previous owner was. Ownership by way of administrative decision shall be considered acquired when possession is transferred in the case of movable property or when the acquisition of title is registered in the land registry in the case of real property unless the administrative decision provides otherwise. In the case of an official auction, the auction buyer shall acquire ownership when possession of the movable property is transferred by the auctioneer or when the acquisition of title is registered in the land registry in the case of real property. Upon the acquisition of ownership of the thing by means of official resolution or official auction, the rights of the third party on the thing shall cease, except when the party acquiring ownership by means of official resolution or official auction did not act in good faith in respect of those rights.

According to the Civil Code's rules, acquisition through an official ruling or an official auction qualifies as an original way of acquiring ownership. These cases of acquiring ownership result in a change in the owner's identity with the participation of the state. An official ruling and official auction terminate the original owner's ownership right and create an ownership right for the new owner.

§1. Official Rulings and Auctions

432. The Civil Code only refers to official rulings and official auctions but does not regulate their specifics. These may include cases in the context of enforcement procedures, liquidation procedures or the termination of joint ownership. According to the rules laid down in the Civil Code, the previous owner's ownership right terminates on the basis of an official ruling or official auction, and the new owner does not acquire ownership through legal succession, i.e., there is no legal relationship between these two entities.

I. Distinction of Official Rulings and Auctions from Transfers

433. The rules of transfer cannot be applied to the acquisition of ownership through an official auction. In the context of judicial enforcement, the buyer at the auction acquires ownership based on the official auction rather than based on a contract; therefore, the provisions governing contractual relationships (invalidity, lack of scope) cannot be applied. There was a somewhat different set of arguments behind the ad hoc decision from the Supreme Court, which ruled that while acquiring ownership of real property through an auction does not qualify as an original mode of acquisition, the ownership right of the buyer at the auction nevertheless does not stem from the subject of the enforcement, but is instead based on the auction as a state-coerced action.[259] The case where the joint property is terminated in exchange for compensation does not qualify as an official ruling.[260]

Purchase at an auction is an original mode of acquiring ownership. Ownership is acquired once the auction minutes are issued. However, if the auction is cancelled, the buyer at the auction may lose his ownership right. If no contractual legal relationship is established between the debtor and the buyer at the auction, the debtor can, therefore, not enforce any contractual rights vis-à-vis the buyer[261] and may only seek redress pursuant to the Act on Judicial Enforcement.[262]

II. Time of Transfer of Ownership

434. Similarly to the rules of transfer, the Civil Code gives a clear definition of the time when the ownership right of a person losing his ownership right ceases, and the new owner obtains the ownership right. For movable property, the time of transfer is linked to the transfer of possession, while for real property, the time of transfer is linked to the registration of the new owner in the land registry, which means that the new Civil Code has created new rules superseding the earlier practice where the transfer of ownership was linked to the issuance of the auction minutes. Within the same topic, in earlier cases, the initiator of an enforcement procedure acquires the ownership right of movable property by taking possession of the property,[263] while the ownership of real property passes over when the property is registered in the land registry.[264] Administrative orders may diverge from this.

III. Fate of Encumbrances on the Thing

435. The new owner acquires the ownership right of the thing free of any encumbrances based on the original mode of acquisition, except if the new owner did not act in good faith with regard to the rights on the thing. For real property, the buyer at the auction only requires an ownership right with regard to the real property constituting the debtor's property. The former owner remaining in the dwelling has the same legal status as a tenant if the auction price was determined, factoring in the decreasing impact of tenancy on the auction purchase price. In this case, the buyer at the auction may exercise his right of termination based on the reasons for termination or termination associated with a replacement home, but free termination or citing the absence of an agreement or the nature of the legal relationship is not permitted.[265] The former owner remaining in the dwelling restricts the owner of

259. BDT 2003/812.
260. BH 2007/405.
261. EBH 2011/2310.
262. Act LIII of 1994 on judicial enforcement.
263. BH 1994/680.
264. BH 2007/405.
265. BH 2004/364.

real property purchased at an auction at a purchase price, factoring in the decreasing impact of tenancy by exercising his right of use and possession; the former owner's position is governed by the rules pertaining to the legal status of tenants.[266]

IV. Assessing the Good Faith of a Person Acquiring Ownership

436. The ownership right of a thing may only be acquired in good faith through an official ruling and via an official auction. A bona fide buyer at an enforcement auction acquires the property's ownership right via auction as an original mode of acquisition, with the restricting condition that the last owner of the property auctioned off was indeed the debtor. If the acquiring party knew or should have known that the official ruling was infringing, he will not acquire ownership.[267] The acquisition of ownership is based on an official ruling if the liquidating court passes the real property forming part of the debtor's estate into the creditor's ownership to satisfy the creditor's claim by virtue of a binding order approving the submitted interim balance sheet. Any person who has acquired a thing in good faith by means of official resolution or official auction shall gain ownership irrespective of who the previous owner was.[268]

V. Unlawful Enforcement and Consequences of an Action for the Recovery of Property

437. If the executor proceeds in an infringing manner in the context of a property auction, the court may terminate the property auction based on the submitted objection. An auction will be deemed invalid, and the buyer at the auction will not acquire an ownership right on the auctioned property if the object of the auction is a business share where the owner launched legal action on account of his exclusion from the company and the lawsuit has not been bindingly concluded, and both the announcer of the auction and the buyer at the auction were aware of this fact.[269]

An action for the recovery of property can be successfully initiated as long as the court proceeding in the enforcement procedure is able to take measures for the release of the seized property or the transfer of the sum generated by the sale of the seized property. After the conclusion of the enforcement procedure, the party who would otherwise have been entitled to initiate an application for the recovery of property cannot take action against the initiator of the enforcement procedure on the basis of a claim for the compensation of unjust enrichment. The party who would otherwise have been entitled to initiate an application for the recovery of property may, after the successful or partly successful conclusion of the enforcement procedure, enforce a claim against the debtor, taking into account that enrichment or the

266. EBH 2000/304.
267. BDT 2006/1380.
268. BDT 2008/1863.
269. BH 2000/114.

shifting of wealth occurred to the benefit of the debtor by virtue of the fact it was not terminated because of the sale of the debtor's item of property, or that the debtor's debt decreased.[270]

The buyer at the auction qualifies as a further acquirer of a right in terms of the legal proceedings for deletion, just as if it had acquired ownership on other legal grounds; therefore, a claim for deletion may be successfully enforced against him.[271]

§2. Acquisition of Ownership by the State Without Indemnification by Means of an Administrative Decision

438. The state may acquire ownership without indemnification either on the basis of legislation or a court or official ruling. In such cases, the state is liable up to the value of the things constituting the basis of indemnification due to third parties vis-à-vis the former owner/creditor. The state liability vis-à-vis such claims applies if the third party acted in good faith and initiated enforcement against the former owner's property, in the course of which its claim was not satisfied. The state shall be liable to a bona fide person for obligations existing on the basis of legislation, court (official) ruling, or a contract for countervalue when a seizure ruling is promulgated, to the extent of the value of property seized. Such obligations may include those prevailing on the basis of the rules of *negotiorum gestio*.

Acquisition of ownership by the state without indemnification does not affect the rights of a bona fide third person listed in the land registry, so these remain in place.

270. BH 2013/274.
271. BH 2013/149.

Chapter 9. Acquisition of Ownership of Products

439. Any person who has a right in respect of a thing of another person, which entitles him to take possession of products, produce, or progeny, shall acquire ownership by separation if he has not previously acquired ownership thereof. If the entitled person does not possess the thing from which the product, produce, or progeny originates, he shall become the owner by taking possession thereof.

If the right of a person entitling him to acquire ownership of a product, produce, or progeny ceases before he acquires ownership thereof, such person may demand – in the absence of an agreement to the contrary – that the owner or the new holder provide compensation up to the value of the products, produce, or progeny under the principle of unjust enrichment, and in proportion to his work, and up to the extent of his expenses that cannot be recovered from elsewhere.

A possessor in good faith acquires ownership of products, produce, or progeny of a thing by separation up to the day on which he becomes mala fide or the object is reclaimed from him before a court or notary.

In the case of produce and progeny, a new thing is created primarily in a natural way, albeit not excluding human interaction. The term product in everyday use primarily refers to a thing produced through human labour; however, the Civil Code addresses manufacturing as a separate rule, so in this legislative context, product means exploited assets rather than a thing created through human labour.

440. The acquisition of ownership of products, produce, and progeny consists of two legal phases. On the one hand, somebody has a right to acquire ownership, while on the other hand, the authorized person takes the thing into possession. On account of the duality linked to the traditional acquisition of ownership in the event of a transfer, literature debates whether it is an original or derivative method of acquisition. The former is corroborated by the argument that the acquiring party must have a right to acquire ownership; in other words, this right must stem from somebody. However, a new, previously non-existent thing comes into existence when the product, produce, or progeny is created, which the acquiring party may acquire independently from the owner, based on the authorization ensuring the acquisition of rights, and that as such, it may qualify as an original method of acquisition.[272]

The Civil Code requires taking the asset into possession in order to acquire ownership. If the producing object is in possession of the party authorized to gain acquisition, the acquisition of ownership materializes via simple separation. Separation is the process through which the physical link between the object forming a constituent of the thing that produced it is broken, and the thing becomes independent. In this case, possession and the right of acquisition give rise to the acquiring person's ownership right. The right to acquisition may be founded on legal grounds such as these. For instance, taking a specific area into possession based on an option contract concluded for standing produce materializes when the buyer concludes a contract for services with the seller for the agricultural work and the harvesting of the

272. Menyhárd, *supra*, 250.

produce to be carried out. The specific area with the standing produce thus comes under the control of the person acquiring the ownership right, so the produce becomes the buyer's property upon separation.[273] A sharecropping contract may provide similarly adequate legal grounds; if such a contract is concluded, the produce's ownership right – if it was not produced on land owned by the contract grower – can only be acquired via separation.[274]

To acquire ownership, besides separation, the person authorized to make the acquisition must be acting in good faith and be exempt from any claims for surrendering the thing made through notarial or judicial avenues.

If the person authorized to make the acquisition does not have possession of the thing which produced the product, produce, or progeny at the time of separation, then the producing object must be taken into possession in order to acquire ownership of the product, produce, or progeny. This essentially means harvesting.

If the right of the person authorized to make the acquisition ceases before the product, produce, or progeny is created, the settlement must be addressed. If the person authorized to make the acquisition invests labour and expenses in creating the new thing, he may claim reimbursement from the owner or other persons authorized to make the acquisition according to the rules of unjust enrichment.

273. BH 2002/28.
274. BH 1998/607.

Chapter 10. Accretions

441. The owner of a parcel of land shall acquire ownership of everything that became part of the land subsequently, except if it belongs to another under any title. The rules governing accretion supplement the rule, which states that things that are constituents of the land share the legal fate of the real property. Accretion defines a clear rule with regard to things in such a constituent relationship with the real property, which prevails on a subsidiary basis. In the event that the object is linked in a constituent relationship to the real property through another statutory definition or legal transaction, such as building on land owned by someone else, incorporating construction, etc., the rules of accretion do not apply.

Part IV. Trust and Fiduciary Mechanisms

Chapter 1. Administration of Property: *Fiducia Cum Amico*

§1. Legal Practice Before the New Civil Code

442. Prior to the adoption of the new Civil Code, the property management contract was not an independent type of contract in the Hungarian Civil Code.[275] Given the contractual nature of property management, the creation of trustee rights, as independent rights in others' ownership, and its regulation in the Hungarian Civil Code is not resolved, either. The new Hungarian Civil Code changed this situation through the introduction of the fiduciary property management contract as an independent type of contract. It is important to note that the legal environment preceding the new Hungarian Civil Code also provided for legal instruments that allowed the implementation of property management in practice.[276] The property management contracts in the private sector contain a combination of substantive contractual elements regulated in the Hungarian Civil Code.[277] Accordingly, the property management contracts predominantly reveal characteristics attributable to agency contracts, contracting agreements and consignment contracts.

275. 'It is worth considering whether it is necessary and possible to devise general norms relating to the concession contract and property management contract in the Hungarian Civil Code.' Concept and subject of the new Civil Code text approved by Government Resolution No. 1003/2003. (I. 25.), which was published as a schedule to this resolution in issue 8 of 2003 of Magyar Közlöny (Official Journal), 109.

276. For property management contracts applied before the new Hungarian Civil Code and a discussion of these issues, *see* Dániel Deák, *A vagyonkezelés pénzügyi joga* (*Financial Law of Property Management*) (Dániel Deák ed., Research Report 1998); Norbert Csizmazia & István Sándor, *A bizalmi (fiduciárius) vagyonkezelés modelljei és a Ptk. reformja* (*Models of Fiduciary Property Management and the Reform of the Hungarian Civil Code*), 4 Polgári jogi kodifikáció 10 ff. (2002); István Sándor, *A vagyonkezelői jog szabályozása* (*Regulation of the Trustee Right*), 55 Gazdaság és Jog 3 ff. (2000).

277. For details relating to property management contracts applied in the private sector, *see* Ilona Németh & László Sík, *A vagyonkezelési szerződések típusai és biztosítékai* (*Types and Security of Property Management Contracts*), 42 Pénzügyi Szemle (1997); Dániel Deák, *A bizalmi vagyonkezelés jogi kérdéseiről* (*Legal Issues Concerning Fiduciary Property Management*), 8 Gazdaság és Jog (1995); Mónika Lukács, István Sándor & Brigitta Szűcs, *Új típusú szerződések és azok gyakorlata a gazdasági életben* (*New Types of Contracts and Their Use in the Economy*) 379 ff. (HVG-ORAC 2003).

Thus, in the legal environment regulated by the old Hungarian Civil Code, the property management contract concluded in the private sector was in itself insufficient to create a right in rem to the entrusted private property for the trustee vis-á-vis third parties, within the contractual relationship between natural persons. This resulted in the weakness of the trustee's economic position, as the trustee was not allowed to dispose of the entrusted thing (or property), sell it in his own name, encumber it within the scope of property management, or assert a legitimate claim for property protection. And if the trustee acquired ownership of the trust property under contract, the settlor could only assert in personam claims against the trustee, while the rights of the beneficiary vis-á-vis third parties were determined solely by the rules of the third-party beneficiary contract. Thus, in such cases, neither the settlor nor the beneficiary could take action against third parties with respect to the trust property. Act CXX of 2009, the Civil Code, approved by Parliament but not entering into force on account of the decision of the Constitutional Court, was the first legislation that tried to regulate property management as an independent type of contract.

§2. The Legal Background

443. The new Civil Code regulates the fiduciary asset management contract (in Hungarian: 'bizalmi vagyonkezelési szerződés') in Chapter XLII, within the scope of agency-type contracts.[278] The Act LXI of 2017 modified the Civil Code and brought some minor changes in the rules of this legal institution. The modifications were drafted as a result of practice in the previous three years. The concept of this new type of contract was drawn up on the basis of the model of the trust in English law and that of the Treuhand in German law.[279] The introduction of fiduciary asset management on a legislative level is necessitated by strong, current demand in the economy. We have observed that several Hungarian investors chose legal regimes of other countries because the institution of the trust provided them with a better legal and economic solution. The Chief Codification Committee of the Civil Code codified fiduciary asset management under contract law, emphasizing, however, the application of the legal instrument of the transfer of ownership, based on the trust-like model. Under the rules of the new Hungarian Civil Code, the fiduciary property management contract is an *in personam* legal instrument that implicitly carries substantial in rem effects. The new Hungarian Civil Code sets out a contractual

278. In connection with the Hungarian regulation in English language, *see* particularly Istán Sándor, *The Fiduciary Property Management and the Trust. Historical and Comparative Law Analysis* 384 ff. (HVGORAC 2015.); István Sándor, *Different Types of Trust from an Ownership Aspect*, 6 Eur. Rev. Private L. 1189 ff. (2016); Ákos Menyhei, *Estate Planning in Hungary: Private Foundation or Trust?*, 21 Trust & Trustees 650 ff. (2015); István Sándor, *The New Hungarian Fiduciary Asset Management Contract (Trust) from Comparative Aspect*, 12 US-China L. Rev. 600 ff. (2015); Charles E. Rounds & István Illés, *Is a Hungarian Trust a Clone of the Anglo-American Trust, or Just a Type of Contract? Parsing The Asset-Management Provisions of the New Hungarian Civil Code*, 6 George Mason U. School L., J. Intl. Commercial L. 153 ff. (2015), Borbála Kolozs, *An Overview of Hungarian Trusts*, 9 Tax Notes Intl. 771 ff. (2015).

279. Lajos Vékás, *Az új Polgári Törvénykönyv Bizottsági Javaslata magyarázatokkal.* (*Committee Proposal for the New Civil Code with Explanations*) 453 (Lajos Vékás ed., Complex 2012).

arrangement, and its validity is bound to a written contract. The regulation is of a general scope, and several details are regulated in two separate pieces of legislation.[280] We have to remark that Hungary did not ratify the Hague Convention; therefore, foreign trusts are not recognized.[281]

444. A new law was enacted in 2019 in Hungary on Asset Management Foundations (hereinafter referred to as: 'AMF'), which was amended in the summer and at the end of 2020. The aim of the legislator was to create a legal background for a new type of asset management where a foundation can fulfil this role, in addition to the existing rules of trust (fiduciary asset management) regulations.

§3. General Rules of the Fiduciary Asset Management Contract

445. As a general rule, regulation is dispositive; contracting is principally for consideration. Under the fiduciary asset management contract, the trustee has the duty to manage the property transferred to his ownership by the settlor in his own name for the benefit of the beneficiary, for which the settlor is obliged to pay a fee.[282] The managed asset can be things, rights, and claims as well.[283] If the settlor and trustee are one and the same person, fiduciary asset management is established by the irrevocable unilateral declaration of the settlor set out in a public instrument. A legal relationship of property management settled by testament is established by the trustee's acceptance of his appointment to such position under the terms set out in the testament. Rules of the fiduciary property management contract are applied as necessary to fiduciary asset management established by a unilateral legal act. Rules of the agency contract are applicable as necessary to fiduciary asset management.

I. Contractual Status of the Settlor

446. The rights of the settlor extend to the definition of the settled property and the appointment of the trustee.[284] This, however, is a bilateral legal act, as it also requires the acceptance of appointment by the trustee. The settlor transfers ownership, rights, and claims or other negotiable goods to the trustee and the settlor issues

280. Such details are regulated in Act XV of 2014 on Trustees and the regulation of their activity, and in Government Decree No. 87/2014. (III. 20.) on certain rules concerning the financial security of fiduciary property management undertakings.

281. Convention on the Law Applicable to Trusts and on their Recognition/Convention relative à la loi applicable au trust et à sa reconnaissance.

282. Pursuant to s. 6:310(1) of the Civil Code.

283. In connection with the regulation, *see* details in Isvtán Sándor, *A bizalmi vagyonkezelés és a trust: Jogtörténeti és összehasonlító jogi elemzés* (*Fiduciary Property Management and the Trust: Historical and Comparative Analysis of Law*) (2nd ed., HVG-ORAC 2017).

284. In English law, three factors need to be defined with reasonable certainty for the establishment of a trust: the trust property, the beneficiary, and the subject of the trust. Alastair Hudson, *Equity and Trusts* 91 ff. (Routledge 2013[7]).

a declaration as to the manner of the management of the property. In the legal relationship of property management, it is also possible to set out other conditions, such as its duration, which is a maximum of fifty years, terms, right of unilateral termination, remuneration of the trustee, appointment of additional trustees, regulation of the delegation of other agents, and the beneficiary's right to transfer. The settlor reserves the right to remove the trustee, appoint a new trustee, replace the beneficiary, modify given parts of the settlor's declaration, and determine or modify the duration of property management.

The settlor may monitor the activity of the trustee falling within the scope of property management, but the costs of such monitoring are incurred by the settlor. It is a mandatory rule that the settlor may not instruct the trustee. The settlor, however, may remove the trustee from office at any time and simultaneously appoint another trustee.

As a general rule, the settlor designates the beneficiary and the conditions that give rise to and terminate the rights of the beneficiary. The beneficiary may also be named by reference to a group of beneficiaries. The settlor may choose to pass on all or part of the trust property to himself, his successors, or designated third parties under certain circumstances or after a certain period of time. The declaration of the trustee as an exclusive beneficiary is void.

II. Rights and Obligations of the Trustee

447. Act XV of 2014 distinguishes professional and ad hoc fiduciary asset management. Only undertakings are allowed to contract on a regular basis for more than one fiduciary property management, and they may carry out fiduciary asset management only in possession of the licence issued by the Central Bank prior to the start of such activity. The professional fiduciary asset managing company can be only a limited liability company or private limited company with a registered office in the territory of Hungary, or the branch – registered in Hungary – of an undertaking based in another contracting state of the Agreement on the European Economic Area, or a law office.

Except for law offices, the fiduciary asset management company may not carry out any activity other than asset management, and its name must make reference to property management. The company must hold the licences required for such activity. The fiduciary asset management company is required to fulfil strict staff and equipment requirements to receive the authorization of the Central Bank.

The fiduciary asset management undertaking has the burden of proving that it duly performed its fiduciary asset management contracts in accordance with statutory requirements for the utmost benefit of its client, in particular. The fiduciary asset management company is obliged to inform the future party of the contract of the risks defined by law prior to the conclusion of the property management contract. In addition, the fiduciary asset management company has the duty to provide information in writing on a monthly basis. If no changes are made to the original information, it is sufficient to make reference to such fact in subsequent information. The fiduciary asset management company is required to maintain records on the fiduciary asset management relationships to support the traceability of fiduciary property management, administrative controls, and administrative assessments of property.

In case of ad hoc fiduciary asset management relationship, the contract or deed shall be registered by the Central Bank. The omission of registration does not affect the validity of the legal relationship, but it causes serious tax and stamp duty consequences. We have to note that the data in the registry is not public, and only courts and authorities specified by law may get information from it.

448. Property management is essentially built on trust, particularly in relation to the selection of the trustee that is beyond their commercial relationship; the relationship between the principal and the trustee is governed predominantly by aspects of the agency contract and less by a general contracting agreement. Under the contract, the trustee may not be the sole beneficiary. The settlor and the trustee, however, may be one and the same person. The trustee has the duty to provide information, manage the property as instructed in the declaration of the settlor, avoid conflicts of interest, and manage the property separately from his own.

If the trustee is authorized to designate the beneficiary under the contract, the trustee has the right to determine the share of the beneficiary.

Due to stricter requirements arising from the fiduciary nature of the legal relationship, the trustee has the duty to act with utmost consideration of the interests of the beneficiary. The trustee has the duty to protect the trust property against foreseeable risks in a commercially reasonable manner.

449. The management of the property includes the exercise of rights arising from ownership, other rights and claims transferred to the trustee, and the fulfilment of obligations arising therefrom. The trustee may dispose of the assets belonging to the trust property under the conditions and within limits set out in the contract. If the trustee breaches his above obligations and illicitly transfers assets belonging to the trust property to a third party, the settlor and beneficiary have the right to reclaim these for the benefit of the trust property if the third party did not purchase the assets in good faith or for consideration. This rule is applicable as necessary to the illicit encumbrance of the trust property.

450. The trustee has a duty to keep confidential any fact, information and other data he becomes aware of during his appointment as trustee or in relation thereto. Such obligation is without prejudice to the establishment of the trusteeship and remains in effect after the termination of fiduciary property management. The settlor and his successors may grant exemption from the confidentiality obligation.

451. The trustee has the duty to inform the settlor or the beneficiary of the trust property upon their request. Such information must cover, in particular, the actual and foreseeable increase in the trust property, the particular assets of the trust property and their value, and commitments charged to the trust property. Upon request, the trustee has the duty to account for the trust property and settle accounts with the settlor and beneficiary. Costs incurred in connection with the provision of information and the payment of invoices are borne by the settlor and beneficiary.

452. The trustee is liable to the settlor and beneficiary for the breach of his obligations in accordance with general rules of liability for damages. If the trustee carries out his duties gratuitously, rules of liability for damages are applicable to his breach of gratuitous contracts. The settlor and beneficiary may claim the management of any financial gain as part of the trust property, which was realized through the trustee's breach of his obligations arising from property management.

453. If the trustee carries out his duties gratuitously, he may claim reimbursement for his regular costs. The trustee may satisfy his claims for the payment of his fees and reasonable costs and other claims arising from property management directly from the trust property.

454. The trustee is liable for the fulfilment of the undertaken obligations with the trust property. The trustee assumes unlimited liability with his own property for the satisfaction of claims arising from commitments charged to the trust property if these cannot be satisfied from the trust property, and the other party was not and could not have been aware that the commitments of the trustee exceed the limits of the trust property.

455. If the settlor appoints several trustees, the actions and decisions of the trustees are taken jointly. If the trustees are also liable with their own property for their commitments, they assume joint and several liabilities for joint decisions toward third parties. Several trustees assume joint and several liabilities toward the settlor and beneficiary for the breach of obligations arising from fiduciary property management.

If the settlor dies or ceases without a successor, and there are no other settlors to the trust property, the court may recall the trustee from his office upon request of the beneficiary and simultaneously appoint another trustee if the trustee seriously breached the contract. Several beneficiaries may exercise such right jointly, provided any of them may request the court to terminate the appointment of the trustee and appoint a new trustee. The court may not appoint a person as trustee, against whom all beneficiaries object.

456. The rights of the trustee are governed by the legal instrument applicable to property management and rules set out in the given property management contract. As a general rule, rights of use and disposition are also conferred on the trustee in the case of property management contracts; that is, the trustee has the right to:

- use and operate the managed thing;
- possess the managed thing, resort to protection of possession under the appropriate title;
- enjoy, that is, utilize the managed thing either by himself or with the collaboration of a subcontractor or agent, if he is authorized to employ such third parties under the property management contract;
- right of alienation (e.g., in the case of portfolio-type asset management);
- right of encumbrance (establishment of, e.g., a lien on assets belonging to the property);

- right of destruction or, rather, right of processing and use (e.g., an entire plant is entrusted, together with its raw materials, and these are processed in the regular manufacturing process).

The issue of rights conferred on the trustee raises an interesting question in relation to the management of company shares. In this case, the trustee may be entitled to exercise membership or shareholder rights.

457. Due diligence is generally applicable to property management contracts. Rules pertaining to remuneration, however, are not necessarily subject to this approach. If, in the process of utilizing the trust property, the parties do not set out the amount of yields at the time of contracting but only the diligence of the trustee, the trustee is required to follow due diligence under the contract to ensure the satisfactory performance of the contract. If, however, the fiduciary asset management contract sets out specific yields and profits, remuneration may be linked to these. Under the asset management contract, the trustee may not be instructed to preserve the assets but must ensure that the property entrusted to him preserves its value. In such cases, the asset management contract fulfils the function of consignment or portfolio management. Obviously, these three elements may be combined in the property management contract; the trustee is obliged to follow due diligence, he receives separate remuneration when realizing a certain level of profits, and, as the case may be, he may sell the entrusted assets on the basis of general or single authorization.

The remuneration of the trustee may be implemented under different schemes.

III. Legal Status of the Trust Property

458. The Civil Code sets out rules on the separation of property.[285] The trust property constitutes property separate from the trustee's own property and other property managed by him, which the trustee is obliged to register separately. The parties' derogation from this rule is void. Assets registered as property managed separately from the trustee's own property and other properties managed by him are deemed to fall within the scope of trust property until proven otherwise. Any assets substituting the managed assets, insurance indemnities, damages, or other value, and profits thereon constitute part of the trust property, whether registered or not. Assets not registered by the trustee as comprising part of the trust property are deemed to be the private property of the trustee until proven otherwise.

The spouse, life partner, personal creditors of the trustee, and creditors of other properties managed by the trustee may not lay claim to the assets of the trust property. The trust property does not constitute part of the trustee's inheritance. The beneficiary and the settlor may take action against the spouse, life partner, personal creditors of the trustee, and creditors of other properties managed by the trustee to secure the separation of the trust property.

285. Article 6:312 of the Civil Code.

The indirect object of the asset management contract may be securities, company shareholdings, real property, personal property, and other rights and claims. Asset management relating to securities essentially comprises a special area of law applicable to securities traders, which we are not exploring in depth.

The management of company shareholdings is a contractual arrangement essentially applicable to companies with share capital, including quotas in limited liability companies and shares in companies limited by shares. Obviously, this is feasible in any case where the transfer of company shares is possible.

IV. Legal Status of the Beneficiary

459. Under an important rule regulating the rights of the beneficiary, the beneficiary may claim the distribution of the trust property and its profits from the trustee under the contract. The creditors of the beneficiary may assert claims for the assets of the beneficiary when the distribution of such assets or the profits thereon to the beneficiary is due.

The beneficiary may also monitor the activity of the trustee falling within the scope of asset management; the costs thereof are incurred by the beneficiary. The beneficiary does not have the right to instruct the trustee, either.

V. Legal Relationships Between the Parties

460. The relationship between the settlor and trustee (also) constitutes the basis of other legal relationships. This is where the trustee's responsibilities and fiduciary obligations, his level of diligence and loyalty are defined. The Civil Code regulates the settlor's monitoring right, right of exemption from confidentiality, right to recall but expressly prohibits him from issuing instructions. With respect to loyalty, the duty of the trustee not to compete is of central relevance. The regulation of rules on the use of the trust property is also important.

461. The beneficiary has the right to legally enforce the fulfilment of the trustee's obligations. Within this context, it is necessary to examine rights exercised by the beneficiary against the obligor in the case of civil third-party beneficiary contracts. The beneficiary has the right to claim the trust property and profits thereon to receive information, while the trustee is entitled to remuneration and the reimbursement of his costs. Similar to the settlor, the beneficiary does not have the right to instruct the trustee.

462. There is no legal relationship between the settlor and the beneficiary. If the settlor is also a beneficiary, obviously, his capacity is relevant in terms of exercising particular rights.

463. In respect of the relationship between several settlors, it is necessary to determine whether they assume joint or joint and several liabilities. This is not regulated by the Civil Code; thus, general rules are applicable.

Joint and several liabilities similarly to Anglo-Saxon law are governing in relation to several trustees. Among the rules of succession, the new Hungarian Civil Code adopts the right of survivorship of the other trustees in relation to the ownership of the ceased trustee.

The relationship between several beneficiaries is principally determined by the contract concluded between the settlor and the trustee. However, the limited possibility of pupillary substitution should be taken into account in relation to succession after the death of the beneficiary.

The rules of the Civil Code do not preclude the transfer of the trust property and the profits thereon from one beneficiary to another upon the fulfilment of certain conditions or after a given time.

§4. The Legal Position of Creditors

464. In terms of liability, the Civil Code does not allow the creditors of the settlor and trustee to assert claims for the trust property. The creditors of the beneficiary, however, may apply for execution of the property, notwithstanding that the distribution of the managed assets and profits thereon to the beneficiary is not due yet. This rule was at first modified by Act XV of 2014 to the extent that the creditors of the settlor might terminate the asset management contract if the judicial enforcement procedure launched against the settlor was unsuccessful or did not produce any results within a foreseeable time. I wish to note that this rule was drawing heavy criticism in Hungarian legal literature, as it ignored differences in time between the exercise of the right of termination and the insolvency of the settlor. Therefore, this rule was repealed, and the modification of the Civil Code with the Act LXI of 2017 made it clear that the settlor may decide to establish the trust as irrevocable. If the settlor decides so, then his creditors have no right to terminate the contract, even in the judicial enforcement procedure. Only the creditors whose claim existed before the establishment of asset management have the right to the managed property and only in case of fraudulent transfer by the settlor. If these conditions are proven, the fiduciary asset management relationship will not have an effect in relation to the creditors of the settlor.

As a general rule, the trustee is liable with the trust property for the fulfilment of his obligations. However, the trustee assumes unlimited liability with his own property toward third parties if their claims cannot be satisfied from the trust property, and the third parties were not and could not have been aware that the commitments of the trustee exceed the limits of the trust property.

I. The Creditors of the Managed Property

465. If the trustee conducts business with the managed property, and third parties' claim arise from it which cannot be covered by the trust property, then the creditors, as a general rule, may not seek satisfaction of their claims against the trustee. The trustee, however, exceptionally assumes unlimited liability with all of his own property if claims asserted for the trust property cannot be satisfied, and the other party was not and could not have been aware that the commitments of the trustee exceed the limits of the trust property.

II. Relationship Between the Settlor and the Settlor's Creditors

466. As a general rule, the creditors of the settlor may not lay claim to the trust property unless the settlor is also a beneficiary. In respect of the contract between the settlor and the trustee, the creditors of the settlor may assert claims in accordance with the modern rules of *actio Pauliana*, under the general rules of the law of obligations. A fiduciary asset management contract (or unilateral juridical act) that partially or fully concealed assets that would satisfy the claim of the settlor's creditor is ineffective towards that creditor if the trustee was acting in bad faith or had obtained gratuitous benefit from that contract. According to the definition in the Civil Code, it is a contract aimed at concealing assets if someone enters into a contract with his/her relative or a legal person in which he/she has a majority control. Furthermore, if a legal person concludes such a contract with its member or executive officer or his relative, bad faith and gratuitousness shall be presumed. Bad faith and gratuitousness shall also be presumed with regard to contracts concluded between legal persons that are controlled by the same natural or legal person, even in the absence of direct or indirect majority control. Upon request from the settlor's creditor, the trustee shall be required to allow satisfaction from the acquired asset or enforcement against that asset. Finally, if the trustee transferred the managed asset through a contract aimed at concealing assets or lost it in bad faith, the trustee shall be personally liable towards the settlor's creditor up to the value of the acquired asset.[286]

III. Legal Relationship Between the Trustee and His Personal Creditors

467. Pursuant to regulation in the Civil Code, which corresponds to the rules of common law, in the event of the trustee's insolvency, the creditors of the trustee may not lay claim to the trust property. This rule is also applicable to the spouse, partner, and successors of the trustee. This regulation provides asset partitioning for the trustee, which resembles the Anglo-Saxon trust rules.

IV. Legal Relationship Between the Beneficiary and His Creditors

468. The creditors of the beneficiary clearly have the right to take action against the trustee, quasi under the legal title of the beneficiary. This is possible under the Civil Code if the right of the beneficiary is due.

It is difficult to determine the claim of the beneficiary's creditors in relation to the beneficiary's claim in the trust property if the trustee holds discretionary power with

286. Civil Code, s. 6:120.

respect to the management of the property because the claim of the beneficiary is also uncertain and unascertainable in such a case.

§5. The Possibility of Tracing

469. The settlor and the beneficiary have the right to take action against third parties to whom the trustee transferred property in breach of the asset management contract, gratuitously or in bad faith. Such regulation essentially corresponds to the rules of common law tracing in English law.

In the case of a third party purchasing property gratuitously or in breach of the requirement of good faith, the Hungarian Civil Code does not provide any guidelines as to whether the settlor or the beneficiary may take action if the property is mixed with the property of the purchaser, its object changes, or the property is transferred further to other persons. Under the principle of equitable tracing in English law, this is possible under certain circumstances. Case law will eventually demonstrate the specific cases in which the claims of the settlor and beneficiary can be enforced.

§6. Termination of the Relationship

470. The fiduciary asset management relationship is terminated:

- if no trust property is left;
- three months after resignation, if the trustee resigns from his position;
- on the termination date of the trustee's engagement, if there is no trustee to manage the trust property for over three months;
- on the date of the settlor's death, if he was the sole beneficiary;
- if the settlor terminates the fiduciary asset management contract.

471. When resigning, the trustee has the duty to act with utmost consideration of the interests of the beneficiary. Under a mandatory rule, the legal relationship of fiduciary property management established indefinitely or for a fixed period of more than fifty years is terminated after fifty years.

Fiduciary asset management is not terminated if the settlor becomes the successor to the trustee. Fiduciary asset management, however, is not terminated upon the death or cessation of the settlor, trustee, or beneficiary.

Upon termination of fiduciary asset management, the trustee remains subject to the accounting and information obligation imposed under effective fiduciary asset management. If the termination of fiduciary asset management poses a risk to the trust property until the settlement of accounts, the trustee has the duty to take the necessary measures required under fiduciary asset management.

Upon termination of his appointment, the trustee has the duty to pass on the trust property to another or new trustee appointed by the settlor, otherwise to the settlor. If the trustee ceases without a successor, the trust property is passed on to another or new trustee appointed by the settlor; otherwise, it is transferred back to the settlor upon cessation of the trustee. The obligations encumbering the trust property are passed on to another or new trustee as part of the trust property; otherwise, they are passed on to the settlor. In case of more than one settlor, the settlors become entitled to the trust property transferred back to them in the proportion of their contribution to the trust property, and they assume the obligations transferred back to them as part of the trust property in the same proportion; they assume joint and several liabilities toward creditors of the trust property. If the contract provides for the distribution of the property in the form of succession in the position of the trustee, the rules defined above are appropriately applicable to the transfer of rights and obligations to the successor.

§7. The Asset Management Foundation

472. The special regulations for AMFs are set out in Act XIII of 2019, and the rules of the Civil Code also apply to some extent.[287] It is important to highlight that the asset management legal relationship established by the AMF does not fall within the scope of the law regulating fiduciary asset management (trust) activities; thus, the legal relationship does not have to be registered by the National Bank of Hungary, for example, unlike the ad hoc trust relationships, and an AMF does not need to be licensed by the National Bank of Hungary, like in the case of profit-oriented trustee companies. Another distinct advantage of the AMF is that it cannot only manage the assets contributed to it by the founder, but it may also enter into a trust contract with third parties and manage several separate assets. The only limitation of this is that the purpose of the trust relationship with third parties must be the same as the original objectives of the foundation. The provisions of the Civil Code concerning trust contracts also apply to these trust relationships; therefore, the trust properties are separated and enjoy protection against creditors of the settlor, the AMF and the beneficiaries.

473. Two subtypes of AMF are regulated, one for the benefit of private beneficiaries and one for public interest. In the case of a public interest AMF, the beneficiaries are not pre-determined persons; the activities of the foundation are aimed at achieving public purpose goals. The law exhaustively defines these activities, and the AMFs performing public tasks are listed in the act as the following: financing or support of educational, higher education, research, health, charitable, social, family, child and youth protection, cultural or sports activities or the maintenance and operation of institutions providing such activities are considered to be public interest objectives. An AMF is considered to be in the public interest if three conjunctive conditions are met: it has been established for public interest purposes listed in

287. In connection with the regulation *see* István Sándor, *Key Features of Private Foundations in a Comparative Law Approach: With Special Emphasize on Asset Management*, European Review of Private Law, Vol. 29, No. 6 (2021): 885–912. István Sándor, *The Transformation of Foundation Law in Hungary, with Particular Regard to Private Foundations*, Trust & Trustees, Vol. 29, No. 6 (July 2023): 553–560.

the act, the range of its beneficiaries is open, and the founder has requested that it be declared in the public interest. According to practice so far, mainly universities have been set up as public interest AMFs in Hungary.

474. Both an existing or a newly established foundation may conduct asset management activities, provided the court registers it as an AMF. AMFs can be established by the unilateral declaration of the founder, who can be a natural or a legal person, domiciled either in Hungary or outside the country. The founder can design the operating rules of the AMF in its charter quite freely. The founder shall provide the AMF with assets corresponding to at least HUF 600 million, which must be made available to the foundation prior to the submission of the foundation's application for registration. In determining the minimum initial assets of AMFs, the legislator assumed that high capital was essential for such foundations to operate. The initial assets must be listed in the deed of foundation in a manner enabling their individual identification. If the founding rights are exercised by the executive body of the AMF, the board of trustees and the founder fail to furnish the part of the assets allocated to the foundation above the minimum capital not yet made available to the foundation by the set deadline; the foundation is entitled to demand payment. If the founder exercises the founding rights and does not fulfil the obligation to make the property available, despite a written request of the board of trustees, the board of trustees is entitled to exercise the founding rights until this happens. The founder may also specify in the deed the amount below which the assets of AMF may not fall; this may not be less than the minimum capital, and in the absence of a definition, the minimum capital shall be considered as such. Below, we look at the AMFs for private usage.

475. As a general rule, an AMF may be established to manage the assets ordered by the founder and the proceeds thereof for the performance of the tasks specified in the charter and for the distribution of assets to the person or persons designated as beneficiaries. One main advantage of an AMF is that it can manage not only the assets contributed by the founder but also enter into other trust relationships with third-party settlors, without any administrative registration obligation. The asset management relationship may be established for an indefinite period, i.e., it is not subject to the general limit of fifty years for trust relationships in Hungary.

476. The founder appoints a board of trustees, which consists of at least three natural persons, but may decide to entrust the task of the board to only one person as well. The founder may vest the founding rights to the board of trustees in the memorandum of association, and in such a case, co-opting may also take place in this body in the event of a vacancy. The board of trustees exercises the founding rights in certain cases in the manner specified by law. If the founding rights are exercised by the board of trustees, the board of trustees, together with the supervisory board, decides on the appointment of the members and chairman of the board of trustees and also the supervisory board. The decision to recall members of the board of trustees and the supervisory board or the chairman of the foundation may be made in the same way as their appointment provided that the right of recall may be subject to conditions or restricted in the memorandum. If the founder establishes the

AMF with a unilateral declaration, then the memorandum may provide that the founder reserves the right to give instructions to the board of trustees. In addition, the election of a supervisory board of at least three natural persons – or a foundation asset supervisor (protector) acting under its authority – and the appointment of a permanent auditor are also mandatory. Furthermore, the charter may lay down qualifications and other professional requirements for the chairman and members of the board of trustees and the supervisory board. The novelty of the regulation is the obligatory position of the protector if the founding rights are exercised by the board of trustees. The auditor of the foundation has the right to inspect and give opinions and operate legally; he may even initiate legal supervision proceedings at the court of registration.

477. Within the scope of the objective of the AMF, the assets of the foundation shall be used to provide services of pecuniary value to benefit the parties designated as beneficiaries in the deed of foundation or, in the absence of such provision of the deed of foundation, by the appropriate body of the foundation.[288] The designated beneficiary shall not be entitled to raise claims against the foundation unless the deed of foundation identifies the beneficiary, specifies the services the beneficiary is entitled to, and the date of performance in a manner required for the performance, or the board of trustees has decided to provide benefits to the beneficiary, communicated this decision to the beneficiary, and the beneficiary has accepted the conditions of receiving the benefits.[289]

478. The charter of the AMF must set out the basic objectives and principles of the management and use of the foundation's assets, but the founder may also attach the investment regulations to the articles of association as part of this. The investment regulations must include a definition of the foundation's asset portfolio, as well as the risk management and decision-making methods applicable for investments. The founder can ensure the flexibility of the operation of the trust fund by empowering the board of trustees to amend the memorandum of association. The founder may specify in the memorandum of association the amount below which the assets of the AMF may not fall; this may not be less than the minimum capital.

479. A private AMF may be dissolved at the request of the founder exercising its right of founder. If the founder makes an application to that effect, the registry court shall therefore establish the cause of the foundation's termination in civil non-litigation. The termination of the foundation shall not affect the fulfilment of obligations already established and due in favour of the beneficiaries. The AMF shall also be wound up if its assets do not reach the minimum amount of capital for three full years, as this shall be deemed an impediment to the foundation achieving its objective. We have to remark that the AMF may not be transformed into another legal person. The foundation may only merge with another foundation and may only be divided into foundations.[290]

288. Hungarian Civil Code Art. 3:385.
289. Hungarian Civil Code Art. 3:387.
290. Hungarian Civil Code s. 3:402(1).

480. The introduction of the AMF in Hungarian private law is another significant step towards adopting asset management schemes established abroad. As a result of the flexible regulation, the AMF may be suitable for managing both Hungarian and foreign family assets and for developing well-considered asset planning and generational asset transfer to preserve them. Finally, it should be noted that there are very favourable tax rules associated with operating AMFs.

§8. Some Comparative Remarks

481. We describe below the main areas where Hungarian fiduciary asset management varies from that of the Anglo-Saxon institution of the trust.

Under the new Hungarian Civil Code, the fiduciary asset management contract mostly resembles the express trust. Conditions give rise to a resulting trust only in exceptional cases,[291] while constructive trust and charitable trust are not regulated. This is, to a certain extent, understandable, as under Hungarian private law, these legal situations are regulated by the institutions of unjust enrichment, foundations, and public donations.

The fiduciary asset management contract must be made in writing, while the Anglo-Saxon trust may be created orally or by implied conduct. In view of the fact that fiduciary asset management is a new legal instrument in Hungarian law, we believe it is reasonable that the contract is bound to a written form to avoid any legal uncertainties.

The new Hungarian Civil Code, after its modification, sets out expressis verbis that the settlor has the right to terminate fiduciary asset management, while in Anglo-Saxon law, the settlor retains this option during his lifetime if he laid this down in the deed of trust.

Under the new Hungarian Civil Code, as a general rule, fiduciary asset management is a contract for consideration, while Anglo-Saxon law presumes gratuity unless provided otherwise. Since fiduciary asset management was drawn up according to the model of the agency contract in Hungarian law, this may be the reason for its regulation as principally a contract for consideration.

Under the new Hungarian Civil Code, the fiduciary asset management contract has a maximum duration of fifty years. A time limit is also applied in English law, with the exception of the charitable trust. International trends, however, increasingly suggest a loosening and elimination of time limits.

According to the principle derived from the *Saunders v. Vautier* case,[292] the beneficiary is entitled to the distribution of the trust property if he is of legal age and does not breach the interests of other beneficiaries. This rule is worth considering for possible application in Hungarian legal practice.

With regard to the fiduciary asset management contract under the new Hungarian Civil Code, legal practice will likely resolve many issues currently not regulated by statutory rules. Such issues include the trustee's option of modifying the rules of the contract if this is necessary in the interest of the beneficiary. The definition of the

291. *See* s. 6:321(3) of the Civil Code.
292. *Saunders v. Vautier* [(1841), Cr. & Ph. 240; 4 Beav 115].

eligibility conditions applicable to the position of ad hoc trustee also raises several questions. The trustee is obliged to carry out his duties in person; that is, additional requirements may be applied to him through further implementing regulations of the new Hungarian Civil Code.

Chapter 2. Security: *Fiducia Cum Creditore* (*See Also* Parts I, II, and V)

482. Regarding the fiduciary transfer of ownership, a practice emerged in the 1990s in Hungary whereby – similarly to the transfer of ownership for collateral purposes – it was defined as collateral for satisfying services arising from contractual relationships, primarily loan transactions. The primary economic justification of this practice lies in the fact that it offers the most efficient form of enforcement of the creditor's claim in the event of the debtor's default. In practice, the enforcement of rights based on lien rules is time-consuming, cumbersome, and bureaucratic, and if the debtor was a business organization, the outcome was particularly uncertain if the debtor was under liquidation proceedings. As a result, sales contracts or agreements granting a purchase option concluded for collateral purposes offered a good alternative to liens. The use of purchase options in a different manner from their original purpose created a significant challenge for courts, particularly in terms of the validity of such use.

483. Different opinions emerged in judicial practice. Certain courts qualified the imposition of fiduciary collateral as explicitly invalid, arguing that they are contrary to the prohibition of *lex commissoria*. In this regard, rulings were brought where the conversion of the fiduciary clause to a lien was ordered. Meanwhile, other courts deemed such clauses as being valid, provided that the person providing the collateral had the intention of transferring ownership. Third, other court rulings qualified the establishment of fiduciary collateral as valid if the creditor settled with the debtor in the event of enforcement of the collateral and took the collateral into account proportionately in the principal debt.[293]

484. When preparing the new Civil Code, the Codification Committee argued in favour of regarding repurchase and purchase rights as valid credit collateral, initially citing the positions that accepted fiduciary collateral as valid and based on the significant financial market role of leasebacks.[294] The 2003 concept still contained the rules governing purchase rights for credit collateral purposes, as well as the introduction of fiduciary asset management.[295] Subsequently, however, in the Codification Committee's draft published on 31 December 2006, the proposal opted instead to regard agreements on the transfer of ownership right for collateral purposes and the establishment of purchase rights as void. Later, the draft drawn up by the Ministry of Justice and Administration permitted the transfer of ownership for collateral purposes under certain conditions, emphasizing, in particular, the proportionality in value.

293. In connection with the judicial practice, *see* István Sándor, *Anmerkungen zur Konkurrenz von Verträgen über die Begründung eines Optionsrecht und des Pfandrechts*, in Magyar kereskedelmi jogi évkönyv (*Hungarian Commercial Law Yearbook*) Vol. 2, 209 ff. (Zoltán Csehi ed., Pázmány Péter Katolikus Egyetem 2010).

294. *The Concept of the New Civil Code*, 15 Magyar Közlöny, Vol. II (Hungarian Gazette) (2002): 145.

295. *The Concept and Theme of the New Civil Code*, 8 Magyar Közlöny (Hungarian Gazette) (2003): 106.

485. There was much debate in Hungarian legal literature on whether the use of fiduciary collateral in practice can be regarded as valid.

The establishment of purchase rights serving as collateral was addressed primarily by István Gárdos and Péter Gárdos. The authors cite five core arguments on why such contracts have no rationale in Hungarian legal practice. The authors cite the fact that there is an absence of publicity, which is adverse for third parties, the settlement obligation stemming from the prohibition of *lex commissoria* is not satisfied, and the purchase price remains below the market value in accordance with conservative lending policy when the purchase option is allowed. The option right can be transferred – or more specifically, the exercise of the option right is transferable – to a third party who will have no interest in selling the thing at its market value, and if the purchase right is exercised, other creditor claims may be averted because the thing at issue is no longer included in the liquidation assets from the time of exercising the purchase right.[296] The legislator does not fully regulate the relationship of a lien to other legal institutions, which gives rise to legal uncertainty. István Gárdos and Péter Gárdos cite the new Dutch Civil Code on the basis of which collateral purposes do not constitute valid legal grounds for the transfer of ownership.[297] The authors also highlighted that an option is a speculative transaction, so the requirement for equivalency in value between service and consideration does not apply in the case of a purchase right; moreover, in the case of collateral transactions, a transaction of this nature, not associated with settlement and containing elements of chance cannot be allowed and is alien to the collateral purpose.[298] The Expert Committee of the new Hungarian Civil Code argues in favour of converting the transfer of ownership for collateral purposes and the establishment of a purchase option into a lien.[299] In the commentary to the pertaining section (on liens), Norbert Csizmazia and István Gárdos first criticize the exclusion of publicity and also argue that the rules on liens afford adequate regulation of the topic of settlement in terms of the enforcement of rights.

László Leszkoven takes a contrary stance, emphasizing that a purchase right concluded for collateral purposes must be distinguished from the transfer of ownership for collateral purposes, and the establishment of a purchase right for collateral purposes does not afford more. At the same time, if the holder of the purchase right acquires the thing at a realistic price when exercising its purchase right – and not only to offset the current debt arising from the loan transaction – there is no prejudice to the debtor's economic interests. According to Leszkoven, a purchase right does not necessarily afford a more advantageous opportunity to the right holder (the creditor) in the course of the liquidation procedure because if the purchase right is exercised later than the start of the procedure, there will be no opportunity to offset in terms of paying the purchase price. Leszkoven argues in favour of the rationale of purchase for the purpose of collateral, citing that the legal transaction under the

296. Gárdos & Gárdos, *Az engedményezés supra*, 18 ff.

297. Section 3:84(3) of the Dutch Civil Code. István Gárdos & Péter Gárdos, *Ismét a fiduciárius biztosítékokról* (*About the Fiduciary Collaterals Again*), 13 Gazdaság és Jog 14 (2005).

298. Gárdos & Gárdos, *Ismét supra*, 17.

299. Vékás, *Szakértői, supra*, 662.

main obligation (e.g., the loan contract) and the sales contract or contract establishing a purchase right concluded as collateral for this legal transaction are not mutually exclusive. If the parties conclude an agreement that does not violate the prohibition of *lex commissoria*, in other words, the debtor does not 'lose' his ownership right for the creditor's benefit in exchange for his current debt, but instead, the parties regulate their legal relationship by imposing a fair settlement obligation, then the two parallel contracts are both valid. Judicial practice also supports the view that the two contracts – even in respect to one another – can be validly concluded if the purchase price is adequately regulated by the parties in the sales contract or the contract establishing the purchase right, and thus, the settlement relationship does not give rise to disproportionality or any cost prejudice to the debtor. In this manner, when exercising the purchase right, the buyer – who is also the creditor according to the loan contract – can apply an offset when paying the purchase price in terms of his claim for repayment of the loan.[300]

486. The new Civil Code strives to resolve these opposing approaches in legal literature and legal practice. The original wording introduced a general prohibition and associated the legal consequences of invalidity if a contract was aimed at transferring ownership right or any other right or claim or at establishing a purchase right as collateral for a monetary claim. Exceptions were allowed in the cases defined in the Directive on financial collateral.

487. However, this did not conclude the debate on the assessment of fiduciary collateral, and one of the latest amendments to the Civil Code[301] slightly amended the original wording of the Civil Code. Under the amendment, the establishment of fiduciary collateral is only void if the consumer undertakes an obligation to transfer its ownership right or other right or claim or to establish a purchase right as collateral for a claim. As a result, the establishment of fiduciary collateral can essentially be regarded as valid once again, except in the context of consumer legal relationships.

300. László Leszkoven, *A biztosítéki célú vételi jog néhány kérdéséről* (*About Some Questions of the Use of Purchase Right as Collateral*), 12 Gazdaság és Jog 17 ff. (2004); László Leszkoven, *A fiduciárius engedményezés jogi természetéről* (About the Legal Nature of the Fiduciary Assignment), 10 Gazdaság és Jog 13 ff. (2002).
301. Act LVII of 2016.

Part V. Security

Chapter 1. Securities in Immovable Property (*See Also* Parts I and IV)

§1. Privileges, Liens, Charges

I. Restraint on Alienation and Encumbrance

488. With a view to safeguarding the right of ownership of a thing, the owner may impose a restraint on alienation and encumbrance or a restraint on alienation in dealings with third parties. With regard to real property, the right secured by the restraint shall also be indicated in the land registry. The restraint on alienation and encumbrance shall cease to have effect when the right thereto terminates.

From the various sub-rights of an ownership right, the restraint on alienation and encumbrance is aimed at limiting the right of disposal and rules out any sale or encumbrance of the ownership right, namely, the thing is not eligible for sale. The restraint on alienation and encumbrance is primarily designed to secure a right and can thus be stipulated alongside maintenance, life annuity, loan agreement, etc. The new Civil Code no longer contains the constraint that a right to alienate and encumber may only be restricted or ruled out in a contract when transferring the ownership right.

A. *Creation*

489. There are three forms of restraint on alienation and encumbrance: legal regulation, court resolution and a contract. A restraint on alienation and encumbrance can only be established to secure some right. Such a right can arise from the transaction underlying the transfer of the ownership right (e.g., payment of a purchase price, granting of a repurchase/purchase option) or in connection with other legal transactions (e.g., loan, credit). We should highlight that if the restraint on alienation and encumbrance is established on real property, it must be registered in the land registry; failure to do so means the holder of the restraint right cannot enforce it vis-à-vis a third party acting in good faith. In the case of a restraint on alienation and encumbrance for real property, further rights – apart from execution rights – may only be registered on the property with the consent of the holder. The restraint on alienation and encumbrance shares the fate of the right it secures, which means it ceases to exist at the same time the secured right is terminated.

The holder's consent is required for any provision contrary to the restraint on alienation and encumbrance. A provision contrary to the restraint on alienation and encumbrance shall be ineffective with respect to the person whose right the restraint protects. A provision contrary to the restraint on alienation and encumbrance becomes effective upon a statement of consent from the person whose right is protected by the restraint, addressed to the person who made the provision. The restraint on alienation and encumbrance shall not apply to any acquisition of right for consideration by persons acting in good faith.

B. *Legal Effect*

490. The provisions regarding restraint on alienation and encumbrance shall also apply if the restraint is limited to alienation or if the right of disposal is not limited in any other way. When transferring a thing affected by a restraint on alienation and encumbrance, the old Civil Code differentiated between restraints based on legal regulations and court resolutions from those established in contracts. Alienations made in spite of a restraint on alienation and encumbrance based on court or official resolutions were considered null and void, with no exceptions. The new rule in the Civil Code uniformly applies the principle of annulment for all cases of restraint on alienation and encumbrance that are based on contracts, legal regulations, or court resolutions.

A restraint on alienation and encumbrance does not prevent a party acting in good faith and paying consideration from acquiring ownership. The Supreme Court has expressed its position on this issue favouring subjective good faith. In the given case, the customer purchased a vehicle from the seller that had a restraint on alienation and encumbrance in favour of a third party. The restraint on alienation and encumbrance was registered in the vehicle's registration card, but the seller alleged he could not present the card to the customer because he had only bought the car subject to the sale five days previously, and so the competent authority had yet to send it to him. Clearly, it is not possible to refer to one's lack of knowledge regarding the restraint on alienation and encumbrance registered in a public registry, but in this specific case, given the circumstances, the customer was at most careless, and carelessness per se cannot be considered bad faith. Consequently, the Supreme Court ruled that the restraint on alienation and encumbrance was obligatory, and the customer acquired ownership.

The holder of the restraint can consent to the sale of a thing under a restraint on alienation and encumbrance, even retroactively. A restraint on alienation and encumbrance does not signify a complete restriction on changing the ownership of real property. A third party may acquire ownership through adverse possession in spite of this restraint, given that adverse possession is an original way of acquiring ownership, and so the ownership situation does not change because of an action by the owner. Adverse possession is an original way to acquire ownership, where this happens regardless of instructions from the owner if the conditions specified by law are met.

C. Statutory Restraint on Alienation and Encumbrance

491. Where the restraint on alienation and encumbrance is invoked by legislation or by a court ruling for the benefit of specific people, the provisions regarding contractual restraint on alienation and encumbrance must be applied. There are many different legal provisions that provide restraints on alienation and encumbrance. Example:

- Section 7:50(2) of the Civil Code governs estates bound by a succession agreement, with particular regard to the restraint on alienation and encumbrance of real property.
- Based on section 67(4) of Act LXIV of 2001 on the Protection of Cultural Heritage, the Hungarian State is entitled to a lien as well as a restraint on alienation and encumbrance to secure claims established in a final and executable resolution.
- The option under section 119(6)(c) of Act CXXVII of 2003 on Excise Tax and the Special Rules on the Distribution of Excise Products to establish a restraint on alienation for settling legally binding excise penalties under part-payment or deferred payment terms.
- The case of a restraint on alienation and encumbrance as governed in sections 8 and 9 of Act CXLII of 1997 on Regulating the Legal Status of State-Owned Property Used by Civil Society Organizations.
- The restraint on alienation granted to the Hungarian State and regulated in section 26(4) of Act XXXI of 1997 on the Protection of Children and the Administration of Guardianship with regard to subsidized purchases of real property.
- The restraint on alienation and encumbrance as governed in section 5(4) of Act LXV of 1996 on the Ownership Status of Real Property for Sporting Purposes.
- The restraint on alienation and encumbrance that may be established by the environmental authority as per section 102/B(1) of Act LIII of 1995 on the General Rules of Environmental Protection.
- The restraint on alienation and encumbrance on movable property seized in accordance with section 104(3) of Act LIII of 1994 on Judicial Enforcement.

492. Restraints on alienation and encumbrance based on law can arise *ipso jure*, if conditions set forth in legislation occur (e.g., in the case of movable property seized during an enforcement procedure), based on an official resolution as per a legislative provision (e.g., resolution from the environmental authority), or by means of an agreement based on a legislative provision (e.g., when granting payment in instalments relief for payment of an excise penalty). In our view, the Civil Code indicates only how a restraint on alienation and encumbrance established by court resolution comes into being, not the legal grounds for it; since the court may not decide arbitrarily to grant a restraint on alienation and encumbrance, it can only adopt such a resolution with the proper legislative support. This means it is not possible for the court to establish a restraint on alienation and encumbrance with a temporary measure; this is only possible in the case of insurance measures and only if the conditions specified in the Act on Judicial Enforcement are met.

In the case of any restraint on alienation and encumbrance registered on real property, or one that applies to a real property invoked on the strength of legislation or by a court ruling in the absence of registration, the change of ownership or any encumbrance of the property may be entered into the land registry if the person whose right the restraint on alienation and encumbrance is intended to protect provides a statement of consent. In the case of a restraint on alienation and encumbrance for real property based on a contract, it must be registered in the land registry for it to be effective towards third parties. A case decision by the Supreme Court emphasized that for leasing contracts, a restraint on alienation and encumbrance prevailing when the contract was concluded renders the contractual provision on the transfer of ownership invalid (under the new Civil Code, this is relative annulment), given that the leasing contract itself contains the parts of the sales contract. However, it is worthwhile noting that in a different case, the Supreme Court upheld the final court order when consent was subsequently obtained from the party entitled to the restraint on alienation and encumbrance with regard to the ownership title redeemed in the lawsuit for the termination of joint property, which is consistent with the rules of the new Civil Code.

It is also important to note that a court cannot take action in a lawsuit for the termination of joint property if the person holding the restraint on alienation and encumbrance objects to this.

II. Mining Right

493. Treasures of the earth may be utilized by means of mining. A mining right is a right given without changing the ownership status of the real property, so the mining site per se is not a right that differs from the ownership right registered in the land registry with regard to the earth's surface, which means the legal status of the minerals and gases under the ground is the same as that of the real property on the surface.[302]

The mining right only enables the entitled party to exploit the fuels or other materials under the property. This activity can be conducted with the permission of the mining authority. For the mined minerals and geothermal energy, mining tax shall be paid to the state. The owner of the land shall tolerate the creation of the mining site but is entitled to adequate compensation.

§2. Mortgage

I. Legal Background

494. The rules on liens have changed several times in recent years. The main aim of the Civil Code with regard to liens is for this institution to help not only lending relationships by providing effective security for the lender but also ensuring proper protection for the ownership interests of the lienee. The new Civil Code book

302. For the detailed regulation of the mining right, *see* Act XLVIII of 1993 on the mining.

on the law of things contains rules not just for own property but also for rights over the property of someone else. What is new in the new Civil Code in terms of liens is that these rules were placed into the book on the law of things instead of under the law of obligations.[303] The law of obligation rules that govern the rights and obligations of the parties became mandatory upon their transfer to the book on the law of things. There are some default rules under the law of things (e.g., neighbour rights, building on land owned by someone else, easement), but the rules previously under the law of obligations became mandatory under liens, without being separately specified by the law. Accordingly, if the parties nevertheless decide to deviate from these rules, then the agreement between them is null and void.

The new Civil Code moved onto completely new foundations with the lien regulations, but the situation brought about by economic life meant that some rules had to be revisited. According to the Ministry of Justice, there was no need for fundamental, piecemeal reform; only a few rules were fine-tuned. The reasoning stated that compliance with EU regulations was part of the drive behind the amendment. According to the Civil Code amended with Act LVII of 2016, the aim of credit collateral is to restore the independent liens that previously existed under Hungarian law instead of the seceded lien introduced two years ago. The reason given was that the seceded lien introduced by the new Civil Code had not worked, while the Hungarian Central Bank had the express objective of increasing the number of participants in the mortgage bond market and thereby stimulating the bank refinancing market. This required the reintroduction of independent liens.

In 2023, the amendment of the mortgage law regulation became necessary again because the previous regulation left a gap in the mandatory content of the agreement for the establishment of the mortgage right. As a result of which the extent of the obligation to restore the mortgaged objects was not available from the registered data, so third parties could only know the fact of the mortgage but not the amount of the encumbrance. And this undoubtedly made it more difficult to practice lending, which feeds economic life. The institution of sub-pledge – especially with regard to the refinancing of financial institutions – is playing an increasingly important role in economic life. As a result, it has become necessary to regulate the institution of sub-pledge, which can be used as well-applied and effective security in this area and which is more conceptual and transparent than before. In this regard, the amendment particularly envisaged a partial revision of the rules governing the enforcement of sub-pledge and the adaptation of these provisions to the emerging needs of economic conditions.

The current Civil Code does not differentiate between the types of lien and instead tracks the stages of the lien from origination to termination. The Civil Code breaks liens down into the following chapters:

303. Several relevant books and articles have been published concerning liens in Hungary, but unfortunately, these are only partly up-to-date because of the changed regulation brought by the new Civil Code and its modification. *See*, e.g., Tamás Zámbó, *A zálogszerződés* (*The Lien Contract*) (KJK Kerszöv 2001); Ibolya Solymosi Salamonné, *A szerződések biztosítékai* (*Collaterals of the Contracts*) (Agrocent 2002); Tibor Anka, István Gárdos & András Nemes, *A zálogjog kézikönyve* (*Manual of the Law of Lien*) (HVG-ORAC 2003).

- creation of a lien;
- claim secured by a lien;
- object of a lien;
- rights and obligations of parties before the effective date of right to satisfaction;
- credit collateral register;
- hierarchy of liens;
- enforcement of liens;
- termination of liens.

II. Creation of a Lien and Related Rules

A. Lien Concept

495. Upon the failure of the obligor of the secured claim to perform, a lienholder shall be entitled to seek satisfaction prior to other claims against the property pledged as security for his claim.[304] The right to satisfaction shall not be affected by any rights to the pledged object acquired after pledging unless otherwise provided for by the Civil Code. It follows from the lien concept that this is a kind of priority satisfaction right that precedes other creditors. It is easiest to describe this concept based on its features. A lien is a right related to things, which enjoys in rem protection; this means that the rights stemming from it are effective for everyone. The owner of the pledged object (the lienee), or any other person who obtains some right over the pledged object, must tolerate the fact that the lienholder can exercise his rights from the lien. The lien offers a preference right to satisfaction for the lienholder vis-à-vis third parties, and the rights of the lienholder are not affected by rights to the pledged object obtained after pledging.

The limited in rem right nature of the lien manifests itself in the fact that the holder gives exclusive authority to someone else over a thing owned by another person. This is a right encumbering the thing that remains in place even when the owner changes and encumbers the prevailing property. The limited in rem right applies to everyone and is binding for everyone, even the owner.

496. A lien is an ancillary right, which means it is always granted to secure some obligation, and its scope is always aligned with the given receivable, while the personal obligor and the lienee do not have to be the same person. This is because a lien is not tied to the debtor but to the claim secured with the lien, and the lien can only be transferred together with the claim. The exception to this rule is the independent lien because a lien can be established in a way that encumbers the pledged object without a personal claim. In this case, the lienholder may only seek satisfaction from the pledged object encumbered by the lien.

As mentioned earlier, a lien is a kind of credit collateral, which means that it constitutes security for contracts or to enforce claims and rights from contracts with a view to mitigating the risks from lending agreements. Among credit collaterals, liens can be found among tangible collaterals. In the case of tangible collateral, the

---

304. According to Art. 5:86 of the Civil Code.

obligor of the tangible collateral is only obliged to meet his obligation with the pledged asset and without a payment liability if the personal obligor does not fulfil his obligation, provided that the personal obligor and the obligor of the tangible collateral are not one and the same.

Finally, a lien is also a preferential right because the lienholder's right to satisfaction takes priority over other claims against the lienee if they want to satisfy such claims from the pledged object.

B. Creation and Establishment of a Lien

497. A lien is created if the lienholder and the lienee establish the lien and the lienee has a right of disposal over the pledged object.[305] The lien is created if these two conditions are fulfilled at the same time. If the lienee does not have a right of disposal over the pledged object, then despite establishing a lien, the lien itself is not created; it is also not created if the lienee has a right of disposal over the pledged object, but the lienholder and the lienee do not establish the lien. The parties enjoy a great deal of freedom when establishing a lien. This means a lien can be established on one or more existing or future claims, and such claims can be conditional or unconditional. To establish a lien, there needs to be a lien contract, and therefore, the lien must be registered in an appropriate registry (mortgage), or possession of the pledged object must be transferred to the lienholder (pledge).[306]

These two legal facts differ from each other in time: the establishment is always the first step before the creation of the lien. So, first of all, the lien is established, which requires an agreement between the parties, a lien contract, and any additional actions required for disclosure (registration, handover of possession). This is why liens cannot be created, established, or registered for real properties over which the lienee has no right of disposal.

C. Lien Agreement

498. A lien agreement is an agreement between the lienee and the lienholder, which governs the lien to secure a given claim on the pledged object.

The Civil Code deals with consumer pledge agreements in a separate section. If a lienee is a natural person and the pledged object is primarily used for a purpose that is not required for the pursuit of professional, private entrepreneurial activities, or business operations of the lienee, furthermore, the claim secured by a lien is not a result of the lienee's profession, private entrepreneurial activities, or business operations, the provisions of the lien agreement shall apply subject to exceptions. One particular rule is that the pledged object may be an individually determined asset owned by the lienee or an asset which the lienee will acquire by means of a loan or payment deferral provided by the lienholder, while the definition of the

305. According to Art. 5:87 of the Civil Code.
306. According to Art. 5:88 of the Civil Code.

secured claim must indicate the amount. This means the lienee can only be a natural person; the pledged object cannot be related to the lienee's occupation or profession (e.g., residential property), while the third condition is that the claim secured by the lien is not the result of the lienee's profession, private entrepreneurial activities, or business operations.

The Civil Code mentions that lien agreements can be replaced by statutory provisions under which a holder of a claim is afforded lien rights. It is important to highlight that only replacements by provisions in legislative acts meet this condition (but a court can replace a legal statement with a ruling).

III. Registration of Mortgages

499. Mortgages can be registered in two ways: in the land registry for real properties and in the credit collateral register for movable property, rights, or claims. Such registration requires the lien agreement or consent from the lienee to the registration if the pledged object is determined unilaterally and the lienee is the owner or authorized person.

IV. Transfer of Possession for Pledges

500. A pledge is indispensable for the pledged object to be handed over, but this transfer of possession is not required if the thing is jointly owned by the lienholder and the lienee or if the thing is held in safekeeping for them by a third party (pledgee). The situation is different if the thing is held by a third party (as a secondary possessor) as then he must be notified about the pledge, and no pledge may be established, even if the lienee keeps the pledged object in spite of the agreement.

V. Lienholder Agent

501. The law enables an agent to be registered in the appropriate registry instead of the lienholders. In this case, the lienholders do not have to be designated, but the lienholder agent must be registered in this capacity. The lienholder agent exercises the rights of the lienholders, but in accordance with this agent status, the assets obtained in this regard do not form part of his own assets, and his creditors may not lay claim to them.

VI. Claim Secured by a Lien

502. A lien assumes a secured claim; the lien is always in favour of the person entitled to the claim and is consistent with the secured claim in terms of size. The secured claim may only be a cash claim, and the amount may be outstanding or a future claim, conditional or unconditional, defined or to be defined. The lien also covers compensation claims or cash claims derived from non-performance of the claim if the lien itself was otherwise not established to secure a cash claim. A lien may not be established to secure a claim that cannot be enforced in court proceedings, and therefore, a lien may not be established on a lapsed claim. Thus, e.g., an existing lien is terminated if the underlying claim lapses.

A. *Scope of Liability Assumed Through Pledged Object*

503. As outlined when defining the overall concept, a lien is an ancillary right, which means it is always granted to secure some obligation; its scope is always aligned only with the given claim, but this also applies to the interest on the claim secured by the lien, costs incurred when asserting the claim and the lien, as well as any costs on the pledged object. The parties can determine a set amount up to which the lienholder may seek satisfaction from the pledged object, but this amount may not exceed such agreement; in terms of the claim above this amount, the lienholder will be the same as a person asserting an unsecured claim.

B. *Transfer of Secured Claims*

504. If a secured claim is transferred to another person or is passed on in some other manner, then the lien also transfers to the new holder of the claim, but this means the transferor must surrender the pledged object or give consent to the lienholder for the registration. It is also possible for only part of the secured claim to be transferred by the claim holder. In this case, the previous and the new lienholders receive the same rank for the lien in proportion to their respective claims. The essence of the lien's ancillary nature is that the lien is not eligible for sale independently (the lien may only be transferred or encumbered together with the claim secured by the lien), but when the secured claim is transferred, the lien passes to the new holder as well. When a secured claim is pledged, the lien securing the claim is also for the benefit of the holder of the lien on the claim (subordinated lien). The object of the subordinated lien is the lien itself and the claim it secures, and the rules on liens apply.

VII. Independent Lien

505. An independent lien is also known as a non-ancillary lien. In the time that has elapsed since the new Civil Code took effect, it has transpired that the seceded lien introduced as a new institution is not really capable of playing the role previously fulfilled by independent liens. The Civil Code in force discontinued independent liens as such, but on 11 July 2016, the National Assembly adopted the amendments to the Civil Code, which changed the lien rules and once again introduced independent liens instead of seceded liens. The amended rules on liens have been in force since 1 October 2016.

Various arguments were put forward for the change, including that bank portfolios need to be cleaned up and the security of the mortgage bond market has to be raised based on the decree of the Central Bank, lending volumes in the banking sector have to increase, and greater competition could contribute to keeping interest rates low, etc. A new feature with independent liens compared to the previous Civil Code is that such liens can only be established on real properties and solely in favour of financial institutions.[307]

506. It is important to highlight that by law, a pledged object may be mortgaged regardless of the secured claim (up to a certain amount); this gives rise to the non-ancillary designation of an independent lien, as in this case, the lien is not ancillary to the secured claim. In the case of an independent lien, a lien agreement must be concluded, which contains the defined amount by which the pledged object is encumbered, and this amount must be indicated in the land registry. A guarantee agreement must be concluded to establish an independent lien, and the minimum content thereof is defined by law. For guarantee reasons, the guarantee agreement must be in writing, similar to a lien agreement.

Since the guarantee contract must contain the conditions for the effective date of the right to satisfaction derived from the real property encumbered by the independent lien and the conditions for exercising this right, without this, the independent lien would relate to an impossible service because the whole purpose of a lien is the ability to seek satisfaction from the pledged object. An independent lien may be transferred and independently of the underlying claim, but this right is limited in that the transfer can only be made to financial institutions. However, the transfer may relate to part of the independent lien, or the lien may be transferred in instalments. Upon transferring the lien, the lienholder withdraws from the guarantee agreement, and the party acquiring the lien enters the contract in the legal position of the former lienholder. So, in this case, it is indeed a transfer of contract based on statutory provisions due to a guarantee arrangement.[308]

507. The most significant change in the amendment in relation to the independent lien is that the law protects the lienee from the risk of double payment since, vis-à-vis the independent lienholder, the lienee can make reference to objections and can offset the counterclaims he is entitled to be based on the guarantee agreement. This means that in the case of an independent lien transfer, the lienee may avail of all the objections that arose against the party transferring the lien based on the guarantee agreement between them and in relation to the claim to be satisfied from the pledged object.

An independent lien can be terminated by both parties in writing to satisfy the lienholder unless otherwise provided for in the guarantee agreement. A provision of a guarantee agreement that does not provide for the lienholders' right to satisfaction but rules out the opportunity to terminate the independent lien is null and void. Unless otherwise agreed, the termination period is six months.

---

307. The definition of financial institution is contained in Act CCXXXVII of 2013 on Credit Institutions and Financial Enterprises.

308. Article 6:211 of the Civil Code.

Since the creation of an independent lien is not subject to the conclusion of a guarantee agreement, it can happen that the parties involved do not fulfil this mandatory element of an independent lien, or they do, but it lapses in the course of the independent lien for any reason. If the guarantee agreement is not concluded for whatever reason, the purpose of establishing the lien has failed, the claim to be satisfied from the pledged object no longer exists, or if a condition resulting in the termination of the independent lien determined in the guarantee agreement arises, then the lienholder is obliged to consent, based on written notice from the lienee, that the independent lien be deleted from the land registry, or alternatively, the lienee or a financial institution designated by same must be registered as the independent lienholder. Similar to the old Civil Code, the regulation makes it possible to convert the lien securing the claim into an independent lien and to convert the latter into an ancillary lien while retaining the ranking of the converted lien.

Finally, with respect to independent liens, the law prescribes the application of the rules for liens securing claims in all issues where there are no other options based on independence from the secured claim or the special provisions relating to independent liens.

VIII. Object of Lien

A. Pledged Objects

508. A pledged object may be any asset: movable property, real property, a right, or a claim.[309] The object of a mortgage can be movable property, real property, a right, or a claim too, while a pledge may only relate to movable property. The requirement in respect of the things (movable property, real property) is that they must be eligible for sale, while in the case of rights and claims, they must be transferable, and the exercising of non-transferable rights must be permitted.

As a main rule, liens may only be established on whole assets (things, rights), while the law designates three exceptions. First, the part of a jointly owned thing owned by the lienee; second, the part owned by the lienee of something owned by several parties; and third, the specific part of a divisible claim. If the pledged object is a right or claim and the law does not provide for otherwise, then the ownership right to the pledged object is the right or claim, and the owner is the holder.

B. Components, Accessories, and Profits of Pledged Objects

509. A lien covers the components, accessories, tangible products, produce, accretions, and other benefits of the pledged object. The Civil Code specifically defines what a component and accessory is; a component is permanently joined with a thing in such a way that separating would cause the thing or its separated part to be destroyed or would significantly reduce its value or usefulness, while for an

309. Assets are defined in the closing provisions of the Civil Code (s. 8:1(1) point 5 of the Civil Code) as follows: '"asset" shall mean tangible property, rights and claims'.

accessory, when in doubt, the ownership shall also cover parts that are not components but are usually necessary or beneficial for the proper use or maintenance of a thing. Components, accessories, and profits of pledged objects may separate after the lien is established. The lien only does not apply to components, accessories, and profits separated from real property (i.e., the lien is terminated) if such separation happens before the effective date of the right to satisfaction and in accordance with the rules of prudent management, while the ownership right to the separated component, accessory, and profit has been transferred and removed from the property. In the case of real property, the lien remains on the components, accessories, and profits where all of these conditions are not met.

C. *Things and Other Valuables in Place of Pledged Objects*

510. If another asset takes the place of the original pledged object or comes in beside it, then the lien remains even if the pledged object is destroyed or the lien above it is terminated. This is because the asset in place of the pledged object substitutes for the pledged object.

If the pledged object is destroyed or its value decreases, the insurance sum, compensation, or other value due as a result takes the place of the pledged object or complements the pledged collateral. Similarly, any indemnification received for the expropriation of the pledged object or the claim thereof shall replace the pledged object. If the pledged object is sold to compensate for damage caused to the lienholder, the consideration from the sale will replace the pledged object. This can be an option for pledges too, as the sale can only take place in possession of the pledged object. According to general statutory rules on indemnification, the aggrieved party, first of all, has an obligation for damage control, prevention, and mitigation.

If the pledged object is in the credit collateral registry and the lienee sells it, abiding by the rules of prudent management, the purchase price received also takes the place of the pledged object. A new thing created upon processing or converting a pledged object, combining or mixing it with other assets takes the place of or comes in beside the original. In this case, the parties do not necessarily have to enter into a new lien agreement, and they do not need to register the lien again in the register. A new pledged object – or an additional pledged object in the event the original depreciates in value – given by the lienee or the personal obligor instead of the original pledged object also takes the place of or comes in beside the original pledged object.

D. *Lien on More than One Pledged Object*

511. If several pledged objects are encumbered with a lien to secure a claim, then the lien will be joint and several. The joint and several nature of the lien must be indicated in the appropriate registry unless the lienee is the same for all pledged objects and the lien is already registered in the credit collateral registry. In the land registry, joint and several liens are indicated on the title deed, while in the credit collateral registry, it is indicated by the lienee if several objects have been pledged as liens to secure the same claim, objects that the lienee has a right of disposal over.

There are two known types of joint and several lien: when the pledged object has more than one owner and when more than one pledged objects securing the claim are owned by the same person (apparent joint and several liability). In the case of a joint and several lien, all pledged objects secure the claim, while the lienholder may determine the order to enforce the liens. However, the right to satisfaction may only extend to the number of pledged objects needed to satisfy the secured claim. In the case of more than one pledged object owned by more than one lienee, it must be determined how the liability between the lienees is handled, and general rules apply here. Accordingly, lienees with joint and several liabilities share the liability between each other in equal measure, regardless of the value of the pledged object in their ownership.

The lienholder may determine the order of the right to satisfaction, which means that he seeks satisfaction from only one of the pledged objects or from more than one. It may be necessary to reach a separate agreement on the detailed issues surrounding joint and several liens, given that current legislation does not govern this area in great detail.

IX. Rights and Obligations of Parties Before Effective Date of Right to Satisfaction

512. As previously mentioned, the definition of pledges and mortgages is based on the fact that while liens become public, in the case of mortgages, when entered into the registry, for pledges, it is when possession of the pledged object itself is transferred. According to the Civil Code, the objects of mortgages are not just real properties but can also be movable property, rights, and claims, while pledges may only relate to movable property.

A. Possessing, Using, and Utilizing Objects of Mortgages

513. With pledged objects encumbered by mortgages, the difference to that outlined above is that in the case of mortgages, the lienee remains the possessor of the pledged object and may use and utilize it appropriately and is also obliged to keep the object in good condition. The public nature of mortgages is derived from registration in the appropriate registry (land registry, collateral registry, credit collateral registry). The lienee may process, convert, combine, mix, and sell the described pledged object that is registered in the credit collateral registry. This means the mortgage on movable property registered in the registry remains; only the pledged object changes. The person acquiring the newly created pledged object gains unencumbered property, provided that he acquired the object in a commercial transaction for consideration and in good faith.

B. Protecting Mortgage Collateral

514. In terms of inspections, the same rules apply to pledged objects encumbered by mortgages as to pledges, with the difference that the inspection costs are payable by the lienholder, but such can be passed on to the lienee if the parties reach an agreement in this respect, and the lienee possesses the pledged object, not the lienholder. In the case of mortgages, the inspection right of the lienholder is supplemented with the rule that if the lienee or a third person is endangering the condition of the pledged object, the lienholder shall be entitled to exercise the rights of the exposed party in order to eliminate the danger. Accordingly, in line with the circumstances of the case, he is entitled to ask the court to prohibit the person causing the risk from such behaviour, to compel him to take the necessary action to avoid damage or to oblige him to provide appropriate security. In terms of selling pledged objects, the rules applicable for protecting mortgage collateral are the same as the rules for protecting pledges.

X. Hierarchy of Liens

A. Hierarchy Based on Establishment of Liens

515. If the same pledged object is encumbered by more than one lien, the lienholders shall be satisfied in the order in which the liens were established, i.e., the pledged object covers claims secured by more than one lien. A distinction must be made between subordinated liens and joint and several liens. A subordinated lien does not have the same object as the main lien, while in the hierarchy, more than one lien is established on the same pledged object. In contrast to joint and several liens, though, it is not more than one pledged object securing a claim but the same pledged object covering more than one claim. The purpose of the hierarchy principle is to coordinate the order in which creditors are satisfied.

Those who obtained their lien later on can only lay claim to satisfaction from the value of the pledged object after the claims of those higher up the hierarchy have been satisfied. If the pledged object is sold, then the claim can be enforced from the amount remaining after those higher up the hierarchy have had their claims satisfied. The hierarchy does not affect the content of the lien; all lienholders enjoy the same rights as those higher up the hierarchy. The only limitation a lien has is related to when it was acquired. There needs to be a lien agreement and an act ensuring public access for the ranking to be established, but it is the act ensuring public access that is significant in terms of timing. It is possible for two lienholders to occupy the same ranking, which happens when registration applications are submitted at the same time. It can also happen if a single mortgage right is shared, and the sub-rights created in this way occupy the same place in the ranking.

B. Ranking of Lien on an Object Provided in Place of a Pledged Object or to Supplement Pledged Collateral

516. The interests of the lienholder are protected by the lien on an object provided in place of a pledged object or to supplement pledged collateral being recorded in the place of the lien on the original pledged object. The content of the lien does not change, nor do the rights of creditors; only the pledged object is replaced. Based on the Civil Code, the lienee may process, convert, combine, or mix the pledged object with other objects, and the newly created pledged object can take the place of the old one. In other cases, when the pledged collateral is supplemented by another object, the new pledged object takes the place of or comes in beside the original.

C. Lien Established by Previous Holder of Right of Disposal

517. The first exception to the ranking principle is liens established by the previous holder of the right of disposal. A lien established by the previous holder of the right of disposal over the object pledged to secure a lien registered in the credit collateral registry shall precede the lien established prior to said lien, but, for lack of the right of disposal, it was only created thereafter.

Here, we have to analyse two liens, the one established by the previous owner and the one established by the lienee without any right of disposal over the pledged object. Despite the lienee establishing his lien earlier, he did not have a right of disposal over the pledged object at that time, and so this lien is preceded in the ranking by the lien created later by the owner of the thing (or the holder of the right, claim). Thus, the lienee acquires the object encumbered with a lien, and it is ranked behind the lien registered by the previous owner.

D. Priority of Lien Carrying Entitlement to Acquire Pledged Object

518. The second exception to the hierarchy principle is the priority of the lien-carrying entitlement to acquire the pledged object. The purpose of this regulation is for debtors to be capable of accessing additional financing even if they have previously pledged all their assets because the law gives priority to creditors financing the purchase of new assets. A lien established to secure a claim for the purchase price of pledged movable property or for the repayment of a loan granted to acquire the pledged movable property shall precede the liens previously established by the buyer or the seller. There are three conditions for this precedence, all of which must be met. Prior to the transfer of the pledged object, the lien must be registered in the credit collateral registry, and the lienholder, in writing, must communicate the lien establishment to the previous lienholders whose liens will cover the new pledged object if acquired by the lienee. Additionally, preference liens secure claims that have a specific purpose, i.e., commodity or cash loans provided to acquire the pledged movable property.

E. *Hierarchy Between Security Deposit and Lien*

519. The third exception to the hierarchy principle is if there is a security deposit and a lien on the same pledged object. In such cases, the claim of the holder of the security deposit is satisfied before that of the lienholder.

There are two types of in rem credit collateral: the security deposit and the lien. The objects of security deposits can be money, securities, dematerialized securities, payment account balances and other assets. Different rules apply to security deposits than to liens; specifically, the right of security deposit holders to seek satisfaction enjoys priority over lienholder rights, even if the lien was established before the security deposit was made.

F. *Ranking Contract*

520. By concluding a ranking contract, it is possible to change the hierarchy of the liens. This requires the consent of all those with interest, and the change must be registered and noted.

Interested means the person whose lien ranking is directly affected by the change in the hierarchy. Another condition in connection with the ranking switch is that exercising a right of disposal over the rankings of entries may not injure the rights of third parties registered when the ranking is changed. A third party is deemed to be not just the other lienholders but also the personal obligor and the surety. Thus, their consent is also needed to change the order of the liens.

In the event the change in the ranking injures the rights of a third party, they may demand compensation; the Civil Code provides for contracts contingent upon approval, under which ranking contracts concluded without the consent of third parties are invalid. The Civil Code stipulates that a lien moved to a higher ranking shall retain its new ranking thus acquired even if the lien moved backwards is terminated.

G. *Prior Arrangement of Lien Ranking*

521. Apart from a ranking contract, the other way of disposing of a lien is with a prior arrangement of the ranking, where the owner may have it registered or noted in the appropriate record (without indicating a specific person or the beneficiary), in order to encumber an object with a lien. The amount up to which the owner wishes to encumber the pledged object must be specified in the application or in the actual registration. The lien is not created when the prior arrangement of the lien ranking is made, but if it is created later, then retroactively, it receives the ranking as provided by the noted or registered lien. A lien registered under a prior ranking arrangement shall be ranked consistently with the ranking of the noted or registered lien.

XI. Enforcing Liens

A. General Provisions on Exercising the Right to Satisfaction

522. The right to satisfaction provides access to the lienee's asset in the event that the lienee does not perform the service under the main obligation, and the lienholder can resort to various legal acts in order to recover his claim related to the pledged object. The right to satisfaction ultimately removes the lienee's ownership right. The Civil Code specifies two conditions that must be met at the same time; the parties may not deviate from this in a contract, so they are cogent rules.[310] The lienholder's right to satisfaction may be exercised when the claim secured by the lien falls due and as a consequence of the failed performance. If the lien secures a future claim, the lienholder may only exercise his right to satisfaction when the claim arises. The personal obligor is responsible for meeting the obligation of the secured claim, but the lienholder may seek satisfaction from the obligor of the tangible collateral or even from the surety. The due date is the same for both the lienee and the personal obligor, while the failed performance must relate to the personal obligor. Thus, the effective date of right to satisfaction is when the secured claim falls due because of breach of contract by the main debtor on account of non-performance.

The Civil Code enables early repayment in the case of a cash debt, on which basis the personal obligor (or even the lienee) can pay at any time. Another feature of the right to satisfaction is the lack of any fall-back option. For the lienholder to be able to claim from the lienee, it is not necessary to first start enforcement proceedings against the personal obligor; he may claim from the lienee at any time if the immediate debtor fails to meet his obligations. There is a time-based limitation to the right to satisfaction so that the lienholder may not postpone the enforcement of his claim against the lienee forever. If the lienholder exercises its right to satisfaction unjustifiably late, and this means that the secured claim raises, the lienee is not obliged to satisfy such a claim. The seceded lienholder may not use funds from enforcing the lien to satisfy the claim of the original lienholder once his right to satisfaction arises, but only when this second claim also falls due and the original lienholder has failed to perform. The lienholder shall have the option to exercise his right to satisfaction either by way of judicial enforcement or by means other than judicial enforcement. The law states that judicial enforcement is the only option for enforcing liens on payment account balances.

A sub-lien can be established by pledging a claim secured by a mortgage. The object of the sub-lien right is the mortgage right and the claim secured by it. The rules regarding the mortgage right are applicable to the sub-lien right, with the exception that in the case of pledging a claim secured by a mortgage, the sub-lien right is recorded for the amount of the claim specified in the mortgage contract that establishes it.[311] In the case of a sub-lien, the right holder – after the opening of his right of satisfaction – at his choice may exercise the rights of the lien-holder securing the pledged claim or may take the place of the lien-holder securing the pledged

310. Section 5:126(1) of the Civil Code.
311. Section 5:99(4) of the Civil Code.

claim. The sub-lien holder notifies the lien-holder, the obligee of the claim secured by the lien, or, if this person is not the same as the obligee of the claim secured by the pledge, the lienee as well, with a written statement addressed to the lien-holder. The sub-lien holder is obliged to exercise the rights arising from this right in such a way as not to jeopardize the recovery of the claim of the lien-holder secured by the lien. As a result of the enforcement of the sub-lien, the sub-lien holder is obliged to settle accounts with the lien-holder and to release to him the sum of money received in excess of his claim secured by the sub-lien or other property that replaces it. If the claim is secured by a lien, the lienee is obliged to transfer the possession of the pledged object to the sub-lien holder at his request. If the sub-lien holder takes the place of the lien holder, the claim secured by the pledge and the right of pledge are transferred to the sub-lien holder, who as the lien holder can demand the transfer of the possession of the pledged object and the issuance of the legal declarations necessary for the registration of the mortgage right transferred to him.

B. Common Rules on Enforcing Liens by Ways Other than Judicial Enforcement

523. Ways of exercising rights to satisfaction other than through judicial enforcement give cause for concern from an EU law perspective.[312] According to the European Court of Justice, the interests of the lienee must also be protected in such cases, so the lienholder cannot decide arbitrarily, and for there to be some control over the lienholder when enforcing rights to satisfaction by ways other than through judicial enforcement.

The lienholder may choose whether to sell the pledged object himself, obtain the ownership right over the pledged object, or enforce the pledged right or claim. The selected method can be changed later on, but any resultant costs must be reimbursed to the lienee unless they were incurred because of the lienee. In the case of consumer pledge agreements, the lienholder may only sell the pledged object publicly, apart from if the parties agree otherwise after the effective date of the right to satisfaction. In consumer pledge agreements, the lienholder may not acquire the ownership right over the pledged object.

The law also states that after starting to enforce a lien, the lienholder shall be allowed to assign the right to enforce the lien to a higher-ranked lienholder by way of a written statement if compensation is provided for the related costs and expenses of the lienholder who began to enforce the lien. The lienholder enforcing the lien must notify the higher-ranked lienholder of developments to date and of costs incurred as a result. If the lienholder breaches the law in the course of exercising his right to satisfaction, then the lienee, the personal obligor or anyone with a legal interest (e.g., surety, holders of other liens on pledged object) may request that the court suspend the exercising of the right to satisfaction, or compel the lienholder to exercise the right to satisfaction properly. This is a new addition to the Civil Code, with the purpose of protecting the lienee and other parties.

312. The European Court of Justice dealt with this issue in cases C-415/11, C-537/12, C-116/13, and C-482/12.

C. Sale of Pledged Object by Lienholder

1. Prior Notification

524. The main thing used to satisfy claims is not the pledged object but the money received as a consideration after selling the pledged object. Prior notification is mandatory when exercising the right to satisfaction in this format. The lienholder must communicate in writing his intention to sell the pledged object towards the lienee, the personal obligor, those undertaking responsibility for the obligation of the personal obligor, the holders of other liens on the pledged object, and in the case of registered liens, then all those who have a registered right to the pledged object, furthermore, to those people who sent a notice in writing claiming to hold some right over the pledged object, with proof attached, more than ten days before the date of the lienholder's notification. The Civil Code specifically does not provide for the legal implications of failing to meet this prior notification obligation, or if such was not sent with the right content or possibly not by the deadline prescribed by the law. In such cases, though, the lienee may ask for the exercising of the right to satisfaction to be suspended or restricted. The prior notification shall be sent at least ten days, or in the case of a consumer pledge agreement, at least thirty days before the sale.

The Civil Code details the content of the notification as well, which is as follows: designation of lienholder and lienee, the pledged object to be sold, the amount of the enforced claim and associated costs, the reason for and effective date of the right to satisfaction, the planned sales method, the place and date of the public sale, or if sold by other means, then the date after which the sale will take place. There are two cases where there is no obligation for the lienholder to notify the defined individuals, and he may sell the pledged object without such notification. If the pledged object is perishable or if its value is likely to diminish considerably upon any delay, the lienholder does not have to give prior notification. Furthermore, if the pledged object is a thing or right traded on the stock exchange, there is likewise no need to give advance notice of his intention to sell.

2. Right of Possession of Pledged Object

525. After the effective date of the right to satisfaction, the lienholder has the right to take possession of the pledged object. Similarly to prior notification, this requires a call from the lienholder; the law does not make any formal requirements in this respect, but we can say that it should probably be in writing. The purpose of the call is for the pledged object to be released into his possession within the specific time. In section 5:132(2) of the Civil Code, it is stated that a deadline of at least ten days must be given in the case of pledged movable property and at least twenty days for pledged real property. If the lienholder wishes to take possession of a vacated residential property, the deadline for this must be at least three months.

It is also prescribed that the lienee shall release the pledged object it possesses to the lienholder, permit him to take possession and refrain from any conduct aimed at preventing the lienholder from carrying out the sale. If the lienee prevents the lienholder from taking possession and withholds the pledged object, then he is considered a wrongful possessor, but this does not prevent the lienholder from making the sale. If the lienee withholds the pledged object because he contests the legal grounds or amount of the secured claim, this is not permitted, and he may not enforce it through judicial channels.

3. Sale of Pledged Object

526. The requirement of reasonable commercial practices has been introduced to the Civil Code. Based on this rule, when selling the pledged object, the lienholder must act with due consideration of the interests of the lienee and the personal obligor. This fact must be assumed if the sale is completed on the stock exchange, at a price in effect at the time of sale, or the sale takes place under normal market terms usually employed in the commercial sale of pledged objects. As mentioned before, the lienholder is entitled to transfer the ownership right over the pledged object even if the lienee withholds the pledged object. The lienholder acts in the name and on behalf of the pledged object's owner but does not become its owner, not even temporarily.

The lienholder may acquire the ownership right over the pledged object if it is publicly sold or if the pledged object is traded on the stock exchange. It is possible to sell the pledged object in its original state or after reasonable processing or conversion, while it can be sold publicly or privately.

4. Settlement, Distribution of Sales Proceeds

527. The lienholder must settle with the other lienholders of the pledged object regarding the remaining amount with the lienee. This settlement must be prepared in writing and sent immediately following notification to the lienee and to those entitled to receive prior notification. The settlement must include the following:

- the pledged object sold;
- the purchase price received;
- the proceeds collected by the lienholder on the pledged object;
- the costs arising in connection with the safeguarding, maintenance, processing, conversion, and sale of the pledged object;
- if available, the hierarchy of the liens on the pledged object and the amounts of the claims secured by such liens.

If there is a dispute on the costs incurred, the lienee and the other lienholders may contest the settlement in court.

The lienholder must, without delay, distribute the purchase price received plus the proceeds collected, minus the costs incurred – taking into consideration the hierarchy of the liens and the amounts of the claims secured by such liens – among the holders of the liens on the pledged object. The amount remaining after satisfying the claims of the lienholders must be paid to the lienee.

If the purchase price received does not cover the claims of the lienholders, then their claims are sustained up to the level of the unpaid parts. There are compensation implications if the settlement is wrong or incomplete, which has to be proven by the other lienholders and the lienee.

XII. Acquisition of Ownership of Pledged Object by Lienholder

528. Any agreement concluded for transferring ownership of the pledged object to the lienholder on the effective date of right to satisfaction shall be null and void (*lex commissoria* prohibition). The lienholder may only acquire the ownership right over the pledged object he sold if it is publicly sold or if the pledged object is traded on the stock exchange.

A. Acquisition of Ownership of Pledged Object by Lienholder after Effective Date of Right to Satisfaction

529. The law permits the lienholder to acquire ownership after the effective date of the right to satisfaction. The lienholder may make an offer to the lienee to accept ownership of the pledged object in whole or partial satisfaction of the secured claim. The offer is accepted in a sales contract. There are elements that the offer must contain, and the law specifies the group of people who must be notified of the offer because they have the right to object to the offer. The offer must include:

- the lienholder and the lienee;
- the pledged object that the offer relates to;
- the amount of the claim secured by the lien;
- the reason and date for the right to satisfaction being exercised;
- the percentage of the claim that the acquired ownership of the pledged object covers, or the amount that the lienholder is willing to pay to the lienee in exchange for acquiring ownership, in addition to the settlement of the secured claim.

530. In the event of an offer, the following must be notified: the personal obligor, those undertaking responsibility for the obligation of the personal obligor, the holders of other liens on the pledged object, and in the case of registered liens then all those who have a registered right to the pledged object, furthermore, those people who sent notice in writing claiming to hold some right over the pledged object, with proof attached, more than ten days before the date of the lienholder's notification.

A sales contract is concluded if the lienee accepts the lienholder's offer in writing within twenty days of receipt thereof. Under this contract, the lienee must transfer possession of the pledged object or give his consent for the registration of ownership. Upon the transfer of ownership, the claim secured by the lien shall cease to exist in part or in whole, depending on the content of the offer.

B. Right to Direct Satisfaction

531. The essence of the right to direct satisfaction is so the lienholder can avoid the procedure required to enforce the lien. The holder of a security deposit is entitled to acquire ownership – by way of a unilateral statement addressed to the lienee – of the pledged object at the effective date of his right to satisfaction, or, if it was acquired previously, he may terminate his obligation to transfer assets of the same type and amount as the security deposit to the lienee. A security deposit can be money, payment account balances, securities traded on the stock exchange or other securities with a publicly traded market price, or securities embodying pecuniary claims whose market price can be determined independently from the parties under conditions fixed in the securities at that time. Another condition of the direct right to satisfaction is that the lienholder shall settle accounts in writing with the lienee immediately after exercising the direct right to satisfaction and pay the amount remaining after the secured claim is satisfied to the lienee. For this purpose, securities must be taken into account at their market value as of the effective date of right to satisfaction, whereas money and payment account balances must be taken into account at their nominal value.

These rules shall also apply if the object of the security deposit is a warehouse warrant. The holder of the warehouse warrant, as the lienee, provides the schedule and the warrant in his possession with a blank endorsement and gives it to the holder of the security deposit. This means the right of disposal over the warehouse warrant of the person providing the security deposit ceases, and the lienholder becomes entitled to enforce them.

XIII. Termination of Liens

532. The two typical examples are when the pledged object or the secured claim is terminated, but there are a few other examples. The secured claim ceases to exist by law if the lien is terminated, and this applies both to pledges and to mortgages. In order to safeguard trade, the law also states that where ownership of movable property, a right, or claim is acquired in good faith for consideration in the context of trade (whether retail or wholesale), this shall be unencumbered ownership. The law also covers the case where the claim secured by a lien terminates, but the person satisfying the claim is due compensation. In this case, the lien remains to secure such. The law defines the obligations of the lienholder, which must be discharged in order for the previous lienee to be able to exercise his ownership rights again without limitation.

533. Liens shall terminate if:

- the lienholder waives his lien and returns the pledged object to the lienee, or if the mortgage is cancelled from the relevant registry;
- the thing pledged under the lien is destroyed, the claim or right pledged under the lien ceases without any replacement in either case;

- the holder of the pledge loses possession of the pledged object, except when the holder brings a protection of possession action or a possessory action without delay;
- the secured claim no longer exists, or any legal relationship which may result in a secured claim in the future is terminated;
- the claim secured by a lien lapses;
- the lienholder sells the pledged object when exercising his right to satisfaction or acquires ownership of the pledged object.

The right of lien is terminated if the transfer of the claim was made specifically to the exclusion of the transfer of the right of lien securing it. However, if the lien secures other claims of the transferor of the claim in addition to the transferred claim, the lien shall remain as security for this claim.

534. There are three cases that constitute exceptions to the ancillary principle. If the claim secured by a lien ceases to exist, the lien shall remain in force nonetheless to guarantee compensation claims from the personal obligor satisfying the claim, the lienee or a third party.

Under the ancillary principle, the termination of the secured claim impacts the lien; with these exceptions, the lien remains in force, despite the termination of the secured receivables. The holder of the compensation claim takes the place of the original lienholder at the corresponding place in the ranking. The lien remains in force to guarantee the claim secured by the lien if the same person becomes the lienee and the lienholder. However, the law states that the lien is terminated even if it was previously transferred.

Unencumbered ownership is acquired when someone obtains an ownership right, a right or a claim free of a lien registered in the credit collateral registry, in good faith, and in the course of trade for consideration. If the pledged object is sold to protect the pledged collateral, the buyer shall acquire an unencumbered ownership right, a right, or a claim. Finally, the Civil Code mentions the obligations of lienholders when liens are terminated. If a claim secured by a lien is terminated or lapses and no other legal relationship exists which may result in a secured claim in the future, the lienholder must, without delay, return the pledged object to the lienee, consent to having the lien cancelled, and notify in writing the lienee's payment service provider or any third party who, as the pledgee has possession of the pledged object, or on whose account the pledged object was credited to the benefit of the lienholder, regarding the termination of the lien. Thus, if the lien is terminated without being enforced, the lienholder faces the obligations outlined above. If the pledged object is held by a third party or credited to the account of a third party for the benefit of the lienholder, the lienholder is obliged to notify the said third party immediately of the termination of the lien. After receiving notification, the third party must return the pledged object to the lienee or transfer the pledged object credited to his account to the account of the lienee.

The law also regulates the termination of seceded liens as well. A seceded lienholder must settle up with the original lienholder when the seceded lien is terminated and when the lien passes back to the original lienholder.

Chapter 2. Securities in Movable Property (*See Also* Parts II and IV)

§1. Privileges, Liens, Charges

535. Restraint on alienation and encumbrance can also be used as collateral for movable property, the rules of which were defined for real property.

§2. Pledge

536. The law distinguishes between the meeting of liabilities under pledges and those under mortgages. The difference between pledges and mortgages is based on the fact that, in the case of mortgages, liens become public when entered into the registry; for pledges, it is when possession of the pledged object itself is transferred. In the case of pledges, possession of or ownership over the pledged object must be transferred, whereas, for mortgages, approval for registration must be granted. For a contract to be made, both the pledged property and the secured claim must be accurately defined so as to allow for identification. This definition can also refer to claims that have yet to emerge. The law also calls for compliance with formality requirements and for the pledge agreement to be executed in writing, except in the case of pledges where the agreement can be replaced by a security (possessory note) issued by the lienholder.

Where ownership of a movable property or right is recorded in a public register, the mortgage shall be considered established if registered in the relevant registry. Under the Civil Code, the public register is also referred to as a registry.

I. Arrangement of Collateral Security

537. Collateral securities constitute ancillary credit collateral for property, and under the new Civil Code, represent a subcategory of liens. The principal feature of collateral security is the right to direct satisfaction, which is derived from the specific nature of the underlying object. Only money, payment account balances, securities, or other properties set out in legislation may be used as collateral securities. Collateral security may be arranged on money and securities in the form of a pledge. Transfer of possession is a typical example; however, with the extension of payment rules, collateral security may also be arranged on money deposited and/or transferred to payment accounts. According to the rules on dematerialized securities and securities held in collective deposit, collateral security may be arranged by debiting or crediting the securities account and/or the safe custody account. In addition, the law also allows for the recognition of payment account balances as collateral security. In this case, the collateral amount remains on the lienor's account, whose rights of disposal will be limited, and the lienholder will acquire the right of disposal. Furthermore, contrary to the general provisions concerning liens established on claims, the lien does not get listed in the collateral register, but the payment service provider is required to declare the collateral security on all balance statements issued for the account. The law has another special provision in place when the lienholder is the payment service provider itself. To facilitate the use of other properties and intangible assets traded in money and capital markets as safeguards, the law extends the list of possible collateralized assets by citing, on an exceptional basis, other legislation. To this end, instead of stipulating the possible method of arrangement for collateral security, the law only provides a general requirement that essentially has to do with the transfer of possession.

II. Pledged Property Identified by Detailed Description

538. Detailed description is not the only way movable property can be identified, for their characteristics and appearance can often change, whether due to transformation, processing, incorporation, or even sale. Stipulating the rules for identifying pledged properties by detailed description, the Civil Code not only allows for the identification of pledged properties but also specifies the consequences of such identification by a detailed description.[313]

The advantage of the detailed description is that it is always the assets owned by the lienor and meeting the description that represents the pledged property, thus allowing the lienor to even process or sell the pledged property – the individual items of which may change – during the term of the lien.

Only pledged properties entered in the collateral register can be identified by a detailed description. These can include things, claims, and rights of which the lienor has the right to dispose. Consequently, real properties or registered movables and rights cannot be recognized as properties identifiable by a detailed description. However, most movable properties include not only things that can be identified by a detailed description but also those whose characteristics or appearance may change, whether due to transformation, processing, incorporation, or sale.

III. Possessing, Use, and Utilization of Pledged Property

539. The lienholder is entitled to keep the pledged property in his possession and is required to retain it in good condition. Based on this, the lienholder is entitled to protection of possession against all parties, including the owner of the pledged property. The parties' rights and obligations relating to the possession, use, and utilization of the pledged property are governed by the provisions on deposits, on the condition that the lienor is not required to pay a fee and may not recover the pledged property during the term of the lien. The pledge holder is under the obligation to safeguard the pledged property and, in accordance with the provisions on deposits, may be entitled to a right of use over the pledged property only in exceptional cases. In order for the lienholder to be able to use or utilize the pledged property, this must be stipulated by the parties in an agreement and is also subject to authorization by the owner. The only exception is when the pledged property is used or utilized in order to prevent damage.

313. Article 5:102 of the Civil Code.

The lienholder is required to keep the pledged property separate from his own assets and in good condition. The lienholder is required to manage the pledged property if that is necessitated by the nature of the pledged property and to collect the proceeds of the pledged property if, by its nature, it is economically viable. A fruit separating from a pledged property is created free of lien, which the lienholder is required to hand over to the lienor or allow the latter to collect and to give account in relation to the fruit he (the lienholder) has collected.

Upon termination of the secured claim, the lienholder is required to return the pledged property to the original lienholder or its legal successor, except if the personal obligor fails to perform when the secured claim becomes due.

IV. Protection of Pledged Collateral

540. As the lienholder is required to keep the pledged property in good condition, the fact that the lienor has the right to check the property has warranty implications. The right to check cannot be abused, and the lienholder cannot be prevented from exercising his rights. If, during the inspection, it is found that the pledged property is not held in good condition, this shall constitute a breach of contract, which the lienor can use as grounds for terminating the contract.

The lienholder is required to inform the lienor of any imminent danger to the pledged property. The lienholder may be entitled to sell the pledged property if any loss in value of the pledged property jeopardizes satisfaction of the claim, and the lienholder fails to restore the condition of the pledged property (despite notice to this effect) or fails to provide an adequate replacement or an additional guarantee to cover the loss of value. The lienholder is not required to notify the lienor if any insurmountable obstacles exist or if any further delay in waiting for the lienor's action is likely to result in further depreciation. Whether these conditions are being met must be proven by the lienholder.

The lienor may offer an appropriate pledged property of the same value and, unless it jeopardizes the right to satisfaction, the lienholder must return the pledged property.

In the case of changes to the value of a divisible pledged property – whose value can be determined beyond a reasonable doubt based on the collateral security and other publicly accessible information – or of the secured claim, the lienor is required to provide additional security and the creditor is required to release any excess collateral to the lienor. The lienor is entitled to use any insurance settlement, compensation or other value received in exchange for the pledged property to restore the pledged property, provided that this does not jeopardize the satisfaction of the secured claim.

V. Protection of Hypothecated Claim as Pledged Collateral

541. After the debtor of a hypothecated claim is notified in writing concerning the establishment of a lien, the amendment to the contract between the lienor and the debtor of the hypothecated claim shall cease to apply to the lienholder. In this case, the object of the lien is a claim. The greatest risk is presented by an agreement entered into between the lienor and the debtor of a hypothecated claim that jeopardizes the enforceability of the claim. Hence, the provision voids the agreement between the lienor and the debtor of the hypothecated claim that would otherwise change and restrict the contract between the two. Therefore, the notice does not constitute an appropriate legal basis for enforcing objections against the hypothecated claim or using the said objections for offsetting.

The debtor of a hypothecated claim must be notified in writing that a lien on the claim has been arranged. As part of the mandatory layout of the written notice, the hypothecated claim and the lienholder(s) must be specified. The only legal consequence of the notice is that the amendment to the contract between the lienor and the debtor of the hypothecated claim ceases to apply to the lienholder.

VI. Rights and Obligations of the Debtor of a Hypothecated Claim

542. The notice in itself does not mandate the debtor of the hypothecated claim to perform to the lienholder. Unless the lienor presents a performance instruction containing the details of the lienholder (name and registered seat, or home address, place of residence, or account number for natural persons), the debtor of a hypothecated claim is liable to perform to the lienor. Thereafter, the debtor may perform as instructed. The performance instruction invokes a legal effect if the instruction is incorporated into the notice of hypothecation and originates from the lienor or if the lienholder is able to verify that the claim has in fact been hypothecated by way of a pledge agreement or other reliable means. If the notice of hypothecation indicated the lienholder but did not contain any performance instruction, a performance instruction may be given only by the lienholder. The lienholder may send a performance instruction once the right to satisfaction takes effect.

At the lienholder's request, the lienor is required to produce the documents necessary for enforcing the hypothecated claim. If whether the hypothecated claim is due depends on the legal statement of the lienholder or on a condition to be met by him, the lienholder shall be entitled to make the legal statement or satisfy the condition necessary for the claim to become due.

The law also stipulates that said performance instruction does not affect the rights and obligations the payment service provider has under the account or deposit contract with the account holder. That means the payment service provider cannot be given any performance instruction but can continue executing the account holder's orders, and the lienholder may not proceed directly against the payment service provider.

VII. Enforcement of a Hypothecated Right or Claim

543. If the object of a mortgage is a claim, the mortgage holder may give performance instructions to the mortgagor and be allowed, after the claim matures, to enforce the claim in place of the original mortgage holder against the mortgagor. As the key legal consequence of a performance instruction, the mortgagor can only perform afterwards as instructed.

Besides a lien, a subordinated lien also covers the secured claim. If the claim subject to a lien is secured by a lien or surety, the lienholder may also exercise the rights of the holder of the claim arising out of, or in connection with, the lien or surety. Therefore, the subordinated lienholder may exercise the rights of the holder of the secured claim arising out of the primary lien and may seek a claim not only in connection with the claim but the lien as well. If the secured claim is also guaranteed by surety, the holder of the subordinated lien may bring action against the surety also. If the claim subject to a subordinate lien is secured by a pledge, the holder of the claim is required to transfer possession of the pledged property to the lienholder upon his request.

The provisions on subordinated mortgages and on the enforcement of a hypothecated right or claim must be applied appropriately even when the object of the lien is a debt security. Accordingly, the lienholder may give performance instructions to the lienor specified in the securities and be allowed, after the claim matures, to enforce the claim in place of the holder of the debt securities against the lienor.

VIII. Collateral Register

A. Core Principles

544. The collateral register contains the mortgages established on non-registered movables, rights, and claims, as well as other security rights. As opposed to the land registry where the mortgage is listed on the title deed of the given real property, the collateral register contains mortgages and security rights listed separately for each lienor. The collateral register system is maintained by the Hungarian Chamber of Civil Law Notaries.[314]

The collateral register is made available to the general public and accessible online, free of charge, without personal identification. Statements in the collateral register can only be made electronically. All other statements are considered null and void.

The register is not an official public register, as it only validates the availability of collateral statements, the content of which is to be considered authentic unless proven to the contrary. If a person suffers any loss or damage from incorrect collateral records, claims may be enforced by way of judicial process. The burden of proof lies with the party having made the collateral statement. Where ownership is acquired in good faith, in the course of trade for consideration, the transferee will acquire an unencumbered ownership right, right, or claim registered in the collateral register.

Unless entered in the collateral register, a lien is not arranged even when the lienor is entitled to dispose of the pledged property. In other words, registration in the collateral register is construed only as a declaration and not the establishment of

314. Its detailed rules of operation are set out in Act CCXXI of 2013 on the Collateral Register.

the lien. In other words. the credit collateral registry authentically certifies that the declarant of the credit collateral statement made the statement in the registry at the recorded time and with the content specified in the registry, but the registry does not certify or prove the existence of any right, fact, or contract.

Other security rights (the registration of which is mandatory) include: retention of title over movable property, factoring, and financial leasing, if the leased asset is a movable property or right. Even in the absence of registration, the transferee acquires ownership over the movable property if such acquisition takes place in good faith and for consideration. For financial leasing, the third party acquiring ownership from the lessee in good faith and for consideration also acquires ownership of the movable property or of the right. For factoring agreements, in the absence of registration, the claim does not pass to the factor in spite of being assigned, and the factor will have the same entitlements on the claim as the lienholder whose lien on the claim has not been entered in the collateral register.

B. Statements Constituting the Basis for the Collateral Register

545. Entries in the collateral register may be made by the lienholder and the lienor in person (whether natural or legal persons), by way of a representative (power of attorney), or by the court bailiff. Said entries in the collateral register may be made, edited, or deleted electronically via a specific website by persons having already been registered in the collateral register as users. In the process of making a statement, natural persons may proceed in the name of legal persons and other organizations registered as users if designated by the relevant organization at the time of registration or, subsequently, as representatives authorized to act in their name and on their behalf. Upon successful submission of a registration request, access is provided by the Hungarian Chamber of Civil Law Notaries. In order to validate his registration, the applicant must make a statement before a notary public concerning the authenticity of data contained in the registration request, the act of which is to be entered in the system by the notary.

The Collateral Register Act contains a list of acceptable collateral statements, which are as follows: lienholder's statement, lienor's statement, seller's statement on sale under retention of title, factoring statement, lessor's statement and any other statutory statement (e.g., statement of consent to modification).

Collateral statements may be considered effective if the registered user has paid the pertaining fee to the Hungarian Chamber of Civil Law Notaries. Afterwards, the lienor – or, in case of a lienor's statement, the lienholder – receives notification immediately via electronic means.

C. Registration of a Lien and Contents of the Statement for the Registration of a Lien

546. If the statement for the registration of a lien is made by the lienor, the lien is registered on the strength of that statement. If, however, the statement for the registration of a lien is made by the lienholder, the lien is registered on the strength of that statement if the lienor consented to the registration by electronic means via the website. Entries in the collateral register do not require submission and are not subject to the availability of a lien agreement.

D. Cancellation of Liens

547. Statements for the cancellation of a lien can be made both by the lienholder and the lienor. If the statement for the cancellation of a lien is made by the lienholder, the lien is cancelled on the strength of that unilateral statement. If the statement for the cancellation of a lien is made by the lienor, the lien is cancelled on the basis of that statement if the lienholder gave consent to the cancellation of the lien or did not make a statement for maintaining the entry within a period of thirty days of the lienor's statement for the cancellation of the lien. The lienholder must consent to the cancellation of the lien and is not entitled to make a statement for maintaining the entry if his claim secured by a lien no longer exists or there is no legal relationship that in the future may result in a claim secured by a lien. If the lienholder did not consent to the cancellation, the lienor may seek judicial redress, as in this case, the statement is based on a contract.

E. Changes in the Pledged Properties Registered in the Collateral Register

548. If a lien registered in the collateral register is secured by more than one asset identified by a detailed description, changes in such things, rights, and claims do not affect the ranking of the lien. This is one of the cases where the Civil Code permits that the lien remain in its original place even when the pledged property is replaced. The pledged property is identified in this case by a detailed description and not by unique identification. Given that assets, things, rights, and claims may change on a permanent basis, identification by detailed description might not always be appropriate. To avoid this, a provision was added to the Civil Code, stipulating that changes in the pledged property must not affect the ranking of individual lienholders.

§3. RETENTION RIGHT, COMPENSATION

I. Retention Right

A. Retention Right in General

549. The Civil Code discusses the right to withhold performance among the general provisions of obligations. Accordingly, the right to withhold performance may be exercised in the event of non-performance (breach of contract). In the event of non-performance, the obligee is entitled to withhold his own performance as commensurate until the obligor has tendered performance or has provided adequate guarantees. The party having the right to withhold performance may withdraw from the contract, or if restitution cannot be provided, he may be entitled to terminate the contract if the other fails to remedy his non-performance within the reasonable time limit provided or fails to provide adequate guarantee for performance. As to other issues pertaining to the rights and obligations of the party that is entitled to withhold performance, the principles of *negotiorum gestio* apply.

B. Retention Right of the Possessor

550. The right to withhold performance is also discussed under rights in rem, among the provisions of possession. Wrongful possessors are also entitled to surrender their possession (retentio) until demands claimed in connection with possession are satisfied. As regards individual demands, the principles of *negotiorum gestio* must be applied. A possessor who has acquired the thing by committing a criminal offence or in another violent or treacherous way may not refuse to surrender the thing.

551. As regards the wrongful possessor's claim for compensation and right of removal, the provisions of the Civil Code are largely based on Roman law. The wrongful possessor is entitled to demand compensation for his necessary expenses related to the thing. Necessary expenses refer to those without which the thing in possession would have perished or physically deteriorated (e.g., reinforcing the foundation of a dilapidated building). As regards the reimbursement of these expenses, the Civil Code does not distinguish between bona fide and mala fide wrongful possessors because these expenses would have also arisen for lawful possessors. Furthermore, the Civil Code does not allow reimbursement of minor expenses normally required for the maintenance of the thing. The legislator has left this category open for interpretation in legal practice. In our view, this includes expenditures without which the thing could not be maintained but are reasonably foreseeable in connection with the possessed thing (e.g., the feeding of live animals).

A wrongful possessor, if acting in good faith, may also be entitled to compensation for his useful expenses that are not covered by proceeds. Useful expenses refer to those without which the thing in possession would not have perished or physically deteriorated but which add value or improve the thing. For instance, this could include retrofitting the heating system or insulation of a building. The bona fide possessor may claim reimbursement of these expenses; however, in the settlement between parties, the proceeds of the thing during possession must also be taken into account and set off against the expenses.

Mala fide possessors may only demand compensation according to the principles of unjust enrichment.

552. As a general rule, the wrongful possessor may exercise his right of removal (ius tollendi) over his investments in relation to the thing. As a condition to the right of removal, it must be possible to separate the investment from the thing without causing harm to the latter.

553. In matters relating to settlement between the parties and to the right to withhold performance, the following court decisions must be applied.

The wrongful possessor's settlement obligation also extends to the proceeds from, and damages to, the thing. As regards the settlement obligation, the Civil Code distinguishes between the possessors' rights and obligations on the basis of good faith. As a main rule, the wrongful possessor is required to surrender the existing proceeds from a thing, thus causing the lawful possessor to recover the thing in the condition it was when surrendered. An exception is when the wrongful possessor takes possession in good faith and for consideration. Within the scope of their settlement obligation, bona fide wrongful possessors are not liable to provide compensation for the proceeds or for the damages caused. Such protection ceases once official means of enforcement are resorted to. From this point on, the legislator will assume that the wrongful possessor acted in bad faith. A possessor acting in good faith is not required to settle up the proceeds collected and damages arisen before official enforcement if such proceeds no longer exist. It is the intention of the legislator that wrongful possessors acting in bad faith be perceived as though possession never took place, thus exposing them to full liability for damages and an obligation of reimbursement for the proceeds. When unreasonably hoping to be entitled to possession under a contract, a wrongful possessor is not acting in good faith. As regards the wrongful possession of real property, proceeds may be reimbursed by way of payment of usage charges.[315] Mala fide possessors, once their bad faith is confirmed, are liable for the proceeds they have consumed or failed to collect without being entitled to set off claims relating to safeguarding.[316]

A wrongful possessor cannot be forced to incur any expenses or damages in relation to the safeguarding of the thing. Applicable provisions are intended to ensure timely re-possession of the thing by the person entitled to possession, who will then be responsible for all related costs thereafter. As a result, in a limited number of justified cases, the wrongful possessor may be entitled to sell or use the thing for other purposes.

Whenever deemed necessary based on the nature of the thing, the wrongful possessor's obligation to indemnify must be applied. Perishable things and things where any delay is likely to induce substantial loss of value must be sold or used by the wrongful possessor. In such cases, the wrongful possessor is required to settle up with the lawful possessor and surrender any proceeds from sale or usage. In other affairs, the provisions of unjust enrichment must be applied to the relationship of the parties; therefore, no delay on the part of the lawful possessor may result in financial gain to the wrongful possessor.

II. Set-Off

554. For regulations on set-off, refer to the provisions of the Civil Code. Set-off is only possible in the event of mutual claims – particularly for monetary amounts – that are analogous and due. The debtor is entitled to settle his debt also by way of

315. BH 2005/359.
316. BDT 2002/554.

setting off his overdue pecuniary claim against his monetary debt by means of a legal statement made out to the creditor. As a consequence, obligations up to the value of set-off will cease.

Time-barred pecuniary claims may also be offset if the pecuniary claim to be offset had not yet expired at the time when the monetary debt became due. The same type of monetary debt may be offset against a pecuniary claim provided for by an enforcement order or composition or if executed in a notarized deed. Only monetary debts originating from the same legal basis can be offset against pecuniary claims, which are exempt from judicial enforcement.

No set-off is permitted against certain listed claims, including child support and benefits (with the exception of overpayments) and pecuniary claims for compensation for wilfully caused damages. Any pecuniary claim that cannot be enforced in court (naturalis obligatio) may not be offset either.

§4. Delegation, Direct Claim (Possibility Created by Statute Law to Claim Payment Directly from the Debtor of One's Debtor)

555. Legal demands and obligations may be transferred by way of assignment, subrogation, assumption of debt, or transfer of contract.

I. Assignment

556. Claims may be transferred by assignment. For the acquisition of a claim by way of assignment, a contract for transfer or other legal title is required, and, in that context, the claim must be assigned. Assignment is an agreement between the assignor and the assignee upon which the assignee takes the place of the assignor. Through the assignment, the rights proceeding from the lien and suretyship are conveyed to the assignee, including interest claims.[317]

A claim may be assigned if the relationship from which the claim originates already exists at the time of assignment. The assigned claim must be identified by indicating the obligor, the legal title, the sum, and maturity, or by other means facilitating identification of the assigned claim at the time of assignment, or no later than the time when the claim is created in the case of future claims. The assignment of any claim that is bound to the person of the obligor is considered null and void.

557. Any term excluding the assignment of a claim is considered null and void in respect of third parties. The assignor is required to make available to the assignee all information that may be deemed necessary to enforce the claim and hand over to the assignee documents in his possession evidencing the existence of the claim. The assignor is required – if so requested by the assignee – to notify the obligor in writing concerning the assignment, indicating the fact of assignment and identifying the claim, or delivering the deed of assignment to the assignee that shows the name of

317. For detailed analysis, *see* Péter Gárdos, *Az engedményezés* (*The Assignment*) particularly 25 ff. (ELTE Eötvös Kiadó 2009).

the assignee. After the obligor is notified, any amendment of the contract between the obligor and the assignor is considered invalid towards the assignee. The obligor is entitled to enforce the objections and offset the counterclaims against the assignee that arise with regard to the assignor on the legal grounds prevailing at the time of notification. The notice of assignment will invoke this legal effect if it originates from the assignor or if the assignee is able to verify that the assignment has, in fact, been affected by way of the deed of assignment or other reliable means.

558. The obligor is required to perform to the assignor insofar as a performance instruction is conveyed indicating the name of the assignee and the place of business or, failing this, the registered office of the assignee, home address or, failing this, the habitual residence or account number of a natural person. Thereafter, the debtor may perform as instructed. The performance instruction will invoke the legal effect if it originates from the assignor or if the assignee is able to verify that the claim has, in fact, been assigned to him by way of the deed of assignment or other reliable means. If the notice indicated the assignee but did not contain the performance instruction, a performance instruction may be given only by the assignee. If the obligor affects performance of the assignor, the assignor is required to keep the assets received in performance of the service separate from his own assets and deliver them to the assignee without delay. The assignor's creditors may not be entitled to lay claim to such assets.

559. If the assignor assigns the same claim more than once, the obligor will be released upon effecting performance as provided for in the performance instruction first received. Should the assignor reassign the claim, the obligor will be released upon effecting performance as provided for in the performance instruction last received. The expenses of the obligor arising from the assignment must be covered by the assignor and the assignee collectively.

If a claim is transferred to another person under law, the provisions on assignment must be duly applied. In that case, the liability of the assignor will remain only if so prescribed by a specific provision.

II. Subrogation

560. The subrogor may transfer his right to another person, provided that the transferability is not ruled out by law, or unless non-transferability follows unambiguously from the nature of the right. For the acquisition of a right by way of subrogation, a contract for transfer or other legal title is required, and, in that context, the right must be subrogated. Subrogation is an agreement between the subrogor and the subrogee upon which the subrogee takes the place of the subrogor. The provisions on assignment shall apply to subrogation *mutatis mutandis*. If the right is verified by a public registry, subrogation will be considered effective – in addition to assignment – if the subrogee is registered in that registry.

III. Assumption of Debt

561. The assumption of debt results in changes in the obligor's position. Debt is assumed on the basis of an agreement between the obligor and the transferee. In this case, the transferee is entitled to all rights to which the obligor was entitled in respect of the obligee under contract. Upon the assumption of debt, the guarantees of the claim cease to exist. The guarantees may remain in place if their obligor consents to the assumption of debt.

In order for the assumption of debt to take effect against the obligee, this must be consented to by the obligee. If the obligee makes a statement required for the assumption of debt in advance, the assumption of debt takes effect after the notification of the obligee. The obligee may instal a clause in the statement reserving the right to withdraw the statement.

562. The assumption of performance is a special case of debt assumption. If a third party agrees with the obligor to assume the obligor's debt, that third party is liable to satisfy the obligor's debt or to enable the obligor to satisfy his debt when it falls due. The obligee may not demand satisfaction of the debt from the third party. The undertaking of debt is yet another particular case. If the parties notify the obligee on the assumption of performance, joint and several liability evolves. Following the undertaking of a debt, the joint and several obligors are entitled to all rights to which the obligor was entitled in respect of the obligee under contract. The person undertaking the debt is not entitled to offset the obligor's other existing claims against the obligee.

IV. Transfer of Contract

563. The transfer of contract is a novel legal concept in Hungarian law. The party withdrawing from, the party remaining in, and the party entering into the contract may reach an agreement for transferring the rights and obligations of the withdrawing party to the party entering into the contract. All rights and obligations of the party withdrawing from the contract conferred under the contract in respect of the party remaining in the contract accrue to the party entering into the contract. The party entering into the contract is not entitled to offset other existing claims of the party withdrawing from the contract from the party remaining in the contract. The party remaining in the contract is not entitled to offset his other existing claims due from the party withdrawing from the contract. The guarantee of a right transferred to the party entering into the contract will continue to exist. The guarantee of an obligation transferred to the party entering into the contract ceases to exist, except if the obligor of the guarantee consents to the transfer of the contract.

If the party remaining in the contract makes a statement required for the transfer of contract in advance, the transfer of contract will take effect after the notification of the party remaining in the contract. The party remaining in the contract may instal a clause in the statement reserving the right to withdraw the statement. If, in advance, the obligor of the guarantee makes a statement of consent that is required for the guarantee of an obligation transferred to the party entering into the contract to remain in effect, the said statement will take effect when the obligor of the guarantee is notified of the transfer of contract. The obligor of the guarantee may instal a clause in the statement reserving the right to withdraw the statement.

Selected Bibliography

Ablonczay, Bálint. *Conversations on the Fundamental Law of Hungary*. Budapest: Elektromédia, 2012.

Anka, Tibor, István Gárdos & András Nemes. *A zálogjog kézikönyve* (*Manual of the Law of Lien*). Budapest: HVG-ORAC, 2003.

Barta, Judit (ed.). *Bank- és hitelviszonyok. Kodifikációs tanulmányok az új Ptk. születése kapcsán* (*Bank and Credit Relationships. Codification Studies related to the Birth of the New Civil Code*). Miskolc: Novotni Alapítvány, 2009.

Baur, Jürgen F. & Rolf Sturner. *Sachenrecht*. München: Beck, 1999.[17]

Bíró, György & József Szalma (eds). *Kötelmi jog kodifikációs tanulmányok (2003–2005)* (*Codification Studies on the Law of Obligations*). Miskolc: Novotni Alapítvány, 2005.

Bíró, Szabolcs. *A magyar földpiac és az új földforgalmi szabályozás várható hatásai* (*The Hungarian Land Market and the Expected Impacts of the New Land Turnover Regulation*). In *Az új magyar földforgalmi szabályozás az uniós jogban (The New Hungarian Land Turnover Regulation in the Law of the EU)*, edited by Ágoston Korom. Budapest: Nemzeti Közszolgálati Egyetem, 2013.

Boóc, Ádám & István Sándor. *Előadásvázlatok a polgári jog általános tanaiból (Lecture Notes on the General Part of the Civil Law).* Budapest: Patrocinium, 2014[5].

Boóc, Ádám, et al. *Csődjog* (*Bankruptcy Law*). Budapest: HVG-ORAC, 2007[2].

Boóc, Ádám. *Észrevételek az új Polgári Törvénykönyv tervezetéhez nemzetközi magánjogi szempontból* (*Remarks to the Draft of the New Civil Code from Private International Law Aspect*). Polgári Jogi Kodifikáció 8 (2008).

Boóc, Ádám. *The Works Contract.* In *Business Law*, edited by István Sándor. Budapest: Patrocinium, 2016.

Brüninghaus, Birgit. *Die Stellung des Tieres im Bürgerlichen Gesetzbuch.* Berlin: Duncker & Humblot, 1993.

Czuczai, Jenő. *A magyar privatizáció alulnézetből. Múltja, jelene, jövője (Hungarian Privatisation Viewed From Below – Its Past, Present and Future).* Budapest: Agrocent, 1994.

Csink, Lóránt, Balázs Schanda & Zs. András Varga (eds). *The Basic Laws of Hungary: A First Commentary*. Dublin: Clarus Press, 2012.

Csizmazia, Norbert & István Sándor. *A bizalmi (fiduciárius) vagyonkezelés modelljei és a Ptk. reformja* (*Models of Fiduciary Property Management and the Reform of the Hungarian Civil Code*). Polgári jogi kodifikáció 4 (2002).

Selected Bibliography

Csoma, Zsigmond. *A magyarországi hegyközségek 20. századi megszüntetése és újjászervezése* (*The Termination and Reorganisation of the Hungarian Wine-Growers' Associations in Hungary*). Acta Acad. Agriensis, Sectio Historiae 38 (2010).

Csöndes, Mónika & Zoltán Nemessányi (eds). *Merre tart a magyar civilisztikai jogalkotás a XXI. század elején?* (*Where Is the Private Law Legislation Going at the Beginning of the 21st Century*). Pécs: Pécsi Tudományegyetem Állam és Jogtudományi Kar, 2010.

Deák, Dániel (ed.). *A vagyonkezelés pénzügyi joga* (*Financial Law of Property Management*). Budapest: Research report, 1998.

Deák, Dániel. *A bizalmi vagyonkezelés jogi kérdéseiről* (*Legal Issues Concerning Fiduciary Property Management*). Gazdaság és Jog 8 (1995).

Eckhard, Ferenc. *Magyar alkotmány- és jogtörténet* (*History of Hungarian Constitution and Law*). Budapest: Politzer, 1946.

Eörsi, Gyula. *A tulajdonátszállás kérdéséről* (*About the Question of Transfer of Title*). Budapest: Légrády testvérek, 1947.

Fábián, Ferenc. *A tulajdon alkotmányos korlátozhatóságáról* (*About the Possible Constitutional Limitation of the Ownership*). In *Ünnepi tanulmányok Sárközy Tamás 70. születésnapjára (Festal Studies to Tamás Sárközy's 70th Birthday)*, edited by Tamás Nótári. Szeged: Lectum, 2010.

Fábián, Ferenc. *Előadásvázlatok a dologi jog köréből* (*Lecture Notes on the Law of Things*). Budapest: Patrocinium, 2015.

Fábián, Ferenc. *Előadásvázlatok az öröklési jog köréből* (*Lecture Notes in the Law of Succession*). Budapest: Patrocinium, 2014.

Faludi, Gábor. *Szerzői jog, iparvédelem és a ptk. koncepciója* (*Copyright, Protection of Inventions and the Concept of the Civil Code*). Polgári jogi kodifikáció 5 (2003).

Fazekas, Judit. *A hazai fogyasztóvédelem jogi szabályozása* (*Regulation of the Domestic Consumer Protection*). (1/2004).

Fézer, Tamás. *Insolvency Law: Bankruptcy and Liquidation*. In *Business Law*, edited by István Sándor. Budapest: Patrocinium 2016.

Földi, András & Gábor Hamza. *A római jog története és institúciói* (*History and Institutes of Roman Law*). Budapest: Nemzedékek tudása, 2015[20].

Földi, András. *A jóhiszeműség és tisztesség elve* (*The Principle of Good Faith and Honesty*). Budapest: ELTE ÁJK, 2001.

Gambaro, Gambaro. *Perspectives on the Codification of the Law of Property: An Overview*. European Review of Private Law 4 (1997).

Gárdos, István & Péter Gárdos. *Az engedményezés és a vételi jog biztosítéki célú alkalmazása* (*The Application of the Assignment and the Purchase Option as Collateral*). Gazdaság és Jog 12 (2004).

Gárdos, István & Péter Gárdos. *Ismét a fiduciárius biztosítékokról* (*About the Fiduciary Collaterals Again*). Gazdaság és Jog 13 (2005).

Gárdos, István. *Fiduciárius biztosítékok az új Polgári Törvénykönyvben* (*Fiduciary Collaterals in the New Civil Code*). Gazdaság és Jog 16 (2008).

Gárdos, Péter. *Az engedményezés* (*The Assignment*). Budapest: ELTE Eötvös Kiadó, 2009.

Gellén, Klára. *Értékpapírjog* (*Law of Securities*). Szeged: Pólay Elemér Alapítvány, 2009.

Gellér, György (ed.). *A Polgári Törvénykönyv magyarázata* (*Explanation of the Civil Code*). Budapest: Közgazdasági és Jogi Kiadó, 2001.

Gimpel-Hinteregger, Monika. *Das Tier als Sache und Ersatz der Heilungskosten für ein verletztes Tier.* Österreichische Juristen-Zeitung 11 (1989).

Gondosné Pusztahelyi, Réka (ed.). *A magánjogi kodifikáció eredményei* (*Results of the Private Law Codification*). Miskolc: Novotni Alapítvány, 2008.

Görög, Márta. *A know-how jogi védelmének alapvető kérdései* (*Fundamental Questions of Legal Protection of the Know-How*). Budapest: HVG-ORAC, 2012.

Grad-Gyenge, Anikó. *Szerzői jog és iparjogvédelem a magyar magánjogban* (*Copyright and Industrial Property in the Hungarian Private Law*). Budapest: Patrocinium, 2014.

Hamza, Gábor. *Az európai magánjog fejlődése* (*Development of the European Private Law*). Budapest: Nemzeti Tankönyvkiadó, 2002.

Hamza, Gábor. *Entstehung und Entwicklung der modernen Privatrechtsordnungen und die römischrechtliche Tradition.* Budapest: Eötvös Lorán Universitätsverlag, 2009.

Hamza, Gábor. *Le dévelopment du droit privé européen.* Budapest: L'Université Eötvös Loránd Faculté de Droit, 2005.

Hamza, Gábor. *Origine e sviluppo degli ordinamenti giusprivatistici moderni in base alla tradizione del diritto romano.* Santiago de Compostela: Andavira editora, 2013.

Hamza, Gábor. *Szent István törvényei és Európa, Sain Étienne et l'Europe (Saint Stephen's Laws and Europa).* Szent István és Európa, edited by Gábor Hamza. Saint Stephen and Europe. Budapest: Magyar Felsőoktatás, 2001^{2}.

Harmathy, Attila. *A polgári jogi kodifikációról* (*About the Civil Law Codification*). In *Liber Amicorum, Studia L. Vékás dedicata*, edited by András Kisfaludi. Budapest: ELTE ÁJK Polgári Jogi Tanszék, 2009.

Hudson, Alastair. *Equity and Trusts.* London, New York: Routledge, 2013^{7}.

Jakab, Éva. *Konzepte des Eigentums im Wandel der Zeit.* In *Geistiges Eigentum und Urheberrecht aus der historischen Perspektive*, edited by Éva Jakab. Szeged: Pólay Elemér Alapítvány, 2013.

Juhász, László. *Csődjog* (*Bankruptcy Law*). Budapest-Pécs: Dialóg Campus, 2003.

Kampis, György. *Telekkönyvi jog* (*Law of Cadastre*). Budapest: Közgazdasági és Jogi Kiadó, 1963.

Kecskés, András & Vendel Halász. *Stock Corporations. A Guide to Initial Public Offerings, Corporate Governance and Hostile Takeovers.* Budapest, Wien: HVG-ORAC, LexisNexis, 2013.

Kemenes, István. *A biztosítéki célú vételi jog egyes jogalkalmazási kérdései* (*Certain Questions of Legal Practice Concerning the Purchase Option for Collateral Purposes*). BDT 2 (2009).

Kisfaludi, András. *Az adásvételi szerződés* (*The Sales Contract*). Budapest: Közgazdasági és Jogi Kiadó, 2003.

Kiss, Gábor & István Sándor. *A szerződések érvénytelensége* (*Invalidity of the Contracts*). Budapest: HVG-ORAC, 2014.

Kiss, Gábor. *A társasházi jog kézikönyve* (*Manual of the Apartments Law*). Miskolc: Novotni Kiadó, 2011.

Koi, Gyula. *A PPP elméleti és terminológiai megalapozásának kérdései a nemzetközi szakirodalom tükrében* (*The Theoretical and Terminological Questions of the Foundation of PPP in the Mirror of the International Literature*). In *XIV. Országos Jegyző-Közigazgatási Konferencia, Államreform-Közigazgatási reform (14th Notary-Administrative Conference, State Reform – Administration Reform),* edited by Ferenc Gyergyák. Budapest: Közszöv-KSZSZ, 2006.

Kolozs, Borbála. *An Overview of Hungarian Trusts*. Tax Notes International 9 (2015).

Koziol, Helmut & Rudolf Weber. *Grundriss des bürgerlichen Rechts*. Wien: Manz 2002.

Lenkovics, Barnabás. *Polgári alanyi jogok – alkotmányos alapjogok (Alapvető kérdések az alanyi és az alapjogok körül) (Subjective Rights – Constitutional Fundamental Rights [Basic Questions Around the Subjective Rights and the Fundamental Rights]).* In *Alkotmányosság a magánjogban (Constitutionalism in the Private Law),* edited by Adrás Sajó. Budapest: Complex Kiadó, 2006.

Lenkovics, Barnabás. *Tulajdonjog* (*Ownership Right*). Budapest: Tankönyvkiadó, 1991.

Leszkoven, László. *A biztosítéki célú vételi jog néhány kérdéséről* (*About Some Questions of the Purchase Option for Collateral Purposes*). Gazdaság és Jog 12 (2004).

Leszkoven, László. *A fiduciárius engedményezés jogi természetéről* (*About the Legal Nature of the Fiduciary Assignment*). Gazdaság és Jog 10 (2002).

Lippold, Rainer. *Über Tiere und andere Sachen – § 285a ABGB als Beispiel zeitgenössischer Gesetzgebungskunst*. Österreichische Juristen-Zeitung 11 (1989).

Lukács, Mónika, István Sándor & Brigitta Szűcs. *Új típusú szerződések és azok gyakorlata a gazdasági életben* (*New Types of Contracts and Their Use in the Economy*). Budapest: HVG-ORAC, 2003.

Mádl, Ferenc. *Privatizáció Magyarországon. Az európai örökség útján (Privatisation in Hungary: On the Route of the European Heritage).* Budapest: Athenaeum, 1995.

Maitland, Frederick William. *The Constitutional History of England.* Cambridge: Cambridge University Press, 1908[1].

Matúz, György. *Nyolcvan éves a társasház (The Apartment Building is Eighty Years Old).* Magyar Jog 52 (2005).

Meier-Hayoz, Arthur (ed.). *Berner Kommentar, Kommentar zum schweizerischen Privatrecht* IV/1. Bern: Schultess 1966.

Menyhárd, Attila. *Dologi jog* (*Law of Things*). Budapest: Elte Eötvös Kiadó, 2010.

Menyhei, Ákos. *Estate Planning in Hungary: Private Foundation or Trust?*. Trust & Trustees 21 (2015).

Mezey, Barna (ed.). *Magyar jogtörténet* (*Hungarian Legal History*). Budapest: Osiris, 1996.

Miskolczi Bodnár, Péter & Gábor Török. *A magyar csődjog alapjai* (*Foundations of the Hungary Bankruptcy Law*). Budapest: HVG-ORAC, 2002.

Németh, Ilona & László Sík. *A vagyonkezelési szerződések típusai és biztosítékai*

(Types and Security of Property Management Contracts). Pénzügyi Szemle 42 (1997).

Olajos, István. *A vidékfejlesztési jog kialakulása és története (The Evolution and History of the Rural Development).* Miskolc: Novotni Alapítvány, 2008.

Osztovits, András (ed.). *A Polgári Törvénykönyvről szóló 2013. évi V. törvény és a kapcsolódó jogszabályok nagykommentárja (The General Commentary of Act V of 2013 on the Civil Code and the Related Legal Provisions).* Budapest: Opten, 2014, I–IV.

Papp, Tekla. *Law of Business Enterprises.* In *Business Law*, edited by István Sándor. Budapest: Patrocinium, 2016.

Petrik, Ferenc. *Elővásárlási jog – dologi jogviszony (Pre-emption Right – In Rem Legal Relationship).* Magyar Jog 55 (2008).

Petrik, Ferenc. *Ingatlan-nyilvántartás, Kommentár a gyakorlat számára (Land Registry, Commentary for the Practice).* Budapest: HVG-ORAC, 2015.

Petrik, Ferenc. *Tulajdonjogunk ma (Our Ownership Right Today).* Budapest: HVG-ORAC, 2007.

Prugberger, Tamás. *Az új társasházi törvény néhány jogalkalmazási problémája (Some Problems of Judicial Practice Concerning the New Apartment House Act).* Gazdaság és Jog 13 (2005).

Pusztahelyi, Réka (ed.). *A magánjogi kodifikáció eredményei (Results of the Private Law Codification).* Miskolc: Novotni Alapítvány, 2010.

Rakvács, József. *A közös tulajdon bírói gyakorlatának elemzése és annak tanulságai. A társasháztulajdon (Analysis of the Judicial Practice of Joint Ownership and Its Experiences. The Ownership of Apartment Building).* Gazdaság és Jog 8 (2000).

Rakvács, József. *Társasházi törvény (Act on Apartments).* Budapest: HVG-ORAC, 1998.

Rey, Heinz. *Dynamisiertes Eigentum.* Zeitschrift für Schweizerisches Recht 96 (1977).

Rounds, Charles E. & István Illés. *Is a Hungarian Trust a Clone of the Anglo-American Trust, or Just a Type of Contract? Parsing The Asset-Management Provisions of the New Hungarian Civil Code.* George Mason University School of Law, Journal of International Commercial Law 6 (2015).

Salamonné Solymosi, Ibolya. *A szerződések biztosítékai (Collaterals of the Contracts).* Budapest: Agrocent, 2002.

Sándor, Istán. *The Fiduciary Property Management and the Trust: Historical and Comparative Law Analysis.* Budapest: HVG-ORAC, 2015.

Sándor, István (ed.). *Business Law in Hungary.* Budapest: Patrocinium, 2016.

Sándor, István. *A bizalmi vagyonkezelés és a trust. Jogtörténeti és összehasonlító jogi elemzés (Fiduciary Property Management and the Trust. Historical and Comparative Analysis of Law).* 2nd ed. Budapest: HVG-ORAC, 2017.

Sándor, István. *Az 1959. évi IV. törvény megalkotása és módosításai 1989-ig (The Creation and Amendment of the Act IV of 1959 and Its Modifications until 1989).* In *Tanulmánykötet az 1959-es Polgári Törvénykönyv előkészítéséről, alapvető intézményeiről és fejlődésmenetéről I–II (Volume of Studies on the Preparation, Basic Institutions and Development of the Civil Code of 1959)*, edited by Tamás Sárközy. Budapest: Magyar Közlöny Lap- és Könyvkiadó Kft, 2018.

Sándor, István. *A vagyonkezelői jog szabályozása (Regulation of the Trustee Right).* Gazdaság és Jog 55 (2000).
Sándor, István. *Anmerkungen zur Konkurrenz von Verträgen über die Begründung eines Optionsrecht und des Pfandrechts.* In *Magyar kereskedelmi jogi évkönyv (Hungarian Commercial Law Yearbook),* edited by Zoltán Csehi. Budapest: Pázmány Péter Katolikus Egyetem, 2010.
Sándor, István. *Different Types of Trust from an Ownership Aspect.* European Review of Private Law 6 (2016).
Sándor, István. *The New Hungarian Fiduciary Asset Management Contract (Trust) from Comparative Aspect.* US-China Law Review 12 (2015).
Sándor, István. *Key Features of Private Foundations in a Comparative Law Approach: With Special Emphasize on Asset Management.* European Review of Private Law, Volume 29, Issue 6 (2021).
Sándor, István, *The Transformation of Foundation Law in Hungary, with Particular Regard to Private Foundations*, Trust & Trustees, Volume 29, No. 6 (July 2023).
Sárközy, Tamás. *Rendszerváltás és a privatizáció joga* (*System Transition and the Law of Privatisation*). Budapest: Közgazdasági és Jogi Kiadó, 1997.
Schadl, György. *The Concept, Importance and History of Judicial Enforcement.* In *Business Law*, edited by István Sándor. Budapest: Patrocinium, 2016.
Siklósi, Iván. *A kincstalálás római jogi, jogtörténeti és modern jogi kérdésköre* (*Treasure Trove in Roman Law, in Legal History and in Modern Legal System*). Budapest: Patrocinium, 2016.
Szabó, Zsolt. *The Constitutional System of Hungary.* In *Business Law in Hungary*, edited by István Sándor. Budapest: Patrocinium, 2016.
Szalma, József. *Kisajátítás – jegyzetek a horvát kisajátítási törvényről* (*Expropriation – Notes on the Croatian Expropriation Act*). Jogtudományi Közlöny 52 (1997).
Szászy, István. *A Szovjetunió magánjogának alapelvei (Basic Principals of Private Law of the Soviet Union).* Kolozsvár: Józsa Béla Athenaeum, 1945.
Szeibert, Orsolya. *A törvényes örökösöknek minősülő hozzátartozók és rokonok köre, tekintettel a polgári jogi kodifikációra (The Group of the Relatives and Cognates Qualified as Intestate Heirs, Regarding the Civil Law Codification).* In *Az új Ptk. öröklési jogi szabályai, tapasztalatok és kihívások (The Inheritancy Rules of the New Civil Code, Experiences and Challenges),* edited by Ágnes Juhász. Miskolc: Novotni Alapítvány, 2015.
Szilágyi, János Ede. *Eredetvédelmi kérdések a borjogban (Questions of Protection of Origin in the Law of Wines).* Miskolc: Novotni Alapítvány, 2009.
Szladits, Károly. *Magánjog. I. Általános Rész, Személyi Jog (Hungarian Private Law, Vol. I, General Part, Law of Persons).* Budapest: Grill, 1941.
Tanka, Endre. *Magyar birtokpolitika az Európai Egyesült Államokban. Földviszonyaink útja Moszkvától Brüsszelig (The Hungarian Agricultural Land Policy in the United States of America. Path of Our Land Relations From Moscow to Brussels).* Budapest: Alterra, 2004.
Tattay, Levente, György Pintz & Anett Pogácsás. *Szellemi alkotások joga (Law of Intellectual Property).* Budapest: Szent István Társulat, 2011.
Tattay, Levente. *A termőföldvásárlás problémái az Európai Unióban (Problems of Purchasing Agricultural Land in the European Union).* Európai Jog 9 (2009).

Téglási, András. *A tulajdonhoz való jog alkotmányos védelme (The Constitutional Protection of the Right to Ownership).* Szeged: Pólay Elemér Alapítvány, 2013.

Téglási, András. *The Constitutional Aspects of Ownership.* In *Business Law*, edited by István Sándor. Budapest: Patrocinium, 2016.

Udvary, Sándor. *The Organization of the Administration of Justice.* In *Business Law*, edited by István Sándor. Budapest: Patrocinium, 2016.

Ujlaki, Miklós. *A magyar jog sorsa az Ausztriához és Lengyelországhoz csatolt területeken (Fate of the Hungarian Law on the Territories Annexed to Austria and Poland).* Budapest: Grill, 1932.

Varga, V. Éva, *Kit terhelhet felelősség az ingatlan szomszédjogi szabályokat sértő beépítése miatt? (Who Is Responsible for Building Real Estate with Breaching Neighbourhood Rights?).* Magyar Jog 57 (2010).

Vékás, Lajos (ed.), *Az új Polgári Törvénykönyv Bizottsági Javaslata magyarázatokkal. (Committee Proposal for the New Civil Code with Explanations).* Budapest: Complex, 2012.

Vékás, Lajos (ed.). *Szakértői Javaslat az új Polgári Törvénykönyv tervezetéhez (Expert Proposal for the Draft of the New Hungarian Civil Code).* Budapest: Complex Kiadó, 2008.

Vékás, Lajos & Péter Gárdos (eds). *A Polgári Törvénykönyv magyarázatokkal (The Civil Code with Explanations).* I–II, Budapest: Wolters Kluwer, 2013.

Vékás, Lajos. *Az új Polgári Törvénykönyv elméleti előkérdései (Theoretical Premises of the New Civil Code).* Budapest: HVG-ORAC, 2001.

Vékás, Lajos. *Az új Polgári Törvénykönyv tervezetének néhány elméleti és rendszertani előkérdéséről (About Some Theoretical and Systematic Preliminary Questions of the Draft of the New Civil Code).* In *Sárközy Tamás ünnepi kötet (Sárközy Tamás Festal Volume).* Budapest: HVG-ORAC, 2006.

Vékás, Lajos. *Az új Ptk. Szakértői javaslatának elvi kérdései (Theoretical Questions of the Expert Proposal of the New Civil Code).* Magyar Jog 55 (2008).

Vékás, Lajos. *Bírálat és jobbító észrevételek az új Ptk. kormányjavaslatához (Criticism and Betterment Comments to the Draft of the New Civil Code).* Magyar Jog 55 (2008).

Vékás, Lajos. *Parerga. Dolgozatok az új Polgári Törvénykönyv tervezetéhez (Parerga. Studies for the Draft of the New Hungarian Civil Code).* Budapest: HVG-Orac, 2008.

Vékás, Lajos. *Történeti visszapillantás a magyar magánjog kodifikációjára (Historical Flashback on the Codification of the Hungarian Private Law).* Jogtudományi Közlöny 66 (2011).

Vékás, Lajos. *Magyar polgári jog, öröklési jog (Hungarian Private Law, Law of Succession).* Budapest: Eötvös József Könyvkiadó, 2014.

Vliet, L.P.W. van. *Transfer of Movables in German, French, English and Dutch Law.* Nijmegen: Ars Aequi Libri, 2000.

Vörös, Imre. *Az új Ptk. tervezetének szakértői javaslata (The Expert Proposal of the Draft New Civil Code).* Jogtudományi Közlöny 63 (2008).

Wellmann, György (ed.), *Polgári jog – Az új Ptk. magyarázata (Civil Law – Explanation of the New Civil Code).* (Budapest: HVG-ORAC 2013) I-VI.

Wieacker, Franz. *Privatrechtsgeschichte der Neuzeit unter besonderer Berücksichtigung der deutschen Entwicklung.* Göttingen: Vanderhoeck & Ruprecht 1996^2.

Wieling, Hans Josef. *Sachenrecht.* Berlin, Heidelberg, New York, Tokyo: Springer 1997^3.

Windscheid, Bernhard & Kipp Theodor. *Lehrbuch des Pandektenrechts.* Frankfurt a. M. 1906^9.

Zámbó, Tamás. *A zálogszerződés (The Lien Contract).* Budapest: KJK Kerszöv, 2001.

Zlinszky, János. *Werbőczy jogforrástana (Werbőczy's Tenet of Legal Sources).* In *Tanulmányok Werbőczy Istvánról, Studien über István Werbőczy*, edited by Gábor Hamza. Budapest: Magyar Felsőoktatás, 2001.

Index

The numbers here refer to paragraph numbers.

Index

Index

Index

www.ingramcontent.com/pod-product-compliance
Lightning Source LLC
Chambersburg PA
CBHW071432230926
51846CB00001B/197
9789403536088